Der Spiegel on the New Testament

Der Spiegel
on the
New Testament

*A Guide to the Struggle
Between Radical and Conservative
in European University and Parish*

Werner Harenberg

TRANSLATED BY *James H. Burtness*

The Macmillan Company

Collier-Macmillan Ltd., London

Library of Congress Catalog Card
Number: 75-99022

The original edition of this book was
published in Germany in 1966 under the
title Jesus und die Kirchen: Bibelkritik
und Bekenntnis, Kreuz-Verlag, Stuttgart · Berlin.

The Macmillan Company
866 Third Avenue, New York, N.Y. 10022
Collier-Macmillan Canada Ltd.,
Toronto, Ontario

First Printing

Printed in the United States of America

Contents

Note
to the Reader

IN THE SERIES of articles in *Der Spiegel* which constitutes the origin of this book, references to sources were omitted. In the book all quotations are fully documented. However, in order not to encumber the pages with footnotes, the notes are given according to the following system: After citations two numbers are given in parentheses. The first is the number of the source in the *List of Works Cited*; the second is the number of the page. For example, (29/284) means p. 284 in Bultmann's *Theology of the New Testament*, vol. 1. All biblical quotations are from the Revised Standard Version unless specifically indicated otherwise in the text. Occasionally a note is added by the author or the translator, indicated by brackets. The note has been made by the author unless it is followed by "Translator."

"Now when Jesus came into the district of Caesarea Philippi, he asked his disciples, 'Who do men say that the Son of man is?'. . .

He said to them, 'But who do you say that I am?'"

MATT. 16 : 13, 15

Foreword

THIS BOOK IS based on the series of articles entitled *Jesus und die Kirchen* that appeared in the spring of 1966 in the German news magazine *Der Spiegel*. I have revised the entire work and have expanded it considerably. I decided, rather than to select new themes, to handle more thoroughly the themes of that series: the virgin birth, miracles, the passion of Christ, the resurrection.

As was the series in *Der Spiegel*, so also this book should be useful to every reader, independent of his intellectual preparation. Yet it is hoped that those at home in theology will detect that efforts have been made to suggest at least some new aspects of familiar problems.

This book is a report about what the "biblical criticism" of modern theology means for the "confession of faith." The quotation marks may indicate the difficulties in the current controversy. There is no agreement, and has never been, about even the fundamental concepts. Mass rallies do not hide the fact that both sides are ill equipped for battle concerning proper faith—and that is precisely what the battle is about! To be of some help in making information available is the chief purpose of this book.

I should like to thank both Professor Rudolf Bultmann of Marburg and Spiegel-Verlag for their consent to publish here the expanded version of a *Der Spiegel* interview with

Pastor Gerhard Bergmann of the "Confession Movement 'No Other Gospel,' " and Professors Hans Conzelmann and Walter Künneth for the interviews with which this book ends.

W. H.

1. Heresy and Superstition?

THERE IS NOT one Jesus; there are at least four: Jesus[0], Jesus[0,5], Jesus[1], and Jesus[2]. This formula is used by Bo Reicke, Protestant professor of theology at Basel. *J* stands for *Jesus* (79/208ff.).

J[0] is the Jesus of those who do not believe in him. Most non-Christians, however differently they may think about J[0], are united with most Christians in believing that Jesus was born in the year 0, that he founded a church, and that he was crucified. Yet the first is certainly, the second probably, an error. No one knows when Jesus was born. That most non-Christians and Christians consider the year 0 to be the birth of Jesus is a result of an error made by the Roman monk Dionysius Exiguus who, in the sixth century, set the birth of Jesus about four to seven years too late. It is also uncertain when Jesus was crucified. According to the New Testament scholar Martin Dibelius, it can be said only "with considerable certainty that Jesus died between 27 and 34, probably in the year 30 or 33" (35/34). Most theologians have decided for the year 30. Jesus did "not bring into being a church in our understanding of that term, namely encompassing Jews and heathens and according to the conviction of many New Testament scholars did not intend it for some future time." So claimed Ernst Käsemann, New Testament scholar at Tübingen, in a lecture in 1963 to the World Conference on Faith and Order in Montreal (57/162).

J^1 is the historical Jesus; J^2, the Jesus of the Bible, the Christ of faith. Yet J^1 is not the same as J^2. That which was written about him from forty to seventy years after his death and which stands in the four Gospels of the New Testament is no historical report but the witness of faith. The great majority of Protestant theologians, and, more recently, many Catholic theologians, are agreed on that. To be sure, they are not agreed as to what degree J^1 and J^2 are to be distinguished from each other. For Catholic New Testament scholars, the two are very nearly identical; for many Protestant New Testament scholars, they are by no means identical.

The Jesus of the Bible was born in Bethlehem of the Virgin Mary. He preached the Sermon on the Mount, healed the sick, and raised the dead. He walked on the sea and made wine out of water. He was condemned to death by the Jewish Council. As the risen one, he ate and drank with his disciples.

ANOTHER JESUS?

The Jesus of many Protestant theologians was born in Nazareth as the child of his parents, Mary and Joseph. He did not preach that Sermon on the Mount, which is recorded in three chapters of the Gospel according to Matthew, on a mountain near the Sea of Galilee. He did not say much of that which stands in the Bible as his word. He worked no miracles. He was condemned, not by the Jews, but only by Pontius Pilate, the heathen from Rome. He did not walk about as the risen one.

The religious scholars who suggest this picture of Jesus believe that they have come closer to J^1 and are of the opinion that they have freed faith in Christ of unnecessary baggage. Yet for other professors of theology this Jesus is only $J^{0,5}$—a Jesus of unbelief rather than of faith.

For years and even decades the professors' controversy concerning Jesus was carried on, for the most part, only between bookcovers and in magazines in which articles were hidden rather than published. Occasionally the Church received the word, yet it said only "to be sure" and "on the other hand." Therefore since everyone understood yes or no, it soon appeared as heresy. This was the way it went, for instance, with the *Reports of the Evangelical–Lutheran Church in Bavaria*, which were written May 10, 1952, after a general synod of the United Evangelical–Lutheran church of Germany. The writers of the report said: "With the decision against the teaching of Rudolf Bultmann we initiate a new epoch in the history of the theology of our church. . . ." Yet they had neither initiated a new epoch nor even made a decision. The synod merely signaled "in great concern . . . the danger . . ." that, through so-called demythologization, "the salvation-deeds of God are first repressed in teaching and preaching, then sublimated, and finally given up." The Christians in the pew, moreover, had little awareness of what was taught at the lectern. "The Church lives, actually, from the fact that the results of scientific research on the life of Jesus are not publicly known," wrote Hans Conzelmann, New Testament scholar at the University of Göttingen, in a 1959 article. Four years later, Protestant jurist Otto Küster, in his book *Glauben müssen?*, consoled him by saying that this information was gradually being made known.

Yet, three years later, in 1966, hope turned to horror. In January, Wilhelm Knevels, professor of theology, announced in West Berlin in *Deutsches Pfarrerblatt* that a bitter Church struggle was approaching. "The assertion that it has to do with non-essentials, differences which do not touch the central issues, rests either on a misunderstanding of this event or on a flight from the facts. Everything is truly at stake here. Radical oppositions have broken out; chasms have opened up." A Church struggle can scarcely still be avoided, unless "in a last hour the hardened fronts are softened and bridges are built" (106/34).

It was already too late. On March 6, 1966, with the sound of a thousand trumpets, the battle was begun: the battle of the congregations against the professors using biblical criticism, the battle concerning Jesus, concerning his words and miracles, concerning belief in the virgin birth and resurrection. Twenty-two thousand Protestants filled the Westfalenhalle in Dortmund for a "great rally" which was, in fact, a combination heresy-trial and prayer-meeting. There were present only judges who condemned; the accused were not there to defend themselves.

Citations were simply read. Not once were names mentioned. The twenty-two thousand did not realize that they were protesting mainly against Rudolf Bultmann, professor of New Testament at Marburg and at that time eighty-one years old, and his students. Bultmann's reaction to this method: "It is unbelievable how many men who have never read a word that I have written presume to judge my work" (8/17).

Over the heads of the Protestants in the Westfalenhalle hung the banners reading "The Lord is risen" and "He is risen indeed." Hymns with lines such as "Enlighten those who are blind" were chosen. Publications with texts such as "His honor is at stake. He calls men into his holy war" (99/41) were selected.

The defenders of the biblical Jesus, who organized this rally in the Westfalenhalle, are united in a "No other Gospel" Confession Movement, which is led by Pastors Rudolf Bäumer of Espelkamp and Paul Deitenbeck of Lüdenscheid. During the course of 1966, associations similar to this one in Westphalia were founded in other parts of the German Federal Republic.

In the Church of Braunschweig an Action Group for Bible and Confession was organized, which approved the

*Braunschweig Theses for the Doctrine and Mandate of
the Church.* In this resolution all Christians were called
upon "not to allow themselves to be 'tossed to and fro and
carried about with every wind of doctrine' (Eph. 4 : 14),
but to remain in the truth" (113/2).

It was demanded in the *Braunschweig Theses* that a
position "be rejected whenever the resurrection of Jesus
Christ as a truly personal and bodily event, and the fact
of the open tomb, is denied; whenever it is contended that
the body of Jesus did not begin the process of decomposi-
tion; whenever the resurrection of Jesus Christ is interpreted only as the meaning of his death on the cross or as
an expression of the Easter-faith of the Christian community, but not recognized and witnessed to as the deed
of God which granted Easter-faith to the community;
whenever the fact of the real resurrection of the Lord
Jesus Christ is said to be irrelevant for Christian faith, or
is understood only as a name for the development of the
preaching of Jesus; whenever the personal identity of the
historical, crucified Jesus of Nazareth with the resurrected
and ascended Lord Jesus Christ is denied; whenever the
report of the ascension of Jesus is labeled as legend and
described as a mythological expression for the confession
of Jesus as Lord" (113/5).

Thus in seventeen paragraphs in all, "the substance of
the Gospel" is set over against that which "to be sure also
wants to be Christian faith, but in the light of the Gospel
is truly unbelief" (113/2). After the sentence: "It must
therefore be rejected, . . . ," there follows sixty-four times
the "whenever." So, in the opinion of the authors and
signers of these theses, a position must be rejected "whenever the real deity of Jesus Christ, the true incarnation of
the pre-existent Logos in him are taken to be only time-
conditioned forms of thought, and his conception by the
Holy Ghost and his birth of the Virgin Mary are denied
as facts of history" (113/4); "whenever the messianic

signs in the life of Jesus of Nazareth, the miracles reported in the Gospels, are considered to be only mythological ways of speaking and their factual historical character is denied" (113/4); "whenever within the writings of the New Testament there is a distinction made between true and untrue, between Christian and extra-Christian preaching materials" (113/8).

DEAD, CHEAP, PHARISAIC CONFESSION

Even the old masters of theology, as well as bishops and other Church leaders, entered into the confrontation: Bultmann with an interview (cf. Chap. 12); Karl Barth with a letter, which was published in the journal *Jungen Kirche* (No. 6/1966) in which he says: "To the 25 organizers and to the 25,000 (?) participants of that huge 'No other Gospel' rally, I should direct the question: Are you prepared and willing to start a similar 'movement' and to call a similar 'rally' against the demand of the West German army to be equipped with atomic weapons? Against the war of the Americans, to whom West Germany has close ties, in Vietnam? Against the repeated outbreak of an ugly anti-Semitism (desecrating of graves) in West Germany? For a peace treaty of West Germany with the eastern European states under recognition of the borders existing since 1945? If your *correct* confession to the Jesus Christ crucified and risen for us according to the witness of Holy Scripture includes that and expresses it, then it is a genuine, costly, and fruitful confession. If it does not include and express that, then it is, in all of its correctness, not a genuine, but a dead and cheap confession which strains at the gnat and swallows the camel and is therefore a pharisaic confession. That is what I have to say to that which happened on March 6, 1966, in the Westfalenhalle in Dortmund."

Bishop Erich Vellmer of Kassel, Superintendent Udo Smidt of Lippstadt ("What we lack now in our churches is not mass meetings, but dialogue"), and Bishop Johannes Jaenikke of the Evangelical church of Saxony, all expressed themselves against rallies. Jaenikke even called rallies an "expression of anxiety concerning the faith and therefore an expression of weak faith."

In Dessau, Church President Dr. Müller warned of the danger that "scholarly theology and so-called parish theology could fall apart from one another." During the preparation period, pastors had requested that special meetings be held for them "since they would not be able to understand the language and problems of modern theology." The Council of the Evangelical Church of the Union welcomed the fact "that even the congregations take part in growing measure in the present conversation concerning questions of evangelical doctrine and that once again God's Word is openly spoken about." President Joachim Beckmann of Düsseldorf prepared a twenty-four page "Word to the pastors, presbyters and fellow workers in church service" over the question "Another Gospel?" Bishop Gerhard Heintze of Braunschweig, in a letter to all clergymen, agreed with the theses, which were put together and signed by pastors of his church. And Bishop Heidland of Baden published at Pentecost a "Word of the bishop to the congregations."

The letter of Bishop Heintze was remarkable in its critical yet understanding analysis of the theses. He writes, for instance, that authors "have not succeeded" in giving a positive solution to the problem of "how the word of man and the word of God are related to one another in the witness of scripture; the theses are rather a very questionable schematization, which is not legitimate for the problems which face us here today." So, to be sure, it would be recognized that biblical research along secular-scientific lines (for instance, the historical–critical method) is justified and necessary (Thesis 15), yet in fact it "is not taken seriously. The theses do not deal thoroughly enough with the stratified layers of the reports of the witnesses, nor with the problem of the intertwining of these reports in thought-forms and modes of expression of a time now completely past, and the inherited tensions and difficulties which accompany that fact." They "endanger therefore one of the most essential and most fruitful exegetical realizations of the last decades, namely that all New Testament reports are written from the presupposition of faith in Christ as the risen Lord and are not at all interested in history in and for its own sake, but are much more interested in leading through that which is reported, both content and style, to faith in Christ as the living present Lord" (105/3).

Heintze, who in his letter asks his pastors "neither to be distressed nor threatened" (105/1), warns in conclusion "not to prematurely cut off the bond of fellowship" (105/6). This request was repeated in almost all written statements by bishops and church presidents. Even President Ernst Wilm of Westphalia, who appears to have set himself as the only leader of a regional church on the side of the Confession Movement, admonished the rally in the Westfalenhalle to brotherliness: "No party against party . . . no split" (12/16).

In Westphalia, the Confession Movement had apparently already become so powerful that Wilm warned of an over-zealous search for heresies: "There are many people who have not come here, who are also to some extent not in agreement with this rally in the Westfalenhalle, of whom we still ought not to say that they want some other Gospel. None of us has the right to make a judgment concerning his brother who has not come to Dortmund, as though that would indicate that he does not have proper faith" (12/16).

The model of the Confession Movement is the Confessing church, in which faithful Protestants, after 1933, united in the struggle against the Nazi-dominated German Christians: There is "today as once before in the time of

the Church Struggle need for a new confession movement,"
called out Professor Künneth in Dortmund, because "we
still have with us Christian talk which refuses to be specific,
a Gospel which is structured, accommodated, altered, and
reinterpreted for the modern world" (12/40f.). And
Gerhard Bergmann, pastor in Halver in Westphalia, evangelist, spokesman for the Confession Movement, author of
numerous articles and of a book with sixty thousand copies
in print entitled *Alarm um die Bibel*, goes even farther.
He is convinced (so he writes in a magazine that was
distributed to all participants in the Westfalenhalle) "that
the theological error of the so-called German Christians
was child's play in comparison to that which we face
today" (99/41). And he calls modern theology a "partisan
of atheism" (102/40).

After reading the book *Alarm um die Bibel*, Künneth,
the sharpest opponent of Bultmann among the German
professors of theology, wrote to Bergmann: "I have read
with innermost sympathy and full, warmest agreement,
your entire excellent presentation" (14/5). Bergmann
writes in his book concerning Protestant professors of theology and their research on Jesus: "Betrayal of the Holy
Ghost" (14/113), "Atomic Demolition of the New Testament" (14/34), "Dogmatic Monstrosities" (14/47), "As-
sault on the Bible" (14/62). According to Bergmann,
Bultmann's Jesus is only risen "in the sense that Goethe
rises from the dead for students in the course of lectures
about him in a university auditorium. Goethe does not
himself live. Goethe is dead. So Jesus also does not himself
live. Jesus is dead" (14/45f.). He calls New Testament
Professor Herbert Braun of Mainz a "heretic and poisoner
of souls" (14/118f.) and says about a lecture of Braun's:
"In an atheistic collection of writings no more basic batter-
ing of Jesus Christ could have resulted than there"
(14/118).

Next to citations out of books by Bultmann and his

students, Bergmann also publishes statements which professors are reputed to have said but are not written. "It
would not unnerve me in any way, if someone should find
today the bones of the body of Jesus" (99/40). Or: "How?
To pray to this man Jesus, who lived about 1900 years
ago? That would be exactly the same as if I would pray to
my dead grandmother. That is ancestor-worship" (14/71).
To "biblical criticism," says Bergmann, "the Christian
congregations say a decisive 'No'" (14/35). And he defines the concept as "when anyone comes and explains, for
instance, that these words of Jesus or these verses are
genuine, those are not genuine, and the rest are probably
not genuine" (14/103).

How great the differences are may also be gathered from
the statements of the other side. Professor Hartmann, who
was cited in Dortmund—as was Bultmann—though not
named, wrote in the Sonntagsblatt, published in Hamburg
(No. 12/1966): "The Confession Movement misunder-
stands Jesus." In the Westfalenhalle you have "turned
against Jesus. Your confession was a confession against
Jesus." Modern theologians would have to realize "that we
now confront a movement which requires of us not aca-
demic instruction but a confession." And with the sentences: "I believe that Jesus was man. And I contest the
belief of the Confession Movement that he became more
than a man," he extinguished the no less decisive rejoinder
of Deitenbeck: "Professor Hartmann testifies to another
Jesus and therefore to another Gospel. . . . Professor
Hartmann's teaching about Jesus is—I realize what I am
saying—antichristian, well-intended though it may be."

It may have been such statements as these which motivated the thirty-one professors and instructors of the theological Seminary of Bethel and of the Universities of
Münster and Bochum (who cannot all be labeled modern
theologians) to publish a clarifying statement. The professors and instructors "see the real danger in the prevent-

ing of the congregations from reaching maturity. It happens wherever one fails to responsibly pass on the results of theological research, or is of the opinion that congregations must be shielded against new knowledge" (*Evangelische Welt*, 1966, p. 334).

GOD IS IN ALL HIS WORDS, EVEN SYLLABLES

It seems as though the differences are irreconcilable. "The two groups," stated the Berlin theologian Knevels, "can increasingly do nothing other than dispute with one another the right of the other group to be in the Church" (106/34).

The leaders of the Confession Movement and the professors of theology associated with them demand, as a matter of fact, an anathema against the alleged heretical scholars, and "heresy" is the party cry. So Künneth: "True doctrine or heresy? This alternative touches the life of faith of individuals, but also touches the meaning of the Christian Church as bearer of the apostolic message. . . . If there is a peaceful coexistence with equal rights granted to true doctrine and to false doctrine, then the church has become merely a place of conversation in which nonbinding religious declamations are invited. The selling out of the church at the cheapest daily price has then become unavoidable" (107/19).

The Catholic canon lawyer Georg May of the University of Mainz has already registered claims on this bankruptcy: "No one will be able to blame Catholic counselors if they alert Protestants, who are thinking of entering into a mixed-marriage, to these unnerving developments. The answer to the question of where the Christian faith is better preserved is today not difficult. To a Protestant for whom the Christian faith is important, against the background of the destruction of Christian Substance by particular theologians, the agreement to the education of his

children in the Catholic Faith is made considerably easier"
(68/65).

"Heresy" is the watchword of one party in the Protestant
faith struggle. The word of the other party is "superstition."
The pious Bible-reading confessors in the congregation
ought—writes Bergmann—"precisely in our present situation . . . to put into motion in our hearts the word of
Martin Luther: 'God is truthful in all his words, even
syllables; whoever does not believe one thing believes
nothing. As Christ says in Matthew 5 : 19.' There we read:
'Whoever then relaxes one of the least of these command-
ments and teaches men so, shall be called least in the
kingdom of heaven. . . .' " (14/88f.). And Pastor Karl
Sundermeier of the West German YMCA said at the rally
in the Westfalenhalle: "I think that with the Word of God
everything which stands between the first and the last
word of the Bible is given to us as the voice of the Good
Shepherd and calls us to discipleship" (12/18).

The faith in words, as it appears in these citations from
Bergmann and Sundermeier, is, according to the conviction
of modern theologians, not only a misunderstanding of
Luther's notion of faith, it is superstition. Käsemann says:
"That which stands in the Bible is certainly *not* all God's
Word. . . . Ultimately the argument today concerns this
sentence, whether it is correct or incorrect. If in the view
of my opponents I threaten or destroy with this sentence
the foundation of the faith, then I see in that my duty, a
duty which an evangelical theologian cannot give up. For
that kind of faith is, in my opinion, and also I think in
Reformation thought, superstition. To separate faith and
superstition is, moreover, the business of the theologian"
(57/279).

Modern theologians also cite Luther, of course, in another place (out of the "Preface to the Epistle of James"):
"And therein agree all righteous and holy books, that they
all preach and bear Christ. And that is the correct criterion

by which to evaluate all books, namely whether they bear
Christ or not. . . . Whatever does not teach Christ is not
apostolic, even if Peter or Paul teaches it; on the other
hand, whatever preaches Christ is apostolic even if Judas,
Annas, Pilate and Herod preach it."

ONE TRUTH OR MANY TRUTHS?

The Protestant church itself, whose most renowned theologians are accused of heresy and whose congregations
are accused of superstition, is neutral in this struggle concerning that about which its members ought to agree—the
Faith. It allows its theologians to make not only different
but contradictory statements.

One can believe that God exists or that he is "the whence
of my security and my obligation toward my fellow men"
(Braun 19/341). Jesus can be only man or also God and
man. One can believe that Jesus is from eternity and came
into the world through a fatherless birth. One can also
believe, however, that he is God's son ". . . through his
special attitude within history . . . by really fearing, lov-
ing, and trusting God above all things" (Heinz Zahrnt,
theological editor of *Sonntagsblatt*, 93/142).

One can believe *in* Jesus, but one can also believe *as*
Jesus: "To believe in Jesus means to believe like Jesus that
God grants prayer" (41a/63). One can think with Künneth
that the resurrection of Jesus is "the principal datum of
theology" and "the act of God, whose significance is not
to be compared with any event before or after" (64/294).
But, according to Zahrnt, it "is to add nothing new to
Jesus. . . . Easter has done no more than reveal—of course
only to faith—what Jesus already was" (93/138).

Theology is—as Knevels contrasts the opposing positions—"Doctrine from God" or "self-understanding of
believing men." Faith "rests on fundamentals and is made
secure through them"; or it "is uncertain and must renounce security." And even with such a straightforward

sentence such as "God is love," the theologians separate. "The subject rules the predicate," says Gollwitzer; "out of the predicate I learn the subject," says Braun (106/35). One can appeal to the fact that "the witnesses of the church fathers" assert "that the disciples Matthew and John as eye- and ear-witnesses of the miracles and preaching of Jesus are the authors of the Gospels named after them, and that Mark and Luke sketched out their Gospels under the editorship or even the dictation of the apostles on their missionary journeys" (Friedrick Wilhelm Ringsdorff in *Schule und Kirche*. vol. 1. Düsseldorf, 1965). But one can also, as does Käsemann, "postulate with certainty that none of the Evangelists himself knew the historical Jesus" (56/95).

Concerning the valuation of history, Gogarten sketches the two views in this way: "This one approach sees its primary task in the establishment of the authenticity of this history in what it usually calls its 'objective' historicity, its 'real factualness,' because, it maintains, this is the only way of preserving the 'trans-subjective' reality of the faith" (47/37). To do that is, to be sure, "to be guilty of a miserable rationalization of the New Testament history" (47/76). Other theologians (and also Gogarten) "differ from this view . . . in that it arises from the conviction that the actual history—and, one must add, the actual historical character (*Geschichtlichkeit*)—of the events recorded in the New Testament is not to be sought in the 'objective' and historically (*historisch*) ascertainable fact of their having taken place, but in the kerygma, the proclamation and witness that in the events of this history God turns with grace towards mankind and their world" (47/37f.).

Whether having to do with God or faith, with Jesus' death on the cross or his resurrection, with the Holy Ghost or eternal life, with the author of the Gospel according to John or the "genuineness" of a word of Jesus—there are always at least two contrary teachings or opinions.

ANGER OVER THE ROTTENNESS OF THE ATMOSPHERE

Both sides appeal to the Bible, even if the issue is the style of the battle. The leader of the Confession Movement, quotes Galatians: "I am astonished that you are so quickly deserting him who called you in the grace of Christ and turning to a different gospel" (1 : 6). And Bultmann refers to Matthew 23 : 13: "But woe to you, scribes and Pharisees, hypocrites! because you shut the kingdom of heaven against men! . . ." (9/8). Bultmann said in 1960 concerning some of his opponents: "In unashamed Pharisaism they summarily condemn as heresy any other opinion than their own in the firm conviction that their opinion alone is the correct doctrine. The awareness that they themselves are capable of error is lost to them. . . . They don't know that Christian understanding is won in inner struggle and in brotherly discussion and must advance step by step. They also demonstrate thereby that they are deaf to the questions which today excite many men in the church— young and old men . . . and so share in the guilt that many men turn their backs on the church. They are like the Scribes and the Pharisees who shut out the Kingdom of God from men." Bultmann adds: "I scarcely need to say that all that does not concern me in so far as it touches me personally. But it disturbs me because it is symptomatic of a certain atmosphere of ecclesiasticism, and together with compassion for those who are blind misled by the blind is mixed an anger over the rottenness of the atmosphere" (9*/8).

On each side there is often a failure to recognize that one side believes as radically and deeply as the other. But how questionable the situation is must be clear to everyone who seeks to grasp it from the viewpoint of one standing on the outside. What Zahrnt wrote about the Bible holds true also for the Protestant church: "Where everything is said to be equally valid, everything becomes indifferent" (93/31).

The Protestant church is very nearly unable to act in matters which relate to problems of the Faith. If a teaching ought to be declared heresy, then the teacher himself must be attended to—no one other than he is responsible for it.

In the struggle over the Faith which broke open in the spring of 1966, no decision is demanded from most Protestants. The Church is schizophrenic. Lectern and pulpit are, and remain, separate worlds, with the exception of those persons who live in one world and feel that they belong to the other. Formerly, people were indifferent. Today, they shout at one another—from a safe distance—the words "heresy" and "superstition." Whoever condemns Bultmann in a pious gathering without having read even one sentence from Bultmann will not be ashamed about his own biblical literalism. In the one world the Star of Bethlehem can shine brightly; we are informed only *that* (not *why*) it is extinguished in the other world. Therefore it is news when a professor of theology (Bartsch) pleads that "Christmas be given up as a church festival" (95). But what Bultmann wrote concerning the message of Christmas remains unknown: "We are the children of light because the light of divine love and grace, which in the birth of Jesus Christ was shed abroad for the world, always shines for us all" (25/78). Such statements do not fit the image of "partisans of atheism" in chairs of theology. Hans Grass, professor of systematic theology, may teach in the University of Marburg that no one can know for sure or must even believe that the tomb of Jesus was empty. In many villages in Westphalia, however, Grass may not enter the pulpit: faith in the empty tomb is for the Confession Movement a criterion of faith in the resurrection of Jesus.

Anyone who wants to change over from the one into the other world must himself be a schizophrenic. He must fear the examination in the university if he cannot enumerate with precision the arguments by which the virgin birth is explained as legend. Before a Confessing congregation will accept him as pastor, he must renounce what he has learned: Faith in a historical, factual virgin birth is an inescapable condition for entrance into a parsonage.

If the pastors who lead the Confession Movement would like to be knowledgeable about that which they condemn, they would first have to learn to understand it. And unbelievers are alienated from the Faith, rather than won for it, not primarily through the multitude of theses, but through the confusing language of conservative, as well as modern, theologians.

The so-called existentialist theology of Bultmann and his students, which is said to bring modern men to Faith, is widely regarded as a curiosity ("that a theologian may talk that way about God . . .") rather than as a call to decision for God. Even if one does not want to judge the situation as radically as does Karl Jaspers, one will have to agree with his statement: "It leaves one who is not committed to a particular faith undisturbed" (55/53). But even Professor Künneth, who accuses the existentialist theologians of an "unclear, scintillating, nebulous way of speaking," himself uses sentences such as this: "The limits of the profane aspects in the knowledge of Jesus must be seen in the elementary fact that the dimension of transcendence is eliminated as a basis for understanding the meaning of the phenomenon of Jesus" (63/43). In clear language that means: Whoever denies the supernatural cannot comprehend Jesus.

A book on the language of German theologians (not *the* German theologians) could easily be filled. There is no lack of material. A few examples may suffice. "Unintelligible and senseless," says Protestant Professor Ernst Heitsch of Göttingen about a key sentence from Tübingen Professor Hermann Diem's book *Der irdische Jesus und der Christus des Glaubens:* "One can encapsulate the entire content of New Testament preaching as: the preaching of

Jesus Christ, who preaches himself. In that way is Jesus Christ the initiator as well as the object, and also the acting subject of preaching." Heitsch further comments on Diem: "If we must understand that in this text, which is typical of innumerable others, an attempt is in fact made to speak in a legitimately Christian, or theological, manner, then there no longer remains any reason for us to busy ourselves with Christianity" (79/63).

How one says nothing in many words and difficult sentences is demonstrated in a book by Bartsch. At times a sentence so cancels out the preceding one that the reader finally ends up with nothing: "The position of Braun, if stated too polemically and too subtly, in spite of all reservations, invites the designation 'atheistic.' Yet Braun ought not to be accused of atheism. But the danger seems unavoidable; that out of the contention that it is impossible to make statements about God arises quite naturally the possibility of making negative statements about God. Has Braun not already succumbed to this danger in that sentence against which most of the opposition to his position has been registered: God is a specific mode of co-humanity" (8/17). And in Bartsch's writings one also finds the arresting formulation that man "cannot receive God securely in his grasp" (8/19). Whoever writes in this way will have to allow the question to be asked: May one write about God and Christians as one would write about a boxing match? Ernst Fuchs, professor of New Testament at Marburg, who knows how to formulate classical sentences with economy and power, such as: "If one believes, one must be able to say what one knows," uses, on the other hand, pictures which one certainly cannot call concrete. To the sentence of Bornkamm: "One would have to turn all the Easter stories upside down, if one wanted to present them in the words of Faust: 'They are celebrating the resurrection of the Lord for they themselves are resurrected'" (18/184), Fuchs comments:

"Goethe hits the mark in spite of Bornkamm's defence" (41/183). But how now does Bornkamm resist Goethe's hitting of the mark?

Professor Gerhard Koch demands that his reader "pay attention to certified encounters with the event itself" (61/24). The demand is made in the context of awkward and stilted expressions such as "combatting" (61/194), "particularness" (61/195), "attestation" (61/197), "confirmation" (61/205), "collation" (61/207). And this book has to do with living issues; for not only persons, but also tombs and concepts, act here. Statements "resist" (61/24); the "empty tomb admits eventfulness and in the service of the event it can only point to the true event, which admits men through itself as through a door" (61/163); and the empty tomb "sets up an insurmountable barrier" (61/166). The tomb and the reader are compared; both may not cross a border: "This border, which is clearly assigned to the tomb in the New Testament, may not be overstepped by the onlooker, even if . . ." (61/164). And one may also read in this book a sentence such as this: "In spite of the mythology which must be overcome, the believer has become free from his sins through the cross of Christ" (61/145).

The manner in which statements are cited is also here and there questionable. That Künneth, for instance, once condensed six pages of Bultmann to twenty lines of citations may be justifiable (26/8–15 and 64/147f.). Yet there is a place which will not bear comparison with the original. In the following text the phrases from Bultmann which are cited by Künneth are set off in italics: "*Of course the doubt as to whether Jesus really existed is unfounded* and not worth refutation. No sane person can doubt that Jesus stands as the founder behind the historical movement whose first distinct stage is represented by the oldest Palestinian community. But how far that community preserved an objectively true picture of him and his message is another question. For those whose interest is in the personality of Jesus, this situation is depressing or destructive; for our purposes it [Künneth inserts here a "but"] *has no particular significance*" (26/13f.).

Künneth shortens this sentence to read: "To be sure, there is no ground for doubting whether Jesus really existed . . . but such doubts are of no essential significance" (64/147). For Bultmann, it is "not of particular significance" whether the community has preserved an objectively true picture of Jesus; for Künneth's "Bultmann," it is "of no essential significance" whether Jesus really existed. . . . Ought Künneth to maintain that he offers in this place a genuine "glance into Bultmann's theological workshop" (64/148)?*

All theologians have in common—understandably—a great interest in definitions. Yet the two groups which at present oppose each another are not able to agree on any. Who stands, for instance, closer to the "rationalists" (whoever may be designated by that label): the scholars of the Bultmann school who are attacked as "neorationalists" or their opponents? Bultmann speaks of a common "viewpoint of rationalism and pietism," even of a "brotherhood of rationalism and pietism" (23/95, 98).

The leaders and the followers of the Confession Movement are called fundamentalists, orthodoxists, biblicists, but are also called positive, true-to-the-Bible, and true-to-

---

* I pointed out this shortened Bultmann citation to Professor Künneth and may report here his explanation: "Certainly it *can* be misunderstood, but the sense, the intention of Bultmann, seems to me to be correctly stated. I do not contest that B. affirms the existence of Jesus, but for B. it has to do with a merely 'historic phenomenon,' whose name is of no consequence. 'Whoever wishes to always set this "Jesus" for himself in quotation marks . . . he is at liberty to do so.' (R.B., *Jesus*, p. 17). That means that the 'personhead of Jesus,' the 'what and how' of his existence, is 'of no particular importance.' His existence squeezes together into a point, the function of which is to bear the proclamation. It is, finally, an unknown X."

the-Confessions Christians. The other theologians are designated liberal, critical, neorationalistic, existentialistic. We wish to avoid getting involved in a dispute over these terms and therefore will designate the first group as the "conservative," and the second as the "modern" theologians.

Theology—modern as well as conservative—has become a garden of confusion (including, to be sure, many well-groomed and much-traveled paths) in which even the experts often no longer know what is going on. It could have an important task to fulfill, that of educating the average man; for, if an investigation were made as to "what the average man of today knows of Christianity and what kind of ideas he has of its nature, then I think that by and large we would find a shocking ignorance" (37/14).

Yet one who is not conversant with the style of modern as well as conservative theologians can scarcely diminish his ignorance in the realm of theology. The genuine or apparent contradictions that exist between opponents and, at times, even within the writings of a single theologian are too great.

Hans Schomerus writes in *Christ und Welt* (No. 17/1966, p. 13) so sharply that one almost imagines one is reading Bergmann: "The 'co-humanity sermon' will become obsolete as quickly as did those sermons on the practice of stall-feeding with which rationalistic pastors fed their congregations." And he asks: "Does anyone who has thrown overboard practically all the content of the creed still retain the right to speak in the name of the Church of Jesus Christ?" A contradiction results when the apparently conservative Schomerus writes in a modern way about the ascension: "What peculiar set of circumstances gave rise to the solemn celebrating of this event by believers, an event in which the God in whom we believe would finally leave the earth and become a distant god, so that we could look up to him only from a great distance, as far as the heaven is from the earth!" (45/25).

Bergmann and Künneth, the two best known spokesmen for the Confession Movement, seem to be in disagreement on an essential point. Bergmann considers it to be "enormously important to ask the representatives of modern theology directly: You speak about the resurrection of Jesus. Do you mean the *bodily* resurrection? Do you mean it as *historical fact?*" (14/79). For Künneth, on the contrary, (as he writes in his *Theology of the Resurrection*) "the definition as historical fact is an untenable shift of accent which cannot be said to be valid for that which the message really intends to convey" (63/24). But does not Künneth contradict himself when he still calls the resurrection a "fact," as he did in Dortmund? (12/38).

The Confession Movement is "observed not without sympathy . . . on the catholic side," as one can read in the *Kirchenzeitung für das Bistum Hildesheim* (No. 12/1966). On the other hand, Anton Vögtle, professor of New Testament at the University of Freiburg, writes in a book that appeared in 1966: "If many hyperconservative, biblicistic, catholic New Testament scholars reject, along with their equally archconservative protestant colleagues of a fundamentalistic-spiritualistic and pietistic stamp, virtually every methodological advance and persist in an historical, perspectiveless interpretation of scripture, then any development in regard to either of them could have been disregarded long ago" (16/48).

As concerning nearly every verse of the Bible, so also concerning every person in the history of the Church—from Jesus to the Jesus-specialist Bultmann—there is a bewildering profusion of opinions. For the leader of the Confession Movement, Bultmann is a heretic; Martin Niemöller, however, said about him: "If half of our church people are as genuine Christians as he, then I should like to thank God for it!" (71/117). Niemöller also writes: "Bultmann is no atheist. Bultmann is also no 'pretending' Christian. He knows Jesus!" (71/118). Catholic theologians, even after basic Bultmann studies, could not agree on the judgment concerning Bultmann as it was formulated by Protestant Christians in the Westfalenhalle during the rally, or, in any case, as it is said to have been formulated. They take him to be a Lutheran (Marlé, Paris), a Calvinist (Adam, Tübingen), a Kantian (Fries, Munich), an unbeliever (Romeo, Rome), or a believer with whose basic ideas Catholics could also agree (Hasenhüttl, Tübingen) (53/12f.).

For the theologians the current dispute about Jesus may concern primarily two opposite directions and definitions of faith. But the simple Christian and many non-Christians want to know "if that which is preached also really happened; if Jesus of Nazareth did live; if his person, his words and his deeds, his suffering and death, are to be taken in only a legendary or mythical way, or if the reports are true, if the message concerning Jesus Christ is correct, if it deserves to be believed or not." That is what Künneth maintains, and every theologian and every Christian (if one does not stress his concept of "true," which many would conceive quite differently) could and would have to agree with him (63/123).

These questions are as dangerous as they are legitimate. May Christians in the parishes be permitted to call a boycott against the pastors? Bergmann writes: "Christians must say to one another: Shun all pastors who deny the incarnation of Jesus, and specifically the incarnation in a pre-existence, exclusive, sense" (15/207). Ought simple Christians to immediately suspect one who considers the report of the wedding at Cana to be a legend? Bergmann makes a case of a pastor who has doubts about the changing of water into wine ("I could give name and place," 14/8) and states without hesitation: "The biblical statements deserve our total confidence with regard to historical authenticity. They cannot be shaken by any research or

method which has appeared to date, not even by historical–critical research" (14/39).

That this has to do with the "life-nerve of the Church"
is established by Bergmann: "The preaching of the Church
of Jesus Christ instantly becomes a mythology itself and a
religion among religions if it is not based on the hard
foundation of historical facticity" (14/77).

Bergmann writes to the congregations that "they do not
have to have the slightest basis for feeling 'old-fashioned'
because of their faithfulness to the Bible, or to be seriously
depressed over subjective rebukes such as 'naïveté' and
'oversimplification,' 'primitive' and 'unscientific.' We choose
to accept these rebukes without excitement or rancour"
(14/11).

Zahrnt writes concerning this attitude: "There is not
only such a thing as a stubborn unbelief; there is also a
stubborn credulity which doggedly and desperately maintains the most improbable and impossible positions and
thinks that in this way it is proving its faith. In reality, by
doing this it praises itself alone, its own work, the self-
satisfying sacrifice of the intellect. This has nothing to do
with faith. It is fearfulness, or pietistic, malicious obstinacy,
or both together . . ." (93/21). Professor Käsemann of
Tübingen is convinced that Protestant congregational piety
"has been standing still historically and theologically since
the 18th century" (57/281).

At any rate, it is certain that the current church struggle
is being carried out after considerable delay. That which
is today stirring up the congregations has been taught by
theologians, in part at least, for several decades. That the
virgin birth is a legend and also that several miracles and
many words of Jesus were added to the record for the first
time following his death had already been established with
the help of historical–critical research, above all by the
so-called form-critical method, and not for the first time
by existentialist theology.

2. Modern Theology
and the Bible

OUR PURPOSE IS neither to give a survey of the history of historical criticism nor to present in detail the methods with which it was first practiced. We are limiting ourselves rather to the method which came into use only recently and which is most controversial, that is, to the form-critical method which was developed after the First World War in particular by Karl Ludwig Schmidt, Martin Dibelius, and Rudolph Bultmann.

The form-critical method takes as its starting point a fact which was unknown to Christians for centuries—or which was contested by the churches—namely, the long history of development of the New Testament. The oldest part, the letters of the Apostle Paul, was written in the fifties, therefore about a quarter of a century after the death of Christ. The oldest Gospel (Mark) was edited shortly before the year 70, the Gospel according to Matthew after 70, the Gospel according to Luke probably between 75 and 80, and the Gospel according to John somewhere around the year 100.

The fact that the Bible contains only four and not more Gospels, and only twenty-one and not more letters, is traceable to a late decision of the Church. For decades other "gospels" and letters by Christians were devoutly read and honored in congregational worship. These, however, were finally declared apocryphal and not included in the New Testament.

The form-critics subject these apocryphal writings to analysis along with the writings of other religions. They also compare the Gospels and the other parts of the New Testament with one another. It is certain that the authors of the Gospels according to Matthew and Luke used as a source the Gospel according to Mark and, in addition to that, a collection made up primarily of the speeches of Jesus—today called Q by theologians—which is no longer extant.

The form-critics begin with the assumption that the evangelists did not want to describe the life of the historical Jesus but to proclaim the lord of the community which believed in him. Willi Marxsen, professor of New Testament at Münster, therefore calls the Gospels "the oldest extant volume of the preaching of the church" (65/85). "This basic reorientation," says the American theologian James M. Robinson, "is to the effect that all the tradition about Jesus survived only in so far as it served some function in the life and worship of the primitive Church. History survived only as kerygma" (80/37).

THE SERMON ON THE MOUNT: A COLLECTION OF SAYINGS

The Gospels as we have them were the last stage of the process. After the death of Jesus, they were essentially only a collection of individual sayings and deeds of Jesus that were circulated, at first, orally, by preachers and missionaries: "this is the fundamental hypothesis of the form-critical method" (Dibelius, 33/306). Furthermore, the "framework" of the Gospels was the creation of their authors. Statements of time and place, such as, "straightway," "and it came to pass that," "in evening," "on the sea," "on the mountain," are at best only editorial helps given by the evangelist. Therefore the Sermon on the

Mount is "not a sermon actually . . . but a collection of sayings"; it "is known neither to whom these sayings were originally directed nor in what circumstance they were originally spoken" (Dibelius, 33/306). Since the framework of the Gospels is artificial, it is "no longer possible to put together the sequence of events in the life of Jesus, to write a biography of Jesus, and to sketch an impression of his personality" (Conzelmann, 32/600).

The form-critics again disconnect the individual pieces from their artificial framework and are able, on the basis of literary and physical characteristics, to ascertain approximately their ages. To be sure, this is not always possible, but often it is. They have thus found that most of the parables of Jesus belong to one of the oldest layers.

This is also true of the paradigms, described by Dibelius as short narrations "not designed to satisfy the curious, but to serve the pious" (33/312). They can often be found in a word of Jesus. An example is the blessing of the children in Mark. The kernel of the portrayal is the word of Jesus: "Let the children come to me, do not hinder them; for to such belongs the kingdom of God" (Mark 10 : 14). The questions of the curious remain unanswered: "Where was Jesus? In a house or on the street? Who brought the children? Why did the disciples want to prevent the children from coming to Jesus? Did Jesus appear to them too excited or too tired to be bothered by the children?" (Dibelius, 33/310f.).

Such paradigms are older than the "Novellen [which] are written in the style which is characteristic of non-Christian *events*" (Dibelius, 33/313). "The less a particular narrative resembles the form and technique of the customary style of narration, the more original its form is, the more certain is the assumption that it originated in the circles of the earliest Christian community; correspondingly the greater is its historical worth" (Dibelius, 35/36f.).

With every individual piece of material an attempt is

made to determine what meaning (*Sitz im Leben*) it may
have had in the message of Jesus or in the early Christian
community. Modern theologians, in countless cases, suppose or feel certain that the words of Jesus have been
omitted, changed, completed, or created according to the
actual situation and the tasks of preaching, of mission, and
of congregational life. The community, says New Testament scholar Käsemann of Tübingen, "if it was indeed
concerned not with the reproduction of a notable happening, but with that decision between faith and unbelief
which was demanded of it, had no alternative but to act
as it did. . . . By acting as it did the community bore
(and still bears) witness to history as being living and
contemporary. It interprets out of its own experience what
for it has already become mere history . . ." (56/20).

A classic example of an event created for the glorifica-
tion of Christ is, for many theologians, the birth narrative
found in Matthew. Almost every detail—the unrest of the
ruler, the advice of the wise men, the murder of the
children, the miraculous escape, the flight into Egypt—is
reported about Jesus with striking similarity to the older
report about Moses. "Because Jesus is the future Saviour,
the traditional and given scheme can be transferred to
him and the events surrounding his birth and infancy must
correspond to the stories already in existence concerning
Moses. In this way an 'historification' of mythical material
is arrived at" (Käsemann, 56/26). And even Bethlehem
is, according to New Testament scholar Hans Conzelmann
of Göttingen, "not the historical place of Jesus' birth, but
a place postulated on the basis of a specific christology"
(32/626). Conzelmann's main argument is that in the
earliest Gospel (Mark) Jesus is always called "Jesus of
Nazareth" (1 : 9; 1 : 24; 10 : 47; 14 : 67; 16 : 6).

On the other hand, Bergmann says: "In the 'Confession
Movement,' with regard to Bethlehem, we are dealing with

the report of a fact, not of a legend" (99/39). And in another place he writes: "I should be happy to allow myself to be laughed at for the sake of this naïveté" (14/59).

THE QUEST FOR THE SITZ IM LEBEN

At first it may seem as though little has changed in theology, for words and miracles of Jesus were in past decades and centuries also declared to be unhistorical. And is it perhaps also true that almost every modern theologian has his own picture of Jesus, that there are therefore about as many pictures of Jesus as there are chairs of New Testament? Occasionally this impression has arisen, and the leader of the Confession Movement seems to be interested in strengthening this impression.

Yet such opinions do not reflect the actual situation. To be sure, there are a huge number of diverse conceptions and interpretations of individual Bible verses and individual words and deeds of Jesus. For instance, the literature concerning the famous word to Peter out of the Gospel of Matthew ("You are Peter, and on this rock I will build my church . . ." Matt. 16 : 18), which even long ago would have filled books, grows continually. But neither the methods of research of modern theologians nor their goals can be compared with those of the earlier liberal generations of theologians.

The first difference is that with the form-critical method statements concerning the historical genuineness or lack of genuineness of a word of Jesus, or of a particular Bible verse, are not said to be of primary importance; they are rather a byproduct of work which serves primarily to determine the *Sitz im Leben* of single situations. It is of importance for contemporary preaching to determine what place a text had in the preaching of the primitive Christian community. The Bible can no more be handled today as a book fallen from heaven than the tradition concerning Jesus could at that time be passed on to others as though it were an essentially undamaged relic.

Another difference is that modern theologians do not attempt, as did their liberal forefathers, to make of a reconstructed picture of the historical Jesus an object of faith alongside the picture of Christ which has impressed itself on Christian dogma. According to Bultmann, "historical science can in general not lead to any result which can serve as a foundation for faith, because all its results have only relative value" (23/3). And there are few theologians who stress the meaning of the kerygma as decisively as does Bultmann and who see to it that the witnesses to this kerygma—the texts of the New Testament—are not used as sources for the reconstruction of the historical Jesus. It is Bultmann's view that "in the Christian message . . . there is absolutely no question of man's being given an historical account of a section of the past, which he might put to the test, or critically affirm or reject. He is told, on the contrary, that in what happened then, whatever the circumstances, God has acted, and that through this action of his the Word of divine judgment and forgiveness which now confronts him is authenticated; this action of God's is to be interpreted as the actual establishment of this Word—as the proclamation of this Word itself. No science of history can verify this assertion —either to confirm or reject it, for it is beyond the sphere of historical observation to say that in this Word and its proclamation God has acted" (24/18).

The historical Jesus, for whom liberal theologians have searched in vain for decades (Albert Schweitzer wrote about the *Quest of the Historical Jesus* in a book which is now justly famous), has, according to Bultmann, virtually no significance for faith. In any case, it is sufficient for faith to know "the incarnation and the early life of Jesus as bare facts" (29/203), as Bultmann stresses again and again in other places.

That which Karl Barth and Rudolf Bultmann once wrote about "the quest of the historical Jesus" may still be true today. Karl Barth said that "critical–historical study means the deserved and necessary finish to the 'fundamentals' of this understanding [of the person of Jesus Christ], which are nothing because they are not given by God himself." Whoever does not yet know (and we always know not *yet*), that we know Christ *no* longer according to the flesh, it may be said of that person in regard to critical and scientific study of the Bible: "the more radically he is frightened the better it is for him and for the whole situation" (7/13). And Bultmann says: "I have never felt uncomfortable in my critical radicalism, but rather entirely at ease. But I often have the impression that my conservative colleagues in New Testament studies feel considerably uncomfortable, because I see them constantly engaged in rescue work. I let it burn peacefully, for I see that that which burns is all fantasy-pictures of the life-of-Jesus-theology, that is, the Christ according to the flesh. But the Christ according to the flesh is irrelevant for us; I do not know and do not care to know the inner secrets of the heart of Jesus" (23/101).

THE MESSAGE OF JESUS IS FOR THE MOST PART
NOT AUTHENTIC

Through the work of the form-critics it was pointed out, according to Käsemann, "that the message of Jesus presented by the synoptic Gospels is for the most part not authentic, but is stamped by the faith of the primitive Christian in its various stages"; the real Jesus tradition is "received only as embedded in the preaching of primitive

Christianity and superimposed by it" (57/188). "Only a few words of the Sermon on the Mount and of the conflict with the Pharisees, a number of parables and some scattered material of various kinds go back with any real degree of probability to the Jesus of history himself" (56/59f.).

To what degree the words of Jesus in the Gospels are genuine is, to be sure, also debated by the modern theologians. Yet the discussion is often made too simple. Among the opponents of modern theology there is made reference almost exclusively to differences in judgment, and in most cases no attention is given to the *grounds* on which the words of Jesus are taken to be unauthentic. We want, therefore, to attempt to make up for this omission with two examples.

Bultmann assigns the following verses, among others, to those pieces which "have been made into dominical sayings in the tradition" (22/102): "For what does it profit a man, to gain the whole world and forfeit his life?" (Mark 8 : 36); "Salt is good; but if the salt has lost its saltness, how will you season it? Have salt in yourselves, and be at peace with one another!" (Mark 9 : 50); "Do not give dogs what is holy; and do not throw your pearls before swine, lest they trample them under foot and turn to attack you" (Matt. 7 : 6); "So be wise as serpents" (Matt. 10 : 16); "So whatever you wish that men would do to you, do so to them; for this is the law and the prophets" (Matt. 7 : 12); "For everyone who exalts himself will be humbled, and he who humbles himself will be exalted (Luke 14 : 11); "He who is faithful in a very little is faithful also in much; and he who is dishonest in a very little is dishonest also in much" (Luke 16 : 10). As a basis for his judgment Bultmann says: "These sayings are hardly if at all characteristic of a new and individual piety that sprang up in Judaism, but are observations on life, rules of prudence and popular morality, sometimes a product of humor or skepticism, full now of sober, popular morality, and now of naive egoism" (22/104).

DID JESUS PREDICT HIS DEATH?

With particular frequency modern theologians are criticized because they, almost without exception, explain the predictions of the passion as supplementary creations of the primitive Christian community. There are the three places in Mark: "The Son of man must suffer many things, and be rejected by the elders and the chief priests and the scribes, and be killed, and after three days rise again" (Mark 8 : 31); "The Son of man will be delivered into the hands of men, and they will kill him; and when he is killed, after three days he will rise" (Mark 9 : 31); "Behold, we are going up to Jerusalem; and the Son of man will be delivered to the chief priests and the scribes, and they will condemn him to death, and deliver him to the Gentiles" (Mark 10 : 33).

The most important grounds for considering these predictions to be unauthentic are the following: The predictions are not yet contained in the source Q, but are first found in Mark and are therefore relatively late. The predictions in the other synoptic Gospels deviate from those in Mark; they presuppose a detailed knowledge of the passion and of the resurrection and stand therefore in contradiction to the resurrection reports in which the Easter events are described as something thoroughly surprising, something which the disciples could scarcely comprehend (cf. Pannenberg, 73/245).

Has now Bultmann, who is probably the most radical critic, obliterated most of the words of Jesus? Has a word which he considers to be unauthentic therefore become meaningless for him?

For modern theologians, the results of their work have a significance quite other than they do for their conservative Christian opponents and for non-Christians—two groups not usually spoken of in the same breath. But non-Christians and conservative Christians are equally convinced that a word which Jesus has not apparently spoken is of less importance than another which he probably or even certainly has spoken.

Bultmann and the other modern theologians disagree. For the Marburg scholar there is no contradiction in supposing, on the one hand as a researcher, that Matthew 11 : 28ff. ("Come to me, all who labor and are heavy laden, and I will give you rest . . .") is a "quotation from Jewish Wisdom literature put into the mouth of Jesus" (22/160) and, on the other hand as a preacher, in preaching on this text in Marburg without even mentioning any doubt as to its historicity. In the pulpit he says simply that it is "the word of Jesus" (28/85). In another place he stresses that it is of particular importance to him whether words, "even if they may formally be constructions of the community, actually reproduce in an appropriate way the views of Jesus" (23/193).

Other modern theologians express themselves in a similar way. Thus Zahrnt says: "The historically unauthentic passages need not necessarily be theologically inauthentic, but can present a legitimate exposition of the historically authentic. Therefore I can in good conscience also preach on so-called historically inauthentic texts" (93/101). Even "a saying which Jesus never spoke," says the American New Testament scholar James M. Robinson, "may well reflect accurately his historical significance, and in this sense be more 'historical' than many irrelevant things Jesus actually said" (80/99n).

The conservative theologian Bo Reicke of Basel, on the other hand, considers the selection of ungenuine words of Jesus to be almost a sacrilege: It will not do "to so limit the revelation and reality of God" (79/217). Künneth of Erlangen is also critical, saying that it evokes "the impres-

sion of the plainly chaotic position of a bankrupt under-
taking" (63/144).

However critically modern theologians may make judgments about the genuineness of the tradition, their faith is
not challenged by it. Marxsen writes: "I will not be
dictated to by historical research concerning what can and
what cannot be valid as a theologically correct expression"
(65/30), which is to say, as Bultmann continually emphasizes: Not the Jesus of history but the Christ of faith is the
Lord.

THE SOVEREIGNTY AND CLAIM OF JESUS

Yet, concerning the problem of whether the historical
Jesus is to be so separated from the Christ of faith, Bultmann seems to be in threefold opposition to his own students. Contested first of all is the manner in which the historical Jesus is to be classified (whether to late Judaism or
not); second, in which sphere the historical Jesus *can* still be
recognized; and third, if and how one *may* ask about the
historical Jesus at all. So it would appear, at any rate, if
one reads the works of Bultmann, Käsemann, Bornkamm,
Ebeling, and others.

Bultmann asks: "Was Jesus—the historical Jesus!—then
a Christian? Now if Christian faith is faith in him as the
Christ, then certainly not. . . . As an historical figure he
stands within Judaism" (21/8). On the other hand, Käsemann writes that "he cannot be integrated into the background of the Jewish piety of his time" (56/38).

Bultmann is of the opinion that we know "almost nothing" concerning the personality of Jesus (26/8). "The
character of Jesus, the plain picture of his personality and
of his life is for us no longer recognizable." On the other
hand, Günther Bornkamm writes that "the Gospels justify
neither resignation nor skepticism. Rather they bring before our eyes, in very different fashion from what is cus-

tomary in chronicles and presentations of history, the historical person of Jesus with utmost vividness. Quite clearly what the Gospels report concerning the message, the deeds and the history of Jesus is still distinguished by an authenticity, a freshness, and a distinctiveness not in any way effaced by the Church's Easter faith. These features point us directly to the earthly figure of Jesus" (18/24).

Bultmann says: "One may . . . not go back behind the kerygma, using it as a 'source' in order to reconstruct a 'historical Jesus' with his 'messianic consciousness,' his 'inwardness' or his 'heroism' . . ." (23/208). On the contrary Ebeling says: "The strange dogma has spread abroad that we must not seek for the historical Jesus beyond the New Testament witness. Who, then, is going to forbid it?" (38/205). And Bornkamm writes: "But it cannot be seriously maintained that the Gospels and their tradition do not allow enquiry after the historical Jesus. Not only do they allow, they demand this effort" (18/22).

We do not wish to investigate how great this opposition actually is. Nor do we wish to examine whether those people are justified in pointing to the contradiction between Bultmann's *dogmatic* interest in rejecting every historical securing of the kerygma and his own extensive pursuit of historical–critical studies. In any case, whatever Bultmann accomplishes in this area serves, not the historical securing of the kerygma, but the destruction of any previously alleged security.

We are much more interested in investigating which picture of the historical Jesus the modern theologians reject. Bultmann states: "With agreed precaution, one will be able to say the following concerning the works of Jesus. Characteristic for him are exorcisms, the breaking of Sabbath laws, the violation of purification prescriptions, the polemic against Jewish legalism, association with low-class persons such as tax collectors and prostitutes, the affection for women and children. Also it is to be recognized that Jesus was not an ascetic as was John the Baptist, but enjoyed eating, and drinking a glass of wine. Perhaps one may also add that he called men to discipleship, and and gathered around himself a small group of followers, both men and women. . . . [No doubt Jesus also appeared] in the consciousness that he was commissioned by God to proclaim the eschatological message of the in-breaking lordship of God, and the demanding but also inviting will of God. One will therefore assign to him a prophetic consciousness, even a consciousness of full power and authority" (21/11).

If one compares the conclusion to which Ernst Käsemann comes with Bultmann's result, then one gains the impression that both agree on essential points. Käsemann says that there is "common exegetical agreement" that of the antitheses in the Sermon on the Mount *only the following are authentic*: "But I say to you that every one who is angry with his brother shall be liable to the judgment . . ." (Matt. 5 : 22); the second: "But I say to you that every one who looks at a woman lustfully has already committed adultery with her in his heart . . ." (Matt. 5 : 28); and the fourth: "But I say to you, Do not swear at all . . ." (Matt. 5 : 34). With his "But I say," Jesus ". . . claims an authority rivalling and challenging Moses [and] has *ipso facto* set himself above Moses; he has ceased to be a rabbi, for a rabbi's authority only comes to him as derived from Moses." Jesus "certainly . . . was a Jew and made the assumptions of Jewish piety, but at the same time he shatters this framework with his claim." Independent of whether he designated himself as Messiah or not, it is "the only category which does justice to his claim." Even the attitude of Jesus to Sabbath laws and purification rites shows that "we can hardly say here that Jesus has left the law as such untouched and merely made its demands more radical. . . . Jesus felt himself in a position to override, with an unparalleled and sovereign freedom, the words of the Torah and the authority of Moses" (56/37f., 40).

Most contemporary theologians are of the same opinion. Ernst Fuchs, for instance, states that Jesus' conduct was "neither that of a prophet nor that of a wisdom teacher, but the conduct of a man who dared to act in the place of God" (41a/156).

IS FAITH A QUANTITY OF SENTENCES?

Modern and conservative theologians cannot agree at the present time on what Christian faith is. Gerhard Ebeling, a theologian of the Bultmann school, formulates, in a slightly exaggerated way, the position of his opponents in these words: "Faith would then be, if I may say so, an empty sack whose nature it is to serve as a container for specific objects. If it contains the prescribed objects of faith, then it is Christian faith. If it contains them complete and undamaged, then it is orthodox Christian faith. But if only a few meagre objects are contained in it, and moreover not in quite correct form, then the faith is in a bad way. For the essential thing about faith is its content. He who is in earnest about faith is intent on filling the sack full . . ." (37/19).

This distinction is not made by modern theologians who want to require only a smaller quantity of sentences in which to believe. It has much more to do with the attempt to show that "faith is something qualitatively different from the acceptance of a larger or smaller quantity of sentences" (Bultmann, 54/61).

Above all—and here the differing views meet one another most decisively—the content of faith consists for modern theologians not of this. The statements of the confession of faith must be accepted as true. "Whoever therefore asks another: 'Do you believe in the virgin birth?' and then disputes the faith of him who does not answer with a spontaneous 'Yes'—and this does happen —this one has not understood that the Apostles' Creed presents us with no doctrine to be believed, that it rather wants to bring to light the God revealed to man in Christ as his lord. But this is precisely what does not happen where a man ties down another with isolated statements" (Rainer Schmidt. *Deutschen Pfarrerblatt* 8 (1966), p. 215). "According to the Reformation view," says Hermann Diem, the confession is "always a human construct, an attempt to express the Gospel, which requires constant checking and touching-up" (36/153).

Yet it is not enough to demolish the concept of faith held by one theologian with the criticism of another. What do modern theologians say about their own concept of faith? Manfred Mezger, a professor of practical theology, points up the distinction in this way: "Many live in the illusion that the true unity of the church would be won if the great majority of Christians would agree to the same dogmatic formula. But identity of dogmatic formulas is of no importance. There must be unity in faith, that is, *in unconditioned trust in the Word of God* [italics mine]. Each one may say it and confess it as he wishes." And Heinrich Ott defines faith as "an existential movement which has to do with man as a totality, in which man is engaged as an entire person, not only the understanding, not only the feeling, but the entire human being in all its dimensions" (86/2 : 42).

Since at this point the debate is far from a genuine conversation in which each side attempts to gain a proper understanding of the other's position, it seems to be appropriate to allow Bultmann to express himself in a detailed way. Few others have expressed themselves about the nature of faith as frequently as he. "Faith is the attitude opposed to that urge for recognition—the radical abandonment of self-glorification, of the desire for recognition by one's own strength and achievement. It is the knowledge that the recognition which makes him secure for himself and in the presence of God can only be gifted" (24/171). "Faith is not a trust in God in general terms— that is that God will help me here and there, in this and that—but it is radical surrender to God's will, which is unknown to me before it happens . . ." (24/175). Faith is not "the gathering of information concerning facts about the world or a declaration of the will, a noteworthy teaching, a dogma which is to be accepted as true. But it is the obedience which obeys God not in general or in the abstract but in the Now" (25/30). Faith does not have "the unequivocal character of a spiritual or psychical attitude; it is not a conviction about general ('eternal') truths, not a once-for-all acceptance of a dogma. Man does not gain through faith a quality to which he can appeal. He cannot appeal to the fact that he believes, but he can only believe again and again,—*may* believe again and again" (23/148). "Faith (the *fides qua creditur*) is the obedient hearing of the word—the word, namely, that I am a sinner and that God in Christ forgives me my sin. Faith is a free act of decision" (23/101).

Bultmann has often stressed that faith must carry "an element of uncertainty in itself" (23/152). He has been and is suspected of robbing faith of all supports, on the basis of an unwritten dogma that faith may not be made secure. Faith may not be a work ("in the case of the 'work' I remain the man I am" 24/175) which can make men righteous before God. "Man always has"—Bultmann emphasizes again and again—"empty hands before God" (27/100). "Men spoil their relation to God because they are not prepared to confess what they truly are in the sight of God: worthless creatures who have nothing which they did not receive from Him, creatures whose lives are without any content or meaning apart from His grace, and who must flee again and again to His grace in order to have any value, creatures who can receive from Him alone that meaningfulness which frees them from the tense struggle to assert their value" (28/132).

Is there any chance that Protestant Christians can achieve a unity concerning what faith is? If any word from a theologian can be of any help, then it is a sentence of Gerhard Ebeling, who seems to think it through from both sides: "For that reason it is a basic presupposition of theological thinking that the question of faith is neither put in the form: what must I believe?—that would be making faith a law to reason—nor yet in the form: what can I believe?—that would be making reason a law to faith. The question of faith must rather be, to turn again to Bonhoeffer's own words: 'What do we really believe—i.e. in such a way as to stake our whole lives upon it?'" (38/118).

IS GOD ALIVE OR IS HE DEAD?

Conservative and modern theologians seem to be in agreement, nevertheless, that "faith must understand God as person," that faith "cannot be faith at all apart from personal encounter with God" (Ott, 86/2 : 43).

Yet this commonalty does not include everyone. At least Herbert Braun, professor of New Testament at Mainz, has given up this point of view. "The New Testament," Braun writes, "reckons naively with the existence of a deity, as does the Old Testament, and Jewish literature, and for the most part also Hellenistic literature. It is therefore separated from us, for we are no longer capable of making this presupposition" (19/325). For Braun, God is no longer "an object who has and who maintains a secure place in a metaphysic of transcendence, guaranteed by a conservative world view. God becomes 'my' God; the whence of my 'I ought' and of my 'I may.' If I hear and understand the New Testament, I realize: it is correct when it fastens this transformation of God to Jesus of Nazareth. In communication with this happening, which is reflected in the New Testament—though through many layers of materials, often encoded in ancient forms of thought—I grasp how true it is that no one comes to the Father, but through Jesus (John 14 : 6). Here the objective metaphysical God becomes my God, the whence of my obligation and of my action. How insignificant in the light of this happening does the atheistic position appear, but also how insipid that which calls itself traditional Theism!" (19/298).

This sentence has made its author famous/infamous. He seems to bring theology (talk about God) to an end. Another passage that has become famous/infamous is here cited and left to the judgment of the reader. "God means the whence of my resolve. But my resolve is characterized by the 'I may' and the 'I ought,' characterized by security and by obligation. Security and obligation, however, come to me not out of the cosmos but from the other, from the neighbour; the word of preaching and the deed of love also reach me, yes really reach me, through the neighbour. God is the whence of my security and of my obligation through the neighbour. . . . I can only speak of God where I speak of man, therefore anthropologically . . . man as man, man in his common humanity, implies God. Out of the New Testament that is discovered over and over again. God would then be a distinct form of co-humanity. The atheist denies *man*. One could well ask: Is there any atheist after all? For does not every genuine experience of humanity already contain something of the oscillation between the 'I may' and the 'I ought' which lies so close to the heart of the New Testament?" (19/341). As Gollwitzer believes, it seems that Braun comes out "without Word and act of God in any serious sense of the term, without revelation and faith in a Lord who encounters us in concrete ways" (50/37). "God and Jesus are dissolved in a humanism for which the New Testament and the proclamation can at most have an anamnestic function" (50/93).

One may well ask whether it does not become completely insignificant what a Christian thinks about the virgin birth and the miracles of Jesus, about the crucifixion and the resurrection, in the light of a position such as Braun's. Is it not even completely insignificant whether Jesus ever lived? In any case, it seems that the current debate concerning Jesus would be completely superfluous if Braun's theology were representative of everyone in the Bultmann school (which, as we have seen, is not the case). The discussion with Braun on this one point and the discussion between modern theologians and parish Christians on the other points are two different things.

3. Catholics and
Biblical Criticism

Is THE OPPOSITION between modern theology and congregational piety also present in the Catholic church? One would tend to think that it is not because there is almost no indication of it that is publicly noticeable. Yet the Catholic dogmatician Josef Rupert Geiselmann of Tübingen wrote in 1965: "Even in university circles, one may suggest only once in a sermon or a lecture a picture of the man Jesus as it confronts us in the Synoptic gospels, and immediately the *sensus fidelium* becomes restless, and there is doubt as to whether the preacher or the speaker still believes in the deity of Christ. So infested is the faith with Monophysitism" (44/17).

And in *Stimmen der Zeit*, Albrecht Locher stated in 1966 that "the typical Catholic believer locates the person —the life, suffering, and death—of the Lord not in the concrete historical reality which he also experiences, but rather in a kind of sacred sphere for which the claim of reality is not made, or is only casually made." One could even "go farther and say that the picture that many believers have of the person and work of Jesus would prove to be heretical, if it could be determined with sufficient precision. The result of such a view is not a man among men, not our brother, subjected as we are to the concrete conditions of human life, but basically a god walking among men. A picture of Christ develops which is loaded with docetic and monophysitic tendencies" (108/220).

We should like to try to state first of all the extent to which Catholic theology has embraced modern historical–critical methods of research.

For a long time the form-critical method was practiced only by Protestant theologians. This is no longer true. Anton Vögtle writes: "The renewal of Catholic exegesis, the general revolution in New Testament research which has become evident particularly since the Second World War, has led in one sphere to mutually accepted methods and results, which a generation ago could scarcely be imagined. In more than one case realization has broken through that contrasts and fences were previously seen where in reality there were none, and that the New Testament appeals to facts which obligate every confession to critical scrutiny of its self-understanding" (16/47). This also affects Protestant theologians. "Whereas there were insurmountable barriers, today we work together," writes Günther Bornkamm, professor of New Testament at Heidelberg. "Instead of a direct opposition, or even a carefully separated association, we now have a highly intensive cooperation, in which one can no longer do without the other, and no longer wants to do without the other" (16/36). Bornkamm refers to the "fact that Catholic and Protestant biblical research were bound together, as a matter of fact, through nothing other than the axioms and methods of historical–critical biblical research, which today is so often despised" (16/38).

The opinion is widespread that the doctrine of divine inspiration of Holy Scriptures is an obstacle for Catholic research. Yet there is much to support the conviction that this opinion has to do rather with the prejudice of the ignorant than with any considered judgment.

Concerning the *doctrine*, Cardinal Bea writes: "Every biblical book is, in form and content, determined by the will of God which so makes use of the holy writer that he writes that and only that which God wills, and as God wills it. The holy writer, however, is not a mere mechanical instrument which writes according to dictation. Rather God works on the writer in such a way that he, with full insight, free will, and full use of his individual talents and powers, writes down that which God wills and as He wills it" (96/705). Concerning the *practice*, Karl Rahner, professor of theology at the University of Munich, writes: "To be honest, we must confess that, on the average, Roman Catholic Scripture scholars, although by no means denying or doubting the inspiration of the Bible, prefer not to touch it at all in their exegetical work. Perhaps they act as if it had little bearing on the performance of their tasks as exegetes" (74/6).

The Catholic exegete did not always have this freedom. The Pontifical Biblical Commission, which enjoys great respect today in both churches, was founded during the struggle against modernism in the Catholic church. In the first years of its existence, the Biblical Commission put out countless decrees in which it, for the most part, rejected theses of historical–critical scholars. Witness the comment of the Jesuit New Testament scholar Norbert Lohfink in 1966: "The situation was perhaps never as unpleasant as in the first decades of our century, for in previous centuries most Catholic biblical scholars were still able to reject the historical–critical method in good faith. That was now no longer the case. Whoever did not want to violate his conscience had to go into the scientific underground and to develop his secret teaching, which could not be presented to the Catholic public or even taught to theological students" (109/334).

EARLIER THESES WITHDRAWN?

One does not, of course, have to go back into the first years of this century. Right into the thirties and forties, interpretations prevailed which today are more or less thoroughly rejected by Catholic theologians. In the publishing houses today, works of Catholic authors, written in the old spirit, stand next to those of modern theologians who are of very different opinions concerning many problems in the New Testament. The development which has come to pass in a relatively short time in Catholic theology becomes clearest if one compares expressions of an earlier time with those of the present. The opinions which Catholic dogmaticians and New Testament scholars publish today sound in part like a withdrawing of that which their colleagues wrote earlier.

We compare first an opinion which Pius X condemned in the year 1907 with a statement which the New Testament scholar Karl Hermann Schelkle of Tübingen wrote in 1963. Condemned was the statement: "John's accounts are not really history but a mystical contemplation of the Gospel. The statements contained in his Gospel are theological meditations about the mystery of salvation, devoid of historical truth" (70/72). Schelkle: "The Gospel of John no longer describes the historical life of Jesus. But the Gospel presents those conditions which had developed at the end of the first century when it was written" (83/86). Now it is true that Schelkle does not maintain that the speeches in the Gospel of John are "devoid of historical truth." Yet, in spite of that, one can easily surmise that at an earlier date such a statement would have fallen under the judgment of the pope.

The development becomes even clearer with another example. In 1941, Professor Joseph Ricciotti of Rome wrote about the four Gospels in the most successful book on the life of Jesus of this century; a book which appeared with the imprimatur of the Vatican. Ricciotti said: "All of them were eyewitnesses of the deeds of Jesus" (78/101). On the other hand, Vögtle wrote in 1965 that of the authors of the Gospels probably "not one was an eyewitness of Jesus" (115/1257).

In 1933, Karl Adam, dogmatician at Tübingen, asserted that the evangelists maintained "fidelity to Jesus, which made them take anxious care that nothing should be added to or subtracted from the words of the Lord current in their midst. Their historical fidelity was the expression of their faith in Jesus" (1/69). On the other hand, in 1965, Geiselmann, also a Tübingen dogmatician (who, to be sure, in the book here cited, namely, *Die Frage nach dem Historischen Jesus*, did not distinguish sharply between the material of other Catholic theologians and his own argumentation), wrote: "The evangelists transposed the words of Jesus into the community situation of that time, expanded it, and formed it when necessary" (44/181).

In 1933, Adam praised the evangelists for their "faithfulness to tradition, extending to the smallest element, the last word. It reveals the anxious pains which the evangelists took to reproduce the deposit of tradition current in the Christian communities, in so far as it contained Apostolic reminiscences" (1/66f.). "The literary personality of the evangelist counts for nothing; the matter delivered is everything" (1/64). On the other hand, Geiselmann wrote in 1965, for example, concerning the distinction between Mark and Luke: "Luke therefore already takes up the brush to paint the apostles as saints. With Mark they are men with weaknesses and strengths" (44/168).

In 1933, Adam wrote that John is the evangelist who "contemplates the interior life of Jesus, with whom his spirit was so interwoven that his very language involuntarily became that of the Master" (1/71). It is in quite a different mood that Schelkle wrote in 1963: "In John the stories are written in the same style as are the speeches of Jesus . . . even John the Baptist speaks in this style in the Fourth Gospel (1 : 29–34; 3 : 27–32). The style is therefore peculiar to the evangelist, even if it is also not totally foreign to Jesus. But the evangelist uses this style exclusively and he allows Jesus also to always think and to speak in this way" (83/84). In 1924, August Reatz, professor of theology at Mainz, wrote about the Sermon on the Mount that it is a "notable speech which he (Jesus) addressed to the Galilean people on the mountain in the northwest region of the Sea of Galilee" (76/61). In 1941, Ricciotti figured that the Sermon on the Mount, according to the text in Matthew, had lasted "about 20 minutes" (78/32). In 1963, Schelkle wrote: "Matthew has created large and impressive speeches out of the words and stories of Jesus which were delivered to him" (83/50).

Hilarin Felder of Freiburg wrote in 1920: "The evangelists lead us into all the places where the Lord walked; they accompany us into every village and city where he preached, into the desert places and on the mountains where he prayed, into the houses and into the places where he healed the sick and raised the dead" (40/212). On the other hand, Vögtle wrote in 1960: "The itinerary of Jesus, although a few places and areas are named, can unfortunately no longer be reconstructed."

In 1933, Adam wrote: "In this chapter we shall attempt a simple description of the interior religious life of our Lord's human soul. . . . We want to discover what holy, quickening forces, what impelling religious conceptions were at work in that miraculous human figure, which so far we have considered only in its formal, mental, and ethical aspects. We want to discover what it was that dominated and animated him" (1/134). Schelkle wrote in 1963: "To wish to fathom and describe Jesus psychologically means to wish to grasp him and explain him, and that means to place one's self above him" (83/61f.).

Concerning the announcement of Jesus that he would rise on the third day, Felder states: "Jesus had repeatedly instructed even the Pharisees about that. When they demanded from him a miracle from heaven he said: '. . . for as Jonah was three days and three nights in the belly of the whale, so will the Son of man be three days and three nights in the heart of the earth'" (40/159). (Felder referred to Matt. 12 : 40.) On the other hand, Geiselmann writes: "The sign of Jonah has been interpreted subsequently, in the light of the salvation event which has now happened" (44/186).

MUCH THAT JESUS DID NOT KNOW

The Holy Office decided in 1918 that "the view of many newer theologians about the limited knowledge of the mind of Christ is not permitted in the Catholic schools" (44/227). In 1961, Karl Rahner wrote: "Why then should we dogmatic theologians restrain exegetes from saying in a true sense (without of course covering even then the totality of Christ's reality) that Jesus did not know certain things—since he himself has said so (Mark 13 : 32) and we do not have any real reason to try to explain such statements away by clever distinctions" (75/82). About the same time, Geiselmann wrote: "First of all let it be said that the decree of the Holy Office is not a matter of an infallible decision. It is certain that the man Jesus, through the hypostatic union, did not become all-knowing. . . . With his human nature it is . . . given that his knowledge as a man, corresponding to his nature, is finite and remains finite" (44/227).

In 1924, Reatz wrote concerning Jesus: "Neither the contemporary philosophers nor the learned rabbis . . .

were his teachers. He remained independent of every school and every line of doctrinal interpretation. That is his uniqueness. We also observe in him not the slightest clue of a gradual development." Similarly, Karl Adam wrote in 1933 "that from the first moment of his public ministry [Jesus was characterized by an] unfaltering certainty, and with a certainty that admitted of no further growth" (1/179). In 1961, Karl Rahner wrote: "To affirm true development, true independence of the religious milieu of his time, unexpected turns in the life of Jesus 'is the right of every Catholic exegete.' "

Catholic New Testament scholars publish in their technical journals works which—if they had been written by Protestant theologians—would, without doubt, be sharply criticized by the leaders of the Confession Movement. So Vögtle defends the thesis that Jesus, prior to his death, spoke not a word of that passage on which the pope bases his priority: "And I tell you, you are Peter, and on this rock I will build my church, and the powers of death shall not prevail against it" (Matt. 16 : 18). Vögtle considers it probable that the risen Christ first spoke these words (116). And Vögtle considers it improbable that the risen Jesus spoke the mission-and-baptism command ("Go therefore and make disciples of all nations, baptizing them in the name of the Father and of the Son and of the Holy Spirit" [Matt. 28 : 19]).

Up until the most recent times, Jesus-research was a very dangerous field for Catholic theologians. The last major action of the Holy Office, which today is called the *Congregation for the Doctrine of the Faith*, demonstrates this. In 1961, it set on the *Index* a book about Jesus by the French abbey Jean Steinmann, eliminated from circulation a similar book appearing in Paris, and warned the exegetes with the following *monitum*:

"Along with the praiseworthy serious work of biblical science have been distributed in various areas thoughts and views which critically placed in question the true historical and objective truth of holy scripture. This applies not only to the Old Testament (as Pope Pius XII already deplored in his encyclical "Humani generis") but also the New Testament, even where it deals with the words and deeds of Jesus Christ. However, since priests and believers are alarmed with that kind of thought and view, the worthy fathers who are responsible for the protection of the faith and the moral life have found it necessary to admonish all those who concern themselves, either in speaking or in writing, with the holy books, to always deal with such important material with skill and wisdom and veneration. They are also admonished to have in their minds at all times the teachings of the Holy Fathers, the interpretation of the Church and the Teaching Office, so that the conscience of believers is not confused and the truths of faith not damaged."

Preceding this *monitum* there had been a controversy carried on in technical publications between teachers of the Lateran University and those of the Pontifical Biblical Institute in Rome, which also allows one to appreciate some of the moot points with regard to the statement about Peter in the sixteenth chapter of the Gospel of Matthew (the Vögtle article, already referred to, appeared before the admonition) concerning the historicity of the appearances of the risen Christ, his ascension, and the birth narratives recorded by Matthew and Luke (114/59ff.).

The *monitum* of the Holy Office was followed in April, 1964, by an *Instruction Concerning the Historical Truth of the Gospel*, released by the Pontifical Biblical Commission. Here quite another note was sounded. The document spoke this way concerning the form-critical method: "As occasion warrants, the interpreter may examine what sound elements are contained in the 'Form Critical method' that can be used for a fuller understanding of the Gospels. But let him be wary, because scarcely admissible philosophical and theological principles have often come to be mixed with this method, which not uncommonly have vitiated the method itself as well as the conclusions in the literary area" (13/82). There is a warning against those who "begin with a false idea of faith, as if it had nothing to do with historical truth," and against those who exaggerate the "creative power of the community" (13/82). Cardinal Bea writes in his commentary on the document that "the Christian community is not an anonymous community, but one which is *well known to us, guided by the apostles* or authorized eyewitnesses" (13/22). But at the same time the Catholic exegete is encouraged "never to lose heart in explaining the divine word and in solving the difficulties proposed to him. Rather, let him strive earnestly to open up still more the real meaning of the Scriptures." According to a word of Pius XII, other Catholics are requested to judge this work "not only with equity and justice, but also with the greatest charity." And they are pointed to the fact that "even illustrious interpreters, such as Jerome himself, tried at times to explain the more difficult questions with no great success (13/79f.).

In the "Instruction" it is stressed that "when the Lord was orally explaining his doctrine, he followed the modes of reasoning and of exposition which were in vogue at the time," and that the apostles also "accommodated themselves to the mentality of their listeners" (13/82f.). The commission also stresses that there "is no reason to deny" that the apostles reported the words and deeds of Jesus "with that fuller understanding" which came to them "after Jesus rose from the dead and his divinity was clearly perceived" (13/83). In addition to that, "from what they had received, the sacred writers above all selected the things which were suited to the various situations of the faithful and to the purpose which they had in mind, and adapted their narration of them to the same situations and purpose. . . . The truth of the story is not at all affected by the fact that the evangelists relate the words and deeds of the Lord in a different order, and express his sayings not literally, but differently, while preserving (their) sense" (13/85f.).

THE BRAUNSCHWEIG THESES IN THE STYLE OF OTTAVIANI?

In another style, a style similar to the *monitum* of the Holy Office, was the first draft of the *Constitution on Revelation* which was offered to the Second Vatican Council. Condemned there were those who place in doubt the historical truth of the Gospel. Norbert Lohfink responded: "If this text were not to die, then Catholic exegesis would die" (117/181).

Thus began a vigorous discussion over this text, a discussion which extended to the last days of the council. The final statement concerning the New Testament reads this way (the italics were inserted shortly before the disbanding of the council in order to meet objections of the conservative minority): "The Holy Mother Church has firmly held fast and continues to hold fast to this, that the four Gospels, *to whose historicity it confesses unhesitatingly* [*quorum historicitatem incunctanter affirmat*], pass on reliably what Jesus, the Son of God, really did and taught in his life among men for their eternal salvation, until that day when he was received up." And further: "But the four evangelists have written the Holy Scriptures and thereby made a selection of many things already transmitted orally or even in written form. These items that they have selected have been put together by them and occasionally, in light of the situation of the Church, further developed. They have done everything in the form of preaching, yet always in such a way that they communicate to us what is true and worth believing about Jesus" (117/181).

With what care and energy the text was worked on and

argued about becomes evident in the conversation concerning the formula of inerrancy and the truth of the Bible. In the first major draft it still says: "Out of the fact that divine inspiration extends to everything in the Bible, there follows directly and necessarily the absolute inerrancy of the entire Holy Scripture." It is a "shameful error" to grant that the Holy Scripture has erred, since its inspiration excludes "every error in every religious or profane matter." The second draft says that God is the author of the entire Scripture and that therefore the entire Scripture must be absolutely free of every error. The third draft states: "The books of the scripture teach as a whole and in all their parts the truth without any error" (*sine ullo errore*).

Following the protests of countless bishops and a speech by Cardinal König, who counted off a few historical errors out of the Old and New Testaments, the last part of the sentence was changed to: ". . . the truth about what is necessary for salvation without any error." The conservative bishops, who saw in those words a limitation of biblical truth to questions concerning faith and moral life, protested against that change. The final text sent out from the council read: "Since therefore everything which the inspired editor or holy writer expressed is to be valued as expressed by the Holy Spirit, it is to be confessed that the books of the scripture teach with certainty, fidelity, and without error the truth which God wants to have set down in the Holy Scripture for the sake of our salvation" (117/18of.).

A Protestant theologian, Hans Geisser, has compared the first edition of the draft for the *Constitution on Revelation* (for which Curia Cardinal Alfredo Ottaviani assumed responsibility) with the eighteenth theses of the Braunschweig Church Meeting. He arrived at the opinion that they agree both in diction and in detail (102/50).

The limits that Catholic theologians set for themselves,

in the light of their allegiance to the wisdom of the teaching office of their church, can be seen in an article by Josef Schmid. On the one hand, he writes: "Biblical criticism is (as the art of the distinction of false and true, of spurious and genuine) the use of historical–critical method on the writings of Old and New Testament. It is a scientific method and carries no 'negative' attitude as over against the religious content of the Bible, nor does it deny its divine origin." Biblical criticism is "the presupposition of a relevant exegesis. Therefore, present-day biblical science rejects also that apologetic method, which merely wants to convey traditional opinion, as irrelevant and unfruitful." Biblical criticism "is capable of solving, through the illumination of the true intention of the biblical author, many problems which can bring a shock to the thinking reader. It therefore serves the renunciation of the heavy-handed method of a false apologetic."

On the other hand, however, Schmid states: "The biblical critic becomes a 'negative' critic at that point where he oversteps the limits of the historical–critical method, attacks the doctrinal content of the Bible as false on the basis of philosophical presuppositions, understands the Bible only as an ancient document of the history of religions, explains the religion of the Old Testament merely as a product of the Semitic spirit and the Christianity of the New Testament as a creation of Hellenistic syncretism, rejects *a priori*, the facticity of the biblical miracles, and represents the New Testament image of Christ as a mere creation of the faith of the primitive Christian community" (113).

4. Born of the
Virgin Mary

IN A WELL-KNOWN work entitled *Jungfrauensohn und Krippenkind* (1932), Martin Dibelius explained that the virgin birth is a legend which originated following the death of Jesus. Church historian Hans von Campenhausen of the University of Heidelberg came to the same conclusion in 1961 in a study entitled *Die Jungfrauengeburt in der Theologie der alten Kirche.*

The two scholars take their most important arguments from the Bible itself. In only two Gospels, Luke and Matthew, is the virgin birth reported. In Luke, in addition to the report of the virgin birth, there are two independent stories, one focusing on the Virgin Mary in which Joseph is mentioned only once as her betrothed (chap. 1), and a second, the so-called Christmas story (chap. 2). Here, according to Dibelius, Mary and Joseph "are introduced according to name, home, and descent, as if they had not yet been mentioned." And, when introduced, they are "parents in the full sense of the word, man and woman travelling together and living together, the young woman of the blessed womb confined at the end of their journey." Even the pictures given of Jesus are different. In the first story the son of the Virgin is proclaimed as the "eternal ruler from the throne of David." In the second he comes as the savior, whose "birth means joy to all people. Power there; salvation here!" The two stories are "competitors and have nothing to do with one another" (Dibelius, 33/9f.).

In order to bind them together, the evangelist undertook two corrections. In the first chapter he inserted Joseph in a single place (". . . betrothed to a man whose name was Joseph, of the house of David . . ." [Luke 1 : 27]), and in the second chapter, likewise in a single place, he refers to the wife of Joseph as his betrothed (". . . Mary, his betrothed . . ." [Luke 2 : 5]).

Dibelius verifies this thesis, which in the meantime has been adopted by many theologians, by referring to two inconsistencies in the first chapter. Mary answers the angel after the promise of the son: "How can this be, since I have no husband?" [German text: "know of no man" Translator] (Luke 1 : 34). To this Dibelius says: "This question is conceivable only if Mary knew no man at all with whom she could in the future have intercourse. A fiancée cannot speak in this way, can at least not be astonished over the fact that a son is promised to her by an angel." And the "question of how the fiancé reacts to the unborn child that is not his is not even mentioned" (33/11f.).

The second story also contains a contradiction as a result of the correction of the evangelist. Mary and Joseph as an engaged couple violate "all probability and the obvious sense of the narrative. They conduct themselves as a married couple" (Dibelius, 33/13). It is reported that Mary and Joseph make a journey together and that the pregnancy of Mary is "not characterized as something extraordinary, not produced by the spouse" (Dibelius, 33/54).

In the Gospel according to Matthew the virgin birth is reported in a style which, according to the conviction of Dibelius and Campenhausen, stems from a later tradition and therefore no longer contains this contradiction. The angel does not appear in order to announce the pregnancy

of Mary (as in Luke) but after Mary is already pregnant.
And he appears not to Mary but to Joseph, who experiences that his wife is pregnant "of the Holy Spirit" (Matt.
1 : 20) and proposes his plan "to divorce her quietly"
(Matt. 1 : 19). Dibelius comments on this passage:
"Joseph, who was betrothed to her but whom he had not
yet touched, must suppose that she has submitted herself
to a stranger. This suspicion is not spoken but clearly
presupposed. . . . The message of the angel . . . announces
the arrival and the name of the child" (33/23). According
to most Protestant New Testament scholars, the fatherless
birth recorded in both Matthew and in Luke stands in
contradiction to the family tree (Matt. 1 : 1–17; Luke
3 : 23–38), which is said to lead from David through
Joseph to Jesus. Campenhausen considers these genealo-
gies to be "early witnesses who do not seem to be aware
of the virgin birth, and who testify to Joseph as Jesus'
natural father. . . . Only in the last link in the chain
have the evangelists attempted an artificial twist by way
of correction, so as to accommodate it to the virgin birth"
(31/11f.)—Matthew with the verse: "Jacob the father of
Joseph the husband of Mary, of whom Jesus was born, who
is called Christ" (Matt. 1 : 16); Luke with the indication
that Jesus merely "was supposed" to be the son of Joseph
(Luke 3 : 23).

Karl Barth attempts, as do other theologians, to remove
this difficulty: "Although Jesus was not the physical or
natural, he was still the legitimate and legal son of Joseph
and therefore of David" (6/175). Campenhausen says
that "subsequent explanation . . . does not help; it is
simply a makeshift for which there is no adequate basis"
(31/11). Yet it is not only these contradictions to which
many Protestant theologians appeal when denying the
historicity of the virgin birth. According to Wolfhart Pannenberg, systematic theologian at the University of Mainz,
a broad spectrum of theologians share the opinion that the

reports of the virgin birth stand "in an irreconcilable contradiction to the Christology of the incarnation of the preexistent Son of God found in Paul and John. For, according to this legend, Jesus first became God's Son through Mary's conception. According to Paul and John, on the contrary, the Son of God was already preexistent and then as preexistent being had bound himself to the man Jesus" (73/143). Paul Althaus (the Erlangen professor of systematic theology who died in 1966) was of a similar opinion: "The christology which fits with the witnesses to the virgin birth knows nothing of pre-existence and the incarnation of a pre-existent, and the two great pre-existence christologies of the New Testament are silent about the virgin birth. This fact drives one to suspect that in the accounts of Matthew and of Luke we have to do not with witnesses of real happenings, but with a Christologumenon and that therefore the accounts are legends" (3/217).

JESUS OF NAZARETH, THE SON OF JOSEPH

The most important argument against the historicity of the virgin birth is that not only in Paul and John, but in the entire New Testament—apart from the aforementioned places in Luke and Matthew—the natural birth of Jesus is openly presupposed or even emphasized.

Reference to this is made by Paul, for instance, in the Epistle to the Romans ". . . his Son, who was descended from David according to the flesh" [Rom. 1 : 3]) and also in the Epistle to the Galatians ". . . God sent forth his Son, born of woman . . ." [Gal. 4 : 4]). According to Campenhausen, however—contrary to the position of numerous Protestant theologians—this text is not a clear witness against the virgin birth; "woman" or "wife" as it is used here does not oppose "virgin" but "simply denotes in a general way the nature of generation, to originate from which is the mark of all human beings" (31/18).

In the Epistle to the Hebrews it is stressed that Jesus was like all men in everything: "Since therefore the children share in flesh and blood, he himself likewise partook of the same nature . . ." (Heb. 2 : 14); "Therefore he had to be made like his brethren in every respect . . ." (Heb. 2 : 17). In the oldest Gospel, that according to Mark, the "beginning of the gospel of Jesus Christ" (Mark 1 : 1) is taken not to be his birth, but his baptism by John the Baptizer. Church historian Campenhausen says: "As far as the *Heilsgeschichte* is concerned, everything that precedes this event is quite unimportant . . ." (31/12). And he adds that even the Gospel written last, that of John (seventy years after the death of Jesus), "neither mentions nor in any way assumes the virgin birth" (Campenhausen, 31/13). Jesus is presented as "Jesus of Nazareth, the Son of Joseph" (John 1 : 45). He is rejected by his opponents with the argument, among others, that Jesus does *not* come from Bethlehem: " 'Has not the scripture said that the Christ is descended from David, and comes from Bethlehem, the village where David was?' " (John 7 : 42). At least three places in the Gospels seem to indicate clearly that even the parents of Jesus were unaware of a divine mission of Jesus, which would be unthinkable if there had in fact been a virgin birth. One place noted is in the text of Luke describing the twelve-year-old Jesus in the temple: "And when they saw him they were astonished; and his mother said to him, 'Son, why have you treated us so? Behold, your father and I have been looking for you anxiously.' And he said to them, 'How is it that you sought me? Did you not know that I must be in my father's house?' And they did not understand the saying which he spoke to them." (Luke 2 : 48–50). This occurs again in the text in Mark: "Then he went home; and the crowd came together again, so that they could not even eat. And when his friends heard it, they went out to seize him, for they said, 'He is beside himself.' " (Mark 3 : 20–21). Just as controversial as these two texts is the text in the Gospel according to John: "He came to his own home, and his own people received him not. But to all who received him, who believed in his name, he gave power to become children of God; who were born, not of blood nor of the will of the flesh nor of the will of man, but of God" (John 1 : 11–13). It is supposed by a few scholars that the last "who," referring to the children of God, was not in the plural originally, but in the singular, referring to Jesus. Yet, even if this opinion were correct, suggests Professor Cullmann of Strasbourg and Paris, it "by no means proves that the author here thinks of the virgin birth. The following translation results from this interpretation: 'He gave power to become children of God to those who believe in the name of him who was born not of blood, nor of the flesh, nor of the will of man, but of God.' . . . Being born of the 'will of man' means simply 'human descent,' which John 1 : 13 contrasts with 'born of God.' This contrast regarding Jesus' origin runs through the whole Gospel of John and has nothing at all to do with the virgin birth." Cullmann continues: All attempts "to find the tradition expressly stated or unquestionably presupposed in other books of the New Testament are too artificial to be convincing" (32a/296f.).

Against the majority of Protestant New Testament scholars, Professor Stauffer of Erlangen is convinced that "the men of the New Testament are unanimous in their testimony that his birth was a miracle" (88/61). For proof he cites the report of the wedding at Cana from the Gospel of John: "When the wine failed, the mother of Jesus said to him, 'They have no wine' " (John 2 : 3). Stauffer comments: "When the Fourth Evangelist relates the story of the wedding at Cana with Mary already counting upon

Jesus' power to work miracles, he appears to take it for granted that the mother knows from the beginning the secret of her son" (88/15f.). A further illustration for Stauffer is Matthew 11 : 19: "and they say: 'Behold, a glutton and a drunkard. . . .' " Stauffer is of the opinion that "among Palestinian Jews this particular insult would be flung at a person born of an illegitimate connection who betrayed, by his mode of life and his religious conduct, the stain of his birth" (88/16). In another place Stauffer explains this phrase not with reference to a "stain of his birth" but to the fact that Jesus took part in the wedding at Cana and on this occasion changed water into wine: "Many henceforth condemned Jesus as a 'glutton and drunkard' " (88/66).

Stauffer also sees a hint to the virgin birth in Mark 6 : 3 ("Is not this the carpenter, the son of Mary and brother of James and Joseph and Judas and Simon, and are not his sisters here with us?"): "The Jews had strict rules governing name-giving. A Jew was named after his father . . . even if his father had died before his birth. He was named after his mother only when the father was unknown" (88/16). This argument of Stauffer's does not convince Campenhausen, who writes: "Nor do the strict laws of the Jewish system of name-giving affect the matter at all" because in this case the opponents of Jesus "mean to reproach him with illegitimate parentage. . . . A son is named after his father as a matter of course, and only in case of illegitimacy after his unmarried mother; but the remarks of the Nazareth crowd are not a record of births" (31/12). Campenhausen is convinced that this passage is read by Stauffer against its clear meaning: If the passage is made to "speak of illegitimate parentage," then the point of Jesus' answer would be spoiled: "A prophet is not without honor, except in his own country, and among his own kin, and in his own house." Campenhausen takes for granted, as do most New Testament scholars, that Joseph is not mentioned because "reference is expressly made to relatives still living in the place" and that "it may be assumed that he was dead" (31/12).

Other theologians who defend the virgin birth contend, contrary to Stauffer, that Jesus passed for the son of Joseph among his contemporaries. Adolf Schlatter, to whom Bergmann and other spokesmen for the Confession Movement frequently appeal, writes that Mary became pregnant as the fiancée of Joseph, "so that Jesus could have from the beginning a human father and that the miracle of God could remain hushed, thereby also guarding against the blasphemies of unbelievers" (84/7). Whoever embraces this argument prepares himself for the designation of Jesus as the son of Joseph; for example, "Jesus of Nazareth, the son of Joseph" (John 1 : 45) and ". . . is not this Jesus, the son of Joseph, whose father and mother we know?" (John 6 : 42). These texts are to be taken, says Otto Rodenberg, who recently has defended the historicity of the virgin birth, "not as an expression of the evangelist against the divine sonship, but as an expression for the hiddenness of Jesus as the son—not of Joseph but of God. Naturally he appears to his contemporaries as the son of Joseph" (81/20). Rodenberg is also not convinced by the argument that the virgin birth is witnessed to only twice in the New Testament. "One might . . . ask how often something must be witnessed to in the Bible in order for it to be true. But then we would not yet have conquered a quantitative way of thinking. We therefore ask further: Must every moment, especially every important moment, of the existence of Jesus be mentioned regularly and expressly and everywhere? . . . Other important confessional expressions, such as 'true man and true God,' or the doctrine of the trinity, cannot be read directly in the text of the New Testament" (81/11f.).

HEATHEN INFLUENCES ON THE LEGENDS OF CHRISTIANS

Martin Dibelius was not satisfied with the analysis of isolated important passages in the New Testament concerning the birth of Jesus. He also attempted to discover how the legends of the virgin birth may have originated. In his research, he estabished three stages and distinguished carefully between Jewish–Hellenistic and heathen influences.

In Hellenistic Judaism there was a "description of a miraculous procreation of one chosen by God . . . in which the Creative Spirit took the place of the begetting father." This doctrine was known by the Apostle Paul, but "he specifically did not make use of it in relation to Jesus! Paul never speaks of the miraculous birth of Jesus, and shows clearly that his interest lies in an entirely opposite direction. He places considerable value on the fact that the earthly being of Christ began as that of other men through a natural birth" (33/29).

Nevertheless, in some areas of primitive Christianity, belief in the spirit-generation of Jesus began to spread. Dibelius is convinced that "the Hellenistic–Jewish idea of a divine generation was made use of by Christians for the procreation of Jesus. That is almost self-evident. For here it serves to ground the origin of the Messiah; if that important title was assigned to the one begotten of God, then it would have to belong properly, first of all, to the one sent by God in the end-time" (33/35).

Dibelius takes for granted that in the first stage "Christians only proclaimed the procreation of Jesus through the Holy Spirit; they did not describe it" (33/35). But it could not become popular "unless the assertion were clothed in a story: out of the proclamation came the legend" (33/39).

Of the second stage, Dibelius says, "The motif which

presented itself for this legendizing was that of a theogony; the idea of the marriage of a god with a mortal wife, which is common in a great number of birth stories" (33/39). This legend was consequently "of heathen origin, but was mediated through Hellenistic Judaism." The legend of the virgin birth, as it is told in the first chapter of the Gospel of Luke, distinguishes itself from the "usual type of theogony" in that "the event of the miraculous procreation . . . is not at all directly described" and in that "it does not speak of a marriage of God with Mary" (33/39).

But Dibelius also considers the "presuppositions for this variety of material" (33/40) to be given in Hellenistic Judaism. Possibly the Septuagint, the Greek translation of the Old Testament— or at least its first reader intended or understood Isaiah 7 : 14 ("Therefore the Lord himself will give you a sign. Behold, a young woman [or 'virgin'] shall conceive and bear a son, and shall call his name Immanuel.") in the sense of a virgin pregnancy. The first teller of our legend would have known, and would have consciously tied into this understanding if he formulated his angel message in Luke 1 : 31 ("And behold you will conceive in your womb and bear a son, and you shall call his name Jesus.") according to the prior picture of Isaiah 7 : 14 (33/40). It "cannot be proved, of course, that the prophet wanted to indicate with this phrase a special miracle of procreation" (33/24).

Only in the third stage is there concern for Joseph, for the "claim of this father to the virgin mother and the divine child." While the spirit-procreation "can be understood in terms of Hellenistic Judaism, the virgin motif shows itself to be of 'heathen' origin, but was communicated by Hellenistic Judaism; for the inclusion of the earthly father only 'heathen' analogies seem to come into question" (33/43f.).

As Dibelius and others point out with reference to Plato (427–347 B.C.), the "motif of the sexual abstinence of the father before the birth of the divine child" was taken over from the "Greek tradition." According to Plato, the Greeks believed that Periktione, wife of Ariston, was still a virgin when "Apollo approached her" (Dibelius 33/45). Dibelius says: "And this motif, so decisive for the entire presentation, which allows the mortal father to step back before the divine, but which also stresses the rights of the earthly father to his wife, finds itself expressed also in Matthew!" Dibelius sees the parallel in the verse: ". . . but knew her not until she had borne a son; and he called his name Jesus" (Matt. 1 : 25). Here is, therefore, Dibelius asserts, "a 'heathen' motif directly taken over into the material of the story told by the evangelist without going through Hellenistic Judaism" (33/46).

Opposing this doubt about the virgin birth, which Dibelius and others trace back to parallels in the history of religion, is Rodenberg. He cites Justin, who, around the year A.D. 150, responds to the Jew Trypho: "Don't you realize, Trypho, that through that which the devil allows the Greeks to say in deceitful imitation, through that which he does via the Egyptian magicians, through the false prophets at the time of Elijah, my knowledge which is created out of the scriptures and my confidence in the scriptures is strengthened." Rodenberg comments: "The reality of the demonic powers is seen in a proper biblical way and their works are clearly recognized. Through anticipated imitations in the form of heathen myths they seek to discredit the divine need of redemption" (81/26f.).

Rodenberg also supports his case on the basis of Tertullian, who, around A.D. 197, wrote that the "spirits of error [were] raised up as falsifications of the doctrine of salvation, that many poetic myths were also invented by them which, through their similarity to the doctrine of salvation, shook faith in the truth, or even secured faith in themselves, so that men thought it not necessary to believe in Christ" (81/27). Rodenberg says: "These witnesses, to whom one may attribute authenticity in spite of the distance of almost two thousand years, may speak for themselves. That they compare a history of dogma research, which overlooks the reality of Satan, to strange whims is not astonishing at all" (81/27). As for theologians who do not consider the arguments of Justin and Tertullian worth discussing, Rodenberg has this to say: "Over against them we ask, realizing that some will simply smile: Why not take their arguments seriously? Beyond that, how else can one operate who proceeds from the Bible and its description of reality? Is it possible to do away with the reality of Satan and his power and craftiness simply with a wave of the hand? Some men may think so, but theologians ought not to! The disavowal of satanic power has produced a demonic fall which becomes evident, in most cases, only after enormous damage has already been done" (81/28f.). "Satan is always the ape of God" (81/26).

SON OF A VIRGIN OR CHILD OF A MANGER?

We return to the work of New Testament scholar Dibelius. The two stories, the son of the virgin and the child of the manger, according to Dibelius, make clear "the two tendencies of Christian preaching. The one is to describe the miracle of redemption as a super-human appearance which sets aside the laws of nature; the other is to describe it as the gift of God within the narrow confines of earthly existence" (33/78).

It is already clear that, in the opinion of Dibelius, the two tendencies do not fit comfortably with one another, that for him Jesus is the son of Mary and of Joseph. He describes the contradiction when he writes about the manger-child: "It is no child of God not humanly born. . . . It is no son of the virgin whose pregnant mother and foster father are astonished, as we have it in the Mary-legend in Luke, or in the Joseph story in Matthew. It is a human child like others. . . . The Gospel of Jesus came

into the world in the milieu of human life, in an abandoned
land with no historical significance and with no political
protection, and yet grew to historic power through the
faith of those who followed him. Here in the Christmas
legend this paradoxical happening is shaped into a symbol.
. . . The power and the greatness of Christianity became
evident in the penetration of the world with the Gospel
which was spoken to the poor in spirit" (33/74).

The Jesus about whom Dibelius wrote in 1939 was not
born of a virgin. And also in the widely-read *Jesus von
Nazareth* by Günther Bornkamm (although one must read
it between the lines) Joseph is described as the physical
father of Jesus.

The Protestant church is divided at this point. Some
believe in the natural birth of Jesus; others, in the virgin
birth. For Ethelbert Stauffer of Erlangen, the virgin birth
is a historical fact (88/18) and even the crowning glory
of the history of Israel: "This people was created by God
and led through the ages in order to bring forth Mary"
(88a/26).

For Karl Barth the virgin birth is a sign "that amid the
continuity of the creaturely world, yet independently of
it, both as regards our understanding of His action and as
regards His action itself, God himself has the initiative"
(6/182). "The virginity of Mary in the birth of the Lord
is the denial, not of man in the presence of God, but of
any power, attribute or capacity in him for God" (6/188).
Man participates here "only in the form of non-willing,
non-achieving, non-creative, non-sovereign man, only in
the form of man who can merely receive, merely be ready,
merely let something be done to and with himself"
(6/191). In reply to this, Pannenberg writes: "With such
an argument does not Barth find himself already on the
path of Roman Mariolatry?" (73/144).

The Rhenish pietist Theodor Haarbeck takes the virgin
birth as a holy event: "With the woman begins redemption.

In her womb the Holy Spirit builds from the beginning of the embryo the new wonderful life" (52/92). And in a widely-distributed book by Hans Dannenbaum, one reads: "As little as a lion can bear a lamb so little could the Son of God come into the world through means of human procreation and reproduction. In the virgin birth the creative Spirit of God was participating powerfully and decisively; but human nature, in the form of Mary the virgin, was only receiving and accepting" (32b/94).

Such theories come very close to those which Paul Althaus of Erlangen considered to be absolutely forbidden; namely, theories which "conceive of the human fatherhood as being in competition to the divine. In such a case, God's fatherhood in regard to Jesus, and Jesus' divine sonship, is misunderstood biologically–naturally— as if the concept 'Son of God' were not only a *picture* for Christ's eternal relationship to God" (3/218). Also, the virgin birth may not be taken as a "condition for the sinlessness of Jesus. . . . Not by the abolition of the earthly father, but by God's miracle of salvation has Jesus taken away our sinfulness, in spite of his origin out of Adam's stock. But if Jesus' sinlessness is said to depend on his originating without an act of sexual intercourse with its sensual lust, then one may well respond that the libido is not *more* sinful than other natural urges and functions of men" (3/219).

According to the view of Pannenberg, those who want to hold to the *natural* sinlessness of Jesus must stand up for the virgin birth. Since even with the virgin birth, there is a connection with the sinful family of Adam, the thought of the natural sinlessness of Jesus leads to the idea of the immaculate conception of Mary, which, although it was vigorously disputed "in the high Scholasticism of the thirteenth century and rejected by the majority of the great Scholastics, was made dogma in the Roman Church in 1854 (Denzinger, 1803). Accordingly, Christ's merit would have been applied in advance to his mother so that she was purified of sin and Jesus himself could be conceived sinlessly—a very artificial construction! But it is only by such artificiality that one can establish Jesus' natural sinlessness with the help of the virgin birth." Pannenberg is of the opinion that the victory over sin has "not been attained before Jesus' birth, but only in the entire accomplishment of the course of his existence." The sinlessness of Jesus is "not an incapability for evil that belonged naturally to his humanity, but results only from his entire process of life" (73/358ff.).

WHAT OUGHT, WHAT MAY ONE BELIEVE?

Is the question of whether Jesus was born of the Virgin Mary or as the son of Mary and Joseph, acknowledged in the Protestant church to be a problem? Where is it discussed? Do conversations concerning it take place among the leaders of the Protestant churches? The debates are carried on—if at all—only between ministerial candidates and congregational vestryboards, and among children.

An elementary school teacher of religion, Renate Ginsberg, writes the following report: "A young school-girl admits that she never joins in speaking the sentence 'born of the Virgin Mary' because she cannot imagine such a thing. Growing laughter silences immediately when I report the same thing of myself. However, I add that since it has become clear to me that I do not have to take it literally, but may understand it as 'Jesus sent from God,' I again join in" (102a/189).

There are basically different views, and it remains unclear to many Protestant Christians what "born of the Virgin Mary" really means. Are both views in agreement with the confession of faith, and are both equally justified? Or is it that one takes it as literally as possible, therefore *ought* to believe it as historical fact, but that one *may* understand it otherwise? One could understand Künneth to be saying this. "The confession of the 'virgin birth' is in no sense an object of primary Christological interest, but is to be maintained as the classical expression, and one not to be surpassed by any modern formula, of the mystery of the incarnation of the Son, which in contrast to every other earthly birth is a miracle not because his physical parentage was apparently qualified by some divine factor, but because *the* man was born who is the 'Son' and as such the coming 'Lord' (64/140).

Or is it, on the other hand, that one *ought* to believe in the natural birth but *may* believe in the virgin birth? One could understand Claus Hunno Hunzinger, professor of New Testament at the University of Hamburg, to be saying this. "The teaching of the virgin birth is intended basically to be a help to understanding and to faith—but if it instead becomes an obstruction to faith, if it makes it more difficult to believe in Jesus, then it must be said clearly that faith does not depend on this doctrine" (*Kristall* 1 [1966] p. 46). Yet, if this is the case, who then is to "say it clearly" to whom?

Rodenberg wants the problem, which has thus far been dealt with openly only by Protestant children and Protestant theologians, to be officially clarified. He demands from his church that which apparently is most difficult for it to make: a decision. "At this point of christological foundation, the church—for it concerns no less than this!—splits wide open, historical–critical theology on the one hand and the faith of the congregation on the other. If one observes the other christological expressions, for instance the resurrection of Jesus Christ, it is clear that even the most extreme positions include in some way or another the resurrection of Jesus in their theology, of course with entirely different interpretations. It should be obvious, then, considering the present discrepancy between theology and parish, that retention of the status quo ought not to be regarded as a

suitable solution. Either, accepting the results of theological research, there must follow at this point a revision of
the confession of faith—which also means a revision of the
liturgy, the catechism, the hymnbook (one need think
only of Luther's Christmas hymn 'a virgin's arms contain
thee now'!), or there must be a clear recognition and expression of this deep-seated error of a theological science
which has obviously not grown at this point in the task of
theological understanding because an entire dimension of
reality has been lost by it" (81/6).

With this demand Rodenberg, for whom it is no "either"
but only an "or," stands almost alone in theological literature. The one closest to him in this regard is Karl Barth.
"There is certainly nothing to prevent anyone, without
affirming the doctrine of the virgin birth, from recognizing
the mystery of the person of Jesus Christ or from believing
in a perfectly Christian way. . . . But this does not imply
that the Church is at liberty to convert the doctrine of the
virgin birth into an option for specially strong or for
specially weak souls. The Church knew well what it was
doing when it posted this doctrine on guard, as it were,
at the door of the mystery of Christmas. It can never be in
favour of anyone thinking he can hurry past this guard. It
will remind him that he is walking along a private road at
his own cost and risk. It will warn him against doing so.
It will proclaim as a church ordinance that to affirm the
doctrine of the virgin birth is a part of real Christian
faith" (6/181). From those pastors who cannot agree, the
Church must at least demand that they deal with their
"private road as a private road, and therefore not in turn
make of it an object of preaching, that if they cannot
personally affirm the dogma and therefore (unfortunately!)
must hold it back from the congregation, that they at least
respect it through silence" (12/198). The Erlangen systematician, Paul Althaus, did not go this far. One can, he
said, "maintain the virgin birth in no way to be necessary

for the incarnation of the Son, the coming of the new man. The 'born of the virgin' does not have the rank of a salvation-event. Therefore the Church bears the question-ableness and diverse judgment on this matter." What, then, does the virgin birth mean? According to Althaus, "the distinction of Jesus from all other men is entirely deter-mined by God's spirit (Luke 1 : 35); insofar is God his father and is he 'conceived by the Holy Spirit.' Whoever, therefore, brings critical judgment to bear on historical questions can regard the "born of the virgin Mary" of the Church's confession as a picturesque expression of that fact, and can confess the sentence in this sense with sincerity" (3/220).

Pannenberg is of a different opinion in this matter than is Althaus: "Theology cannot maintain the idea of Jesus' virgin birth as a miraculous fact to be postulated at the origin of his earthly life. To that extent it is problematic that the virgin birth found entry into the Apostles Creed. . . . Two functions that dogmatically cannot be given up but that can be handled more adequately in another way [are] that Jesus had been what he is from the beginning as God's work alone" and "that Jesus' origin, his birth, was a truly human event." Only for this reason "is it tolerable that the virgin birth has its place in the liturgical confession of the church" (73/149f.).

Still sharper is the judgment of Grass of Marburg. He counts the virgin birth, and also the ascension, "among the elements" of the New Testament witness to Christ "about which one must ask whether they really belong to the ground of faith, whether they now represent some ideas of faith" (51/274).

5. Attested with
Works and Wonders

THE PUBLIC DISCUSSION about the virgin birth is still carried on only by Protestant Christians. However, the discussion about the miracles of Jesus has spread also to Catholic Christians. "Even in Catholic circles, unfortunately, the position of Rudolf Bultmann, according to which Biblical reports of the miracles of Jesus are seen in connection with ancient myths, has entrenched itself; it can no longer be demanded that they be valued as historical events," complained Prelate Josef Brosch of Aachen. (*Echo der Zeit,* VOL. 10, NO. 6, March 1966).

The question is almost exclusively whether the New Testament reports of miracles are "objectively valid and generally binding matters of fact, which as such cannot be contested" (Otto Michel of Tübingen 79/228) or whether "the great majority of the Gospel miracle-stories must be regarded as legends" (Ernst Käsemann, also of Tübingen, 56/50).

Even this limiting of the problem of historicity is considered by many theologians to be flawed. The miracle reports can—as, for example, Gerhard Gloege writes—scarcely be correctly understood "if Jesus is considered only as a miracle worker. Jesus would then really be on a level with ancient and modern fakirs and dervishes, whose powers are beyond dispute. Faith healers of our own day, such as Hermann Zais and Bruno Gronning . . . can compete with the Galilean charlatan (John 8 : 48)" (46/218f.).

The miracle question has already been brought before the Synod of the Evangelical Churches in Germany. On that occasion Doctor E. H. Edmund Bieneck, an engineer and president of the YMCA of Germany, cited Rudolf Bultmann: "One cannot use electric light and radio, get sick and make use of modern medicine and clinical help, and at the same time believe in the spirit and miracle world of the New Testament." Bieneck's own comment was this: "I travel about a good bit in the world, and daily make use of many technical devices in addition to electric lights and radios, but that does not mean that I must doubt that Christ did the signs of which the Gospels speak. . . . Otherwise he would not be the 'Lord' but only one founder of a religion among many. Otherwise also I could not pray to him, for prayer presupposes that he can do a miracle. It presupposes that all power is given unto him in Heaven and on earth. . . . The Christian knows that Jesus had power, and has power and might over all things" (100/13f.).

In the *Braunschweig Theses*, which we mentioned in the first chapter, there is reference to The Acts of the Apostles (". . . Jesus of Nazareth, a man attested to you by God with mighty works and wonders and signs which God did through him in your midst . . ." [Acts 2 : 22]) and also to the Gospel of Matthew ("And Jesus answered them, 'Go and tell John what you hear and see: the blind receive their sight and the lame walk, lepers are cleansed and the deaf hear, and the dead are raised up, and the poor have good news preached to them. And blessed is he who takes no offense at me'" [Matt. 11 : 4–6]). The *Braunschweig Theses* demand: "It must therefore be rejected . . . whenever the messianic signs in the life of Jesus of Nazareth, the miracles reported in the Gospels, are conceived only as mythological ways of speaking, and their factual-historical character is denied" (113/4).

The significance of this problem is also underscored by modern theologians; as, for instance, by New Testament scholar Klein of Kiel: "The manifold intellectual difficulty with which men who are prepared for serious hearing and thinking meet Christian preaching is nowhere clearer today than at the point where this preaching attempts to speak to them about the miracles" (59/55). Klein thinks that "blind acceptance of the miracles as true—simply because they 'stand in the Bible' or because 'God can do everything' —is now no longer possible. Whoever today believes in miracles must be able to articulate clearly what he understands by miracle and by faith, and he must be able to demonstrate that the man who believes as he does is not schizophrenic but undivided" (59/9).

Before we turn to the New Testament material in detail, it may be worth pointing out the different interpretations of miracles made by men (not only Christians) at the time of Jesus and by men (not only Christians) today. At that time a miracle was not seen as a transgression against the laws of nature. The whole notion of causality, accepted today by nearly everyone, was unknown. The Christian did not distinguish himself from the non-Christian by the fact that he "believed" in miracles. *All* men believed in miracles. Miracle workers were everywhere, and every deity of every religion was claimed to have brought forth great wonders. Today, one has only the alternatives of believing the miracles of Jesus or rejecting them. At that time, there was also a third possibility, namely, to explain the deeds of Jesus, as well as those of the other doers of miracles, as deeds staged by the devil. The modern Christian is of a mind, says Dibelius, "to recognize God's activity in normally explainable events, indeed chiefly in such." The hearer of Jesus, on the other hand, "supposed that God's working was to be seen precisely in the inexplicable" (35/80).

HEALING POWER AND MAGIC SHADOWS

According to the New Testament, Jesus cast out demons and healed, among others, the blind, the lame, the crippled, the moonstruck, the paralytic, the hemorrhaging woman, and the fever-ridden mother-in-law of Peter. In addition to that, the evangelists report nature miracles. Jesus raised the dead, stilled a storm (". . . And he awoke and rebuked the wind and the raging waves; and they ceased, and there was calm" Luke 8 : 24), fed five thousand with five loaves and two fishes, walked on the water (". . . and he came to them, walking on the sea. He meant to pass by them, but when they saw him walking on the sea they thought it was a ghost, and cried out" Mark 6 : 48–49), helped the unsuccessful fisherman Peter to bring in a "great shoal of fish" (". . . and they came and filled both the boats, so that they began to sink" Luke 5 : 7), and changed water into wine at the wedding of Cana.

Just as the words of Jesus recorded in the Gospels often do not agree with one another, so also the reports of his deeds often contain discrepancies. Occasionally a miracle is "softened." The healing of the hemorrhaging woman, for instance, is pictured differently by Mark than it is by Matthew. According to Mark, "She had heard the reports about Jesus and came up behind him in the crowd and touched his garment. For she said, 'If I touch even his garment, I shall be made well.' And immediately the hemorrhage ceased; and she felt in her body that she was healed of her disease" (Mark 5 : 27–29). Käsemann comments: "The idea that the garment of the miracle-worker imparts divine power which is transmitted by touch and has healing properties is a popular Hellenistic conception.

It occurs again in the accounts of Peter's healing shadow and Paul's miraculous handkerchief (Acts 5 : 15; 19 : 12) and in later ages is at the root of the cult of relics" (56/96f.). Käsemann appeals to two passages in the Acts of the Apostles ("So that they even carried out the sick into the streets, and laid them on beds and pallets, that as Peter came by at least his shadow might fall on some of them" Acts 5 : 15; "So that handkerchiefs or aprons were carried away from his body to the sick, and diseases left them and the evil spirits came out of them" Acts 19 : 12).

In Matthew, on the other hand, the woman is healed, not through the touching of the garment, but through the word of Jesus. "And behold, a woman who had suffered from a hemorrhage for twelve years came up behind him and touched the fringe of his garment; for she said to herself, 'If I only touch his garment, I shall be made well.' Jesus turned, and seeing her he said, 'Take heart, daughter, your faith has made you well.' And instantly the woman was made well" (Matt. 9 : 20–22). In the Gospel of Luke, the story is again similar to that in the Gospel of Mark, and it is again through a word of Jesus that the healing power of the touch of the garment is underscored: "And a woman . . . came up behind him, and touched the fringe of his garment; and immediately her flow of blood ceased. . . . But Jesus said, 'Some one touched me; for I perceive that power has gone forth from me' " (8 : 43–46).

More often, the number and the intensity of the miracles are increased. So, according to Mark, Jesus walks alone on the water. In Matthew, Peter also attempts it (". . . so Peter got out of the boat and walked on the water and came to Jesus" Matt. 14 : 29). The servant of the centurion from Capernaum, whom Jesus heals, is in the Gospel of Matthew only "lying paralyzed at home, in terrible distress" (Matt. 8 : 6). But in the Gospel according to Luke (Luke 7 : 2) and in the Gospel according to John (in which he is not a servant of a centurion, but is described as the "son" of an "official" [John 4 : 47]), he is "at the point of death."

In Mark, Jesus heals only *"many* who were sick" (Mark 1 : 34), but in Matthew, he "healed *all* who were sick" (Matt. 8 : 16). In Mark, "five thousand" are fed (Mark 6 : 44); in Matthew, it is "five thousand men, besides women and children" (Matt. 14 : 21).

In the latest Gospel, that according to John, more precise statements are made concerning the sick than in the earlier Gospels. According to the reports in the synoptic Gospels, the dead are raised by Jesus shortly after their death. Lazarus, however, has already been "in the tomb four days" (John 11 : 17) before Jesus raises him: "He cried with a loud voice, 'Lazarus, come out.' The dead man came out, his hands and feet bound with bandages, and his face wrapped with a cloth. Jesus said to them, 'Unbind him, and let him go'" (John 11 : 43–44).

FROM A WORD ABOUT FISHERMEN TO A
MIRACULOUS CATCH

In one example—the miraculous catch of Peter—it is clear just how critically modern theologians deal with those biblical miracles which develop from one Gospel to another and how, at the same time, they stress their theological meaning.

In Mark, it is reported in one passage that Jesus began "to teach beside the sea" and that, because of the press of the crowd, he had to get "into a boat" (Mark 4 : 1). In another passage, it is reported that Jesus spoke to "Simon and Andrew the brother of Simon and said: 'Follow me and I will make you become fishers of men'" (Mark 1 : 16–17).

In the Gospel of Luke, the sea is no longer spoken of in general but is named as the "lake of Gennesaret," and Jesus enters not into *any* boat, but into "one of the boats, which was Simon's" (Luke 5 : 1–3). The word spoken to Simon and Andrew is, according to the Gospel of Mark, spoken only to Simon: "Do not be afraid; henceforth you will be catching men" (Mark 5 : 10). Yet between the sermon by the lake and this word to Simon stands the report of a miraculous catch of fish. Jesus orders Simon to throw out the nets, and Simon answers: " 'Master, we toiled all night and took nothing! But at your word I will let down the nets.' And when they had done this, they enclosed a great shoal of fish . . ." (5 : 5f.). The pericope ends: "And when they had brought their boats to land, they left everything and followed him" (Mark 5 : 11). According to the Gospel of John, the catch of fish happens after the resurrection of Jesus, and the word about "fishers of men" is not reported at all.

Modern theologians are convinced that the word about becoming fishers of men stands at the beginning of the development, that it "was illustrated subsequently by this story of the miraculous catch of fish" (Klein 60/24), and that, finally, in John's Gospel, the miracle entirely supplants the word.

This transformation is, according to Klein, an "exciting chapter in the history of faith . . . a movement in the continuous progress of the Christian community toward new understanding. The Church never came to rest under this text, nor did it allow the text to wither away. Rather the text constantly drove the Church to new insights" (60/26). Yet, while this process of growth brought no anxiety at all to the early Christians, it finds contemporary Christians in quite another situation. "The living growth of the tradition seems to us to be an obstruction to faith, to them it was a help to faith, even an expression of their faith" (60/25).

Klein thinks that the story which originates from the word was first told as an Easter story and then read back into the earthly life of Jesus. It was supposed to show "that

Peter heard the word at Easter which bound him to the mission" (60/25). For Klein it is "in the strongest sense of the word a miracle" that the sinner Peter was called to be a missionary. "It is possible only because this Jesus, who after his death presses men into his service, is stronger than death" (60/26). The story is "the yes of faith, enclothed in a parable, to the miracle that God through the preaching of improbable men desires to work faith in the hearers" (59/27).

Similar to the manner in which Klein has spoken on this text, both in a 1960 lecture and in a 1965 Kirchentag address, is the way Bultmann preached on it in a 1941 sermon in Marburg. "The story teaches us that the wonder-working word of Jesus comes to us precisely when our own resources are exhausted" (28/162). "The one and the true miracle is that the word of God's saving grace which meets us in Jesus Christ creates us anew, freeing us from the fetters of ourselves and our old sinful way of life, thereby making us a 'new creation'" (28/164).

STRANGE TALES ASSIGNED TO JESUS?

A few of the miracles, such as, the walking on the water and, above all, the raising of the dead, can, as various theologians argue, have been attributed to Jesus only after his death because they presuppose faith in his resurrection. Emanuel Hirsch says that "the awakening of a stinking corpse (Lazarus) out of the grave would be, if it really happened, the greatest of all the deeds of Jesus. . . . No Gospel could have overlooked this event" (54/274). In fact, however, this miracle is recorded only in the Gospel according to John. Stauffer, on the other hand, takes it to be a fact that Jesus performed it at the end of his earthly life. "The witnesses of the raising of Lazarus went about everywhere proclaiming what they had seen. The resur-

rection of the dead upon the Mount of Olives had begun"
(88/110).

Several parallels to the miracles can be pointed out,
moreover, in Jewish and in heathen religion. That the first
Christians "appropriated to themselves and transferred to
their Saviour not only foreign motives but also whole
stories of foreign origin," seems to Martin Dibelius to be
certain in three instances (35/85f.): the changing of water
into wine at the wedding of Cana, the story of the coin in
the mouth of the fish (Jesus to Peter, according to
Matthew: ". . . Take the first fish that comes up, and
when you open its mouth you will find a shekel" [Matt.
17 : 27]), and the report about the demon whose name
was Legion, whom Jesus allowed to come out of the
possessed man (". . . and the unclean spirits came out, and
entered the swine; and the herd, numbering about two
thousand, rushed down the steep bank into the sea, and
were drowned in the sea" [Mark 5 : 13]). Two of these
stories seem strange to Dibelius on other grounds as well.
With the story of the changing of water into wine, it is
noticeable "that Jesus does not bring aid in a case of stress,
but helps them out of a quandary; moreover this help is by
no means necessary and may even be doubtful, for it has
nothing at all to do with the Gospel ethos. The over-
whelming amount of wine, between five and seven quarts,
may illustrate the greatness of the miracle, but in no way
does it fit in with the special quality of the Gospel"
(34/101). And in the coin story "a hint of miraculous
self-help is hidden, but the reader senses instinctively that
this is an essentially foreign element" (33/351).

Other New Testament scholars count among the stories
derived from heathen sources the walking on the water and
the stilling of the storm. The systematic theologian Gloege
considers both to be mixtures of poetry and truth: "Historical narratives undoubtedly lie behind these narratives"

(46/151). Concerning the herd of swine and the demons he writes: "However much fantasy has contributed to the shaping of the story, the situation is so uncontrived and unique that the historical basis is obvious" (46/155).

In the healing stories mentioned, Dibelius considers it possible—others consider it certain—"that the method of such healings is simply transferred to Jesus." The classic example of this is the report of the healing of the blind man of Bethsaida by "spittle manipulation," as it is called by the Catholic theologian Vögtle (115/1260): "And he took the blind man by the hand, and led him out of the village; and when he had spit on his eyes and laid his hands upon him, he asked him, 'Do you see anything?' " (Mark 8 : 23). Dibelius writes: "The procedure of the healing, one could almost say, begins the cure" (33/341).

Also undoubtedly historical are, according to critical New Testament scholars, the exorcism stories (with the exception of the herd-of-swine story already mentioned) and a few healings in which the action is not described in detail, but in which a word of Jesus and the faith of the sick person are central. Yet, even in the question of how to judge this historical residue, opinions vary considerably.

For Bultmann "the demon stories of the New Testament are, if they live on or are repristinated in the modern world, mere superstition." Gerhard Gloege states that they "seem particularly strange to us," and that there is "fairly unanimous agreement today that demonic possession is a form of nervous disorder" (46/155f.). Walter Künneth of Erlangen, on the other hand, complains that the "struggle of Jesus with the demons is not taken seriously" and that "these scenes in the life of Jesus, which are so basic to the eschatological message of the New Testament, are felt to be embarrassing, explained mythologically, actually disposed of, or not taken to be Christologically true at all" (63/228).

The healings are also no longer regarded by many

Protestant theologians as miracles. Dibelius, for instance, writes: "What is certain in the case of the 'possessed' is probable in other cases of illness: we have to do with psychically conditioned maladies which are healed by means of an impact upon the psychical life of the patient. And this impact is frequently by means of a command which brings about a psychical reaction: 'Arise, take up your bed and go home!' Such curative commands are also known to modern medicine. Use has been made of them in cases of lameness caused by war, e.g., as the result of pressure on a nerve or something similar, and we now speak of a therapy by means of sudden inspiration [*Uberwaltigungstherapie*]" (35/82f.).

"The great majority of the Gospel miracle-stories," says Käsemann, "must be regarded as legends. The kind of incidents which in fact commend themselves as being historically credible are harmless episodes such as the healing of Peter's mother-in-law from a fever . . . [and] the healing of so-called possessed persons. . . . We can no longer employ them as objective proofs for the intervention of God in history" (56/50f.). Similarly, Bultmann says that "the *miracles of the New Testament* have ceased to be miraculous, and to defend their historicity by recourse to nervous disorders or hypnotic effects only serves to underline the fact" (9/5).

FOR CHILDREN A MAGICIAN AND FIRST-AID MAN?

Although such professional opinions are by no means new in German universities, the problem of how to handle the miracle stories in religious instruction in German schools seems to go unsolved. No theologian and no teacher of religion will contradict the statement of Martin Niemöller: "I am personally convinced that in religious instruction we ought to teach nothing which we ourselves cannot consider to be 'authentic' " (71/120). Yet there is uncertainty about what requirements to set for the teachers and what to consider authentic. A teacher must "show his colors" to his students. He cannot escape out of the difficulties of history into theology. The religion teacher is probably more aware of the helplessness of the Protestant churches in regard to questions of faith than are many pastors.

Professor Klaus Wegenast, a teacher in Lüneburg, has formulated the problem in an impressive way: "Whoever would tell only simple Bible stories or would tell about the Jesus who went around helping in every situation of life" runs the danger of a total misunderstanding of Jesus. "Such a Jesus is too easily associated, by the end of elementary school, with Santa Claus, with the stork who brings babies, and with other fairy tales. But what can I do? What and how ought I to teach so that the child can be armed against our often godless world and established with courage and confidence so that the Bible and its message will not be dismissed along with magical thought?" (92/75). In the magazine *Evangelische Unterweisung*, Wegenast states that "the majority of our children live today under the strong influence of a society for which miracle can no longer be even a symbol for anything significant, for which miracle belongs either in the realm of fairy tale or of 'clergy humbug.'" The result is that "children today often even in the first year of school, after hearing of a miracle story, ask whether it is true." And usually the teacher responds that the miracle stories in the Bible are "now buried in legends and sometimes misunderstood as reports to be taken as true" (103/40).

In the same magazine, the Dortmund professor of pedagogy, Walter Hartmann, reports some experiences which indifferent Christians should allow to shock them out of their complacency. "The following experiences are almost universal. Children very generally think of Jesus as the great magician. He is not taken seriously. I once asked children in the seventh grade to name those biblical characters whom they would most like to bring with them if they went on a difficult and dangerous expedition. Moses won first place and was followed by Isaiah and Amos, and even Pastor Niemöller entered the circle of biblical characters (because he was once a submarine commander). Jesus did not appear on the list. To my carefully-worded question came the answer, in the midst of general snickering, that one could perhaps use him as a reserve first-aid man" (103/42).

Hartmann indicates a solution in the following passage, for which he was criticized by Bäumer in the Westfalenhalle, although without the mentioning of his name): One must have the "courage to set the situations of Jesus constantly in parallel to present-day situations, and the deeds of Jesus in parallel to the deeds of present-day men. That presupposes that we finally begin to grasp Jesus as a real man, and no longer consider him to be a god who was changed into a man. This raises a semantic problem. What Jesus means for us can no longer be expressed in the formula "true God–true man." . . . We must say openly and clearly that Jesus was a man and nothing other than a man. . . . Everything which men are basically not capable of, Jesus also could not have done, for he was a man. Here is a criterion for the critical understanding of miracle which we must use with children, carefully asking and doubting with them" (103/44).

TO BE SURRENDERED COMPLETELY TO CRITICISM

Finally, there are three generally held observations of modern theologians which are worth considering. Klein advises that, with every miracle story, one should make this test: "To hold as true that hundreds of men were once healed through a word does not help me personally at all. I know for certain that in my life the same thing does not happen. But to believe that I, in all my profanity

and without any religious talent, may learn in confrontation with Jesus to surrender to God without reservation,
and that in such unconditioned trust I will be delivered
throughout all of life's difficulties—such a faith will change
my entire life" (59/29). Bultmann summarizes his position
on the miracles of Jesus in this way: "If all of them were
historically secured, then it would still be true that as the
deeds of a man of the past they would mean nothing to us
directly. Seen in this way, they are no works of Christ,
insofar as we understand the work of Christ to be the
work of redemption. Therefore the 'miracles of Jesus',
insofar as they are events of the past, are to be surrendered
completely to criticism. And it must clearly be stressed that
the Christian faith has simply no interest in proving the
possibility or the reality of the miracles of Jesus as events
of the past, that on the contrary, this would only be a
mistake" (23/227). And in another place Bultmann writes:
"In any case we might say about belief in New Testament
miracles what the apostle Paul says about the eating of
meats sacrificed to idols: 'We are no worse off if we do not
eat and no better off if we do'" (I Cor. 8 : 8) (28/158).

For Catholic theologians the life of Jesus without miracles—without events which according to present-day
knowledge violate natural law—is unthinkable. The First
Vatican Council decided in 1870 that the biblical miracles
are "most certain proofs of his divine revelation adapted to
the intelligence of all men" (70/33). The council forbade,
under the threat of excommunication, that a Catholic
should explain the miracles "contained in Holy Scripture
[as] fabulous or mythical" (70/39).

Until a few years ago it seemed to be an unshakable
conviction of Catholic theologians that no miracle of Jesus
could be diminished or doubted. Nevertheless, the discussion about their facticity has now begun in Catholic theology.

In not a few articles—for example, in one by New Testament scholar Anton Vögtle of Freiburg—the same ideas have emerged as did among Protestant theologians a few decades before. Many miracles are said to have only a "substantial historicity"; others bear "certain hints of a Jewish resurrection story"; or healing methods of that time are said to have influenced the presentation (115/1259f.).

Vögtle considers it to be a task of Catholic theology to clarify whether, in the intention of the early Church, many miracle reports "describe an experienced happening, or rather express the redemptive–historical and divine majesty of the person Jesus" (115/1260).

If the miracle of the storm which Jesus stilled may be explained by Catholic theologians as "a non-experienced happening" and may therefore be declared to be a legend, then Vögtle would be free from having to reflect about this miracle. It would have, "under the presupposition of facticity," the "strange consequence that its unhindered decline would at the same time have meant the end of the life and revealing work of Jesus" (115/1260).

6. Suffered under Pontius Pilate, Was Crucified, Dead, and Buried

THE CRUCIFIXION of Jesus was a mistake.

It was—according to the Catholic dogmatician Josef Rupert Geiselmann of Tübingen—a "mistake of those who delivered and condemned him, because they misunderstood his preaching as a political act" (44/112).

Just as the Jews misunderstood Jesus in the year 30, so for nineteen centuries have Christians misunderstood a passage in the passion narrative of Jesus, namely, the self-curse of the Jews before the eyes and ears of the Jew Jesus of Nazareth and of the Roman Pontius Pilate, as recorded in the Gospel according to Matthew: "His blood be on us and on our children!" (Matt. 27 : 25). The report concerning the suffering of the Lord of the Christians created suffering for the people of the Jews everywhere this people had to live with and among Christians. "The days of Holy Week were the most dangerous ones of the year for medieval Jewry. The people, excited by the liturgy depicting the crime of 'the Jews' would, on leaving the churches, molest and maltreat the Jewish population" (Gregory Baum, 11/24).

It was Rudolf Bultmann who stated in 1921, with the help of the form-critical method which he had developed, that this curse was never spoken (22/282). It was also Bultmann who, in 1959, suggested the thesis of "misunderstanding," which Geiselmann and other theologians have made their own. Jesus suffered the "death of a political criminal" on the cross, "on the basis of a misunderstanding of his work as a political act" (21/12). And it is Bultmann who, at the same time, compels Christians to reflect on what the end of the life of Jesus means to them. Did Jesus "seriously consider the possibility of execution by the Romans, or did he only think of the coming of God's lordship?" Is it a "fact that we cannot know how Jesus understood his own end, his death?" May one not conceal from himself "the possibility that he simply suffered a collapse?" (21/12).

Must one (as Bultmann wrote even in 1927) "say openly: It is not clear what advantage the historical Jesus, who goes in obedient love to his death, has over all those who, for example, have also gone this way in obedient love in the world war, and whose sacrifice says much more to us not only because of its great vividness, but above all because we were bound together with them in personal friendship. To want to build such experiences on a person of the past seems to me to be artificial and to lead to sentimentality. Jesus Christ, who has the full power to forgive sins does not become visible in this way. I have done nothing to make him suffer and he has done nothing to forgive me" (23/96f.).

GOD'S GRACE IS REVEALED ON THE CROSS

Künneth considers Bultmann's "inner solution of the passion story" to be "unsurpassed." But does not modern theology really end up, Künneth maintains, "by handling this event as the tragic fate of an honorable man, the fiasco of an idealist, the martyrdom of a witness" (12/31f.)? Must every Christian be seized by the *horror vacui* when he reads the following sentence of Bultmann (or hears it as a citation in the Westfalenhalle): "What a primitive mythology it is, that a divine Being should become incarnate, and atone for the sins of men through his own blood!" (Bultmann 10/7 as quoted in 12/32). Has the cross of Jesus Christ for Bultmann, as the hearers in the Westfalenhalle must have supposed, nothing more to do with the sins of men? Is it in fact denied by modern theologians, as Künneth asserts, that God "has reconciled the world to himself" through Christ, that Jesus Christ "bears the sins of the world" (12/33)?

Let us allow Bultmann himself to speak: Christ "is God's gift to the world, in which his grace, gratuitous and prevenient to all our works, becomes visible. And Paul preaches the crucified Christ—to the Jew a stumbling-block and to the Greeks foolishness. God's grace is revealed in the cross. God raised him to be Lord who was nothing on his own account and knew no desire for recognition, and whom self-surrender and love brought to the cross, and so God has set the law of the cross over the world—the liberating law of the cross" (24/173). Can one say that for Bultmann the death of Jesus on the cross was only "the fiasco of an idealist"?

Bultmann writes: "And this is the meaning of the Christian message: God has revealed himself in the cross of Christ as the God of forgiving grace; Christ is the Word of forgiving grace" (24/160). "Now this message is a message of forgiveness—a forgiveness which does not simply mean that God forgives us this or that moral failing. . . . It declares rather that God forgives and has forgiven the fundamental sin of our whole existence, the one essential sin which is that we have separated ourselves from God and have as it were cut ourselves off from Him in order to live independently in our own strength. In Christ He has created a new humanity . . ." (28/48). Ought one to say that Bultmann denies that God has reconciled the world to himself through Christ? Ought one to allow his listeners to be unclear about how closely the cross and sin are bound together by Bultmann?

And is it possible to say more concerning "participation in the cross of Jesus" than Bultmann has said when he asserts that it means "to surrender our wishes and plans to the will of God, so that we place under the shadow of the cross all that concerns us, both our hopes and our work. This means that we enter the ultimate solitude of man before God, and, as Paul says, that we decree the sentence of death on ourselves, so that we put our trust not in ourselves but in God who raises the dead" (2 Cor. 1 : 9) (28/195).

However false or correct the theses of Bultmann about the knowledge or lack of knowledge that Jesus had concerning his approaching death may be, the Christian who rejects them simply on the basis of a pious feeling (because Jesus *cannot* have suffered a collapse) has not thereby demonstrated his faith. And no one ought to consider himself qualified to condemn them on the basis of two or three citations.

IS THE PASSION NARRATIVE A FACTUAL ACCOUNT?

That which is written by Bultmann and his students about the last episode in the life of Jesus sounds to many Christians like a series of impious or entirely un-Christian denials.

The proclamations of the passion of Jesus "do not present a clear picture of the situation; they are much more *dogmatic* expressions concerning the *necessity* of the passion, as it was understood by the Christian community after his death," writes Conzelmann (32/623). The speech of Jesus on the night of his betrayal could scarcely be about the institution of the Lord's Supper "as an act to be cultically repeated," writes Marxsen (65/268). The biblical report of the trial of Jesus before the council "is not authentic. It was formed by the community" (Conzelmann 32/630); "concerning the legal detail there is scarcely any account" (32/647). The report of the trial before Pilate (Mark 15 : 2–15) is "by far the most artificially constructed piece" of the passion narrative, says Bartsch of Frankfort (94a/454). The saying of Jesus on the cross, "My God, my God, why hast thou forsaken me?" (Mark 15 : 34), was "placed into the mouth of Jesus" by the Church (Conzelmann 32/647). Günther Bornkamm of Heidelberg makes the general statement concerning the biblical records, that it is necessary to understand "that we have little certain knowledge in the proper historical sense about the last chapter of the life of Jesus" (18/157).

This is almost directly contrary to that to which many believing Christians adhere. They are convinced that, on the basis of the Bible, the historical sequence of the last days of Jesus can be experienced in detail.

First impression seems to indicate that this view is correct. The Gospels, including John, agree here more closely than they do in the reports of the life of Jesus up to the entrance into Jerusalem. In addition to that, numerous days and hours are specified, so that many theologians state that Jesus died on the seventh of April, A.D. 30, at three o'clock in the afternoon. (Other researchers indicate the year 33 or 32 [Stauffer]; 31, 29, 28 [Goguel]; 27 and occasionally 21, 24, and 36 [cf. 17/55f.].)

Whereas men in the company of Jesus otherwise remain nameless or are described in only a sketchy way, in the passion narrative there appear historical personages: the Roman governor Pontius Pilate, the high priest Caiaphas, and the Jewish ruler Herod Antipas.

This confidence in the historicity of the details of the passion narrative is encouraged by the work of conservative theologians and, above all, by the flood of books, brochures, and articles written in the style of the best seller *Und die Bibel hat doch recht.* These writings make of the passion narrative a factual account, which can be proved and elaborated with further facts.

Along these lines, Josef Blinzler, professor of New Testament in the Philosophical–Theological Seminary in Passau, and author of a widely distributed book, *Der Prozess Jesu,* writes about the dimensions of the cross: "The cross of Jesus must also have been higher than the normal cross, because the soldier reached him the sponge soaked in vinegar not by hand but on a reed (Mark 15 : 36: 'And one ran and, filling a sponge full of vinegar, put it on a reed and gave it to him to drink'); one can therefore take it that the feet were at least a yard above the ground" (17/249).

As "a technical book for theologians and theological students, but also as a compendium for interested laymen" (43/111), professor of pedagogy Hans-Jochen Gamm wrote *Sachkunde zur biblischen Geschichte,* which lays out a similar position in great detail.

In Gamm's book, one finds the following about Gethsemane: "The place which is regarded as Gethsemane lies so close to Jerusalem that the evening shadow of the city wall falls on it. The garden with ancient olive trees is now an irregular square and is about 60 yards in length and breadth. 'Gethsemane' in translation means 'oil press.' In the garden therefore there would have been an oil press to which the dwellers of the Mount of Olives brought their olives. The olive tree grows as high as 30 feet, the trunk 9 feet high and 6 feet thick. The leaves are about 2 inches long and 3/8 inch wide, the fruit 1 inch long and 3/8 inch thick" (43/209f.).

In reference to the denial of Jesus by Peter before the second crow of the cock, Gamm says, "The keeping of chickens was allowed in Jerusalem only if the animals were given no opportunity to flock together. Otherwise it was feared that worms would come out of the ground. If that happened the holy city would be profaned, for worms belong, according to Mosaic Law, to the 'unclean animals' " (43/213).

Concerning the thirty pieces of silver which Judas is said to have received for the betrayal: "The piece of silver was a coin which weighed half an ounce. Thirty pieces of silver would weigh, therefore, about one pound, which corresponds to a silver ball of about one and a half inches diameter. Thirty pieces of silver had a value of about twenty dollars" (43/205).

Concerning the purchase of the potter's field with the thirty pieces of silver which Judas is said to have thrown away: "Perhaps the potter's field was a place from which one got clay. In the southern part of Jerusalem, by the brick gate, there is a clay field. The potter's field is therefore probably at that place . . ." (43/214).

In reference to Jesus' crown of thorns: "The crown was perhaps made of the 'Christ thorn' or perhaps of the 'Beaker plant,' which covers upper Palestine and is found in lime kilns and in rustic hearths, and which is related to the 'goat thorn' which grows in the immediate neighborhood of Jerusalem, or perhaps of the napweed . . ." (43/216).

Concerning the "hyssop," which is said to have been put on a sponge and given to Jesus on the cross: "The hyssop (*hyssopus officinalis*) does not exist in Palestine. Therefore one might suppose that Biblical hyssop was a form of majorana (*Origanum maru*). It belongs to the family of the labiate flower and thrives everywhere in Egypt and in Palestine . . ." (43/221).

Whether majorana and the cross have anything to do with one another, each Christian may decide for himself. Yet even he who wants to prove, as does Gamm—and Werner Keller before him—with coins and spices that the Bible is still correct, ought not to falsify the truth. It is simply untrue to say, as does Keller, that "the descriptions of the trial, sentence, and crucifixion in the four gospels have been checked with scientific thoroughness by many scholars and have been found to be historically reliable accounts even to the last detail" (58/371).

Actually, the report of the trial is, as is the entire presentation of the way from the entrance into Jerusalem to the crucifixion, much more a proclamation of the Christ than a report about the historical Jesus. And of the "many scholars" who have checked the reports "with scientific thoroughness," most have come to the conclusion that they are *not* "historically reliable accounts."

The single meaning of the passion narrative is to describe the defeat of the crucified Jesus as his victory. What the Jews, and also the disciples, had at first considered to be a catastrophe is now interpreted—in the context of faith in the resurrection—as an accomplishment of God's will and as the opening phase of his coming lordship. At the same time, the guilt of the Jews in connection with the death of Jesus must be maintained and proved. They had rejected the Messiah who was sent by God.

Whoever reads these texts ought neither to take notice of historical facts nor to feel sympathy for the crucified. He ought to be called to a decision for Christ. There is in the accounts of the entrance into Jerusalem and the cleansing of the temple, as also in the passion narratives, scarcely a sentence which was not written exclusively for this purpose.

To many, the indifference of the authors to historical detail may appear strange. For many modern theologians, however, it is a proof of that meaning which the first Christians assigned to these events, how much they worked over them, and how they again and again attempted to bring new meaning to them.

If it is true that the passion narratives in the Gospels agree with one another more thoroughly than does the

presentation of the words and deeds of Jesus prior to his
final days in Jerusalem, they still by no means coincide.
Here also one may speak of a development.

According to the Gospel of Mark, Jesus submits silently
to the kiss of Judas, who addresses him only as "rabbi"
(Mark 14 : 45). According to Matthew, Judas says before
kissing him, "Hail, Master!" and Jesus asks, "Friend, why
are you here?" (Matt. 26 : 49f.). According to Luke, Jesus
says, "Judas, would you betray the Son of man with a
kiss?" (Luke 22 : 48). The reader is given the impression,
on the strength of the above, that Judas decided not to
try to kiss him. And, according to John, there is apparently
no act at all required on the part of Judas—greeting or
kiss—after he had led the "band of soldiers and some
officers from the chief priests and the Pharisees" to Jesus
(John 18 : 3). Jesus himself does the acting: "Then Jesus,
knowing all that was to befall him, came forward and said
to them, 'Whom do you seek?' They answered him, 'Jesus
of Nazareth.' Jesus said to them, 'I am he.'" (John
18 : 4f.).

The tradition concerning the two thieves who were
crucified with Jesus developed in a similar way. In Mark,
there is only a small comment: "And with him they crucified two robbers, one on his right and one on his left."
(Mark 15 : 27). In Matthew, we find: "And the robbers
who were crucified with him also reviled him in the same
way." (Matt. 27 : 44). In Luke, it is only "one of the
criminals [who] railed at him, saying, 'Are you not the
Christ? Save yourself and us!'" (Luke 23 : 39); the other
did not insult or blaspheme, but argued: ". . . this man
has done nothing wrong" [Luke 23 : 41] and asked:
"Jesus, remember me when you come in your kingly
power" (Luke 23 : 24). Jesus "said to him, 'Truly, I say
to you, today you will be with me in Paradise'" (Luke
23 : 43).

ON THE SEARCH FOR WITNESSES

How little the evangelists were interested in the portrayal of historical details also becomes clear if one compares the various interpretations of theologians. Concerning almost every event there are opposing opinions because the scanty and contradictory statements of the Bible are interpreted differently.

The entrance into Jerusalem was "a messianic demonstration only for the disciples of Jesus, [and his] entrance is almost unnoticed by the crowd," writes the French scholar Maurice Goguel (49/276, 281). According to Bultmann, "he seems to have entered Jerusalem with a crowd of enthusiastic adherents; all were full of joy" (26/29).

Concerning the cleansing of the temple, "it must have been an unheard-of attack by Jesus on the rights of the temple-state" in the opinion of Gerhard Gloege of Bonn (46/260). According to Goguel, it was "only a simple objection against the handling of the affairs of the Temple" (49/276).

"A small army of a thousand soldiers" arrested Jesus, according to New Testament scholar Ethelbert Stauffer (88/120). New Testament scholar Josef Blinzler, on the other hand, writes that ". . . even a squad of twelve men can be called a great crowd when it sallies forth to arrest one single, unarmed person, not determined to resist" (17/61).

Doubt over the historicity of the reports of the final days of the earthly life of Jesus is as old as the Gospels themselves. What had happened up to the time of his arrest could have been reported by the disciples. However, much of that which happened between the arrest and the crucifixion could scarcely have been experienced by the disciples as eyewitnesses because by that time, they had fled.

Theologians of all persuasions are convinced that the evangelists were also acquainted with this skepticism and have given hints in a few places about their sources of information. This is perhaps Mark's purpose in referring to a young man who, after the arrest of Jesus, fled naked out of Gethsemane (Mark 14 : 52).

And to this day countless New Testament scholars attempt to find in the Gospels witnesses for the events of the passion—with differing results.

Concerning the dialogue which, according to John's Gospel, Jesus and Pilate are said to have had with one another, according to Blinzler, there "would have been present in any case the official lawyers and attendants of the procurator" who could have reported it or else Jesus himself, after the resurrection, must have "informed (his disciples) of them" (17/185f.).

Concerning the trial before the Sanhedrin, according to Blinzler, "it was not difficult . . . to obtain information . . . , as at least one member of the Sanhedrin, namely Joseph of Arimathea, was favorably disposed toward Jesus" (17/47). Blinzler recalls a passage in Luke: ". . . who had not consented to their purpose and deed" (Luke 23 : 51). Yet another Bible passage deprecates Blinzler's reference. According to Mark, the council unanimously agreed on the death sentence. Blinzler is not entirely consistent in his use of references, but he is forced to hold that Joseph of Arimathea either "absented himself completely from the trial or left before the verdict was given. We cannot say" (17/95).

Peter often is named when witnesses to the accuracy of the reports of the trial are searched for. At this time the disciples sat, to be sure, only "below in the courtyard" (Mark 14 : 66) when "the high priest and all the chief priests and the elders and the scribes were assembled . . . in the courtyard of the high priest" (Mark 14 : 54f.).

According to Martin Dibelius, eyewitness reports could

have been taken into consideration—assuming the most favorable situation—only for the Last Supper, the arrest, the denial and the crucifixion, scarcely for Gethsemane and certainly not at all for the procedures in the Sanhedrin and before Pilate" (33/279f.). But "if one must deny the notion of information from witnesses for the entire episode of the passion story, the psalms and prophets still could report more about the suffering of the Lord than fleeing disciples and shrieking women. They told more and were better authenticated, for this was revealed by God, that only handed on by men" (Dibelius 33/223). "The Old Testament passages on suffering were read as normative sources for the Passion story" of Jesus (34/188). For "this Easter faith guaranteed the assurance that the very Passion of Jesus was in accordance with God's will, and God's will was to be found in scriptures" (34/184).

Jews and Christians were divided (and are divided) on the Old Testament. The Jews hoped (and hope) on the Savior promised there who will still come; the Christians believed (and believe) that he has come (and is coming) in Jesus. The preachers and missionaries of the primitive Christian community described the last chapter in the life of Jesus as the fulfillment of the words of the prophets and the verses of the psalmist. "Precisely the offensive moments of the passion—the betrayal, the flight of the disciples, the torment of the cross—could be explained from the beginning only as the fulfillment of Old Testament prophecy" (Dibelius 33/249).

IS THE PASSION FORETOLD IN THE OLD TESTAMENT?

Every stage of the way, from the entry into Jerusalem all the way to the cross, is reported in the Gospels in the context of the Old Testament. It is often cited, as, for example, in Matthew's report of the crucifixion: "And they crucified him, and parted his garments, casting lots: that it

might be fulfilled which was spoken by the prophet, (Ps.
22 : 19) 'They parted my garments among them, and upon
my vesture did they cast lots' " (Matt. 27 : 35). [King
James version is here cited in agreement with the German
text of Matthew used by the author. RSV does not contain
the quotation for the Psalms.—Translator.] In a few places
the fulfillment of scripture is hinted at without a citation,
as for instance in the report of the Lord's Supper: ". . .
for the Son of man goes as it is written of him" (Mark
14 : 21). But often the Old Testament verses and sayings
are inserted into the text and are not recognized by the
reader who is not familiar with the Old Testament.

It may be uncontested that the sources of the scriptural
proofs—above all, the Psalms 22 and 69 and Isaiah—
"contain a number of features which are not exploited
either directly or indirectly in the story of the passion"
(Blinzler 17/42); it is also certain that the verses of the
Psalms and the speeches of the prophets are, in part, used
contrary to their clear meaning in order to point to Jesus.

Yet, in other respects, opinions and counter-opinions
compete with one another here also. Bergmann, for instance, writes: "Because Jesus is already promised in the
Old Testament, and the promises are fulfilled in him, God
shows his Word itself to be God's Word" (15/41). For
Bultmann, on the contrary, "it is clear that what is already
known is derived from reading of the texts. But people
want to find it in the old texts so that it can count as
authoritative truth" (24/183); such a "scriptural proof is
in fact impossible. These prophecies of the Old Testament
are in part, properly speaking, not prophecies at all, and
many do not point to Jesus and the Christian community,
but simply contain the Israelitish-Jewish picture of the
future hope. Most references must—perhaps with the help
of the allegorical method—be understood contrary to their
original meaning if they are to deliver a suitable prophecy.
But that only shows that faith is established without the

proof of prophecy; faith discovers the prophetic proof subsequently. It is not therefore only the case that, in fact, the proof from prophecy, particularly today, can convince no one; it *ought* also to convince no one. Faith which would believe on the basis of such evidence is not genuine faith at all. The 'scriptural proof' of the New Testament must fall, not primarily because of rational–historical criticism, but because it can only serve to distort the character of faith" (23/335).

Let us look at a few examples of how the Old Testament has influenced the passion narratives in the Gospels. "Blessed is he who enters in the name of the Lord!" says Psalm 118. With the same words the people greet Jesus when he enters into Jerusalem (Matt. 21 : 9). The Prophet Zechariah announces: "Lo, your king comes to you . . . riding on an ass, on a colt the foal of an ass" (Zech. 9 : 9). It is reported of Jesus in the Gospel of Mark: "And they brought the colt to Jesus, and threw their garments on it; and he sat upon it" (Mark 11 : 7). In Matthew the text agrees even more closely with the verse from Zechariah: "They brought the ass and the colt, and put their garments on them, and he sat thereon" (Matt. 21 : 7). Here, according to the commentary of New Testament scholar Marxsen, "he brings the quotation from the Old Testament to bear upon the fragment of tradition itself, which is sometimes altered in the light of the Old Testament" (67/148).

The report of the cleansing of the temple in John 2 : 15, "He drove them all . . . out of the temple; and he poured out the coins of the moneychangers," has its parallel in the second book of Kings: "And the king commanded Hilkiah . . . to bring out of the temple of the Lord all the vessels made for Baal" (2 Kings 23 : 4).

All the details of the betrayal, as it is recorded in the New Testament in relation to Judas, can be found in the Old Testament—if perhaps in another connection. There is talk of "thirty pieces of silver" by the Prophet Zechariah

(Zech. 11 : 12) as well as by the evangelist Matthew
(Matt. 26 : 15). In Psalms, there is a passage: "Even my
bosom friend in whom I trusted, who ate of my bread, has
lifted his heel against me" (Ps. 41 : 9), which matches
almost exactly one in the New Testament: "And as they
were at table eating, Jesus said, 'Truly I say to you, one
of you will betray me, one who is eating with me' " (Mark
14 : 18).

The Judas-kiss ("And he came up to Jesus at once and
said 'Hail, Master!' And he kissed him" [Matt. 26 : 49])
is, in the Old Testament, a Joab-kiss which likewise brings
death to the one kissed: "And Joab said to Amasa, 'Is it
well with you, my brother?' And Joab took Amasa by the
beard with his right hand to kiss him" (2 Sam. 20 : 9).
That Judas threw the thirty pieces of silver "into the
temple" (Matt. 27 : 5) is a motif which already appears in
Zechariah: "So I took the thirty shekels of silver and cast
them into the treasury in the house of the Lord" (Zech.
11 : 13). And in both the Old Testament and the New
Testament there is a verse which states that soiled money
does not belong in the temple: "You shall not bring the
hire of a harlot, or the wages of a dog, into the house of
the Lord your God" (Deut. 23 : 18); "But the chief priest,
taking the pieces of silver, said, 'It is not lawful to put
them into the treasury, since they are blood money!"
(Matt. 27 : 6). In Zechariah the thirty pieces of silver are
given "to the potter" (Zech. 11 : 13), in the Gospel according to Matthew they are used to buy "the potter's field"
(Matt. 27 : 7).

Even the flight of the disciples could be described as
the fulfillment of an Old Testament prophecy: "Strike the
shepherd, that the sheep may be scattered" (Zech. 13 : 7).
Even the young man, mentioned in Mark's Gospel, who
fled naked at the arrest of Jesus ("But he left the linen
cloth and ran away naked" [Mark 14 : 52]) has an ante-
cedent in the Old Testament: ". . . and he who is stout of

heart among the mighty shall flee away naked in that day, says the Lord" (Amos 2 : 16).

The author of the Gospel of Mark describes the discharge of the hearing before the Jewish council in the style of the Old Testament: "Now the chief priests and the whole council sought testimony against Jesus to put him to death; but they found none" (Mark 14 : 55). Psalm 31 : 13 reads: "Yes, I hear the whispering of many—terror on every side!—as they scheme together against me, as they plot to take my life."

And to the question of Caiaphas, whether he is "Christ, the Son of the Blessed" (Mark 14 : 61), Jesus answers: "I am; and you will see the Son of man sitting at the right hand of Power, and coming with the clouds of heaven" (Mark 14 : 62). This answer corresponds to two places in the Old Testament: "The Lord says to my Lord: 'Sit at my right hand'" (Ps. 110 : 1) and "and behold, with the clouds of heaven there came one like a son of man, and he came to the Ancient of Days and was presented before him" (Dan. 7 : 13).

"But Jesus made no further answer, so Pilate wondered" reads the Gospel of Mark (Mark 15 : 5). The parallel in Isaiah (Isa. 53 : 7) is unmistakable: "He was oppressed, and he was afflicted, yet he opened not his mouth; like a lamb that is led to the slaughter, and like a sheep that before its shearers is dumb, so he opened not his mouth." In Ps. 73 : 13, the proof of innocence is described which, according to the Gospel of Matthew, was given by Pilate, the Roman heathen: "All in vain have I kept my heart clean and washed my hands in innocence." A similar passage stands in Ps. 26 : 6: "I wash my hands in innocence . . ."

That a man gave Jesus wine mixed with gall and vinegar while he was on the cross (Matt. 27 : 34, 48) corresponds to Ps. 69 : 21: "They gave me poison for food, and for my thirst they gave me vinegar to drink." Garments are torn and distributed in Ps. 22 : 18: "They divide my garments among them, and for my raiment they cast lots" and in Matt. 27 : 35: "And when they had crucified him, they divided his garments among them by casting lots." Dibelius comments: "The authors of this memorandum are not eyewitnesses who remembered unessential details with secretarial exactness and then passed them on, but teachers who read the classic passion narratives of the psalms with opened eyes. It was useful to the preacher not as a disagreeable episode, but only as fulfilled prophecy" (33/229).

The reports about the crowd under the cross contained in Luke's Gospel: "But the rulers scoffed . . ." (Luke 23 : 35) and in Matthew: "And those who passed by derided him, wagging their heads" (Matt. 27 : 39). Correspond to Psalm 22. Dibelius comments: "Why did the people who mocked the crucified one wag their heads? . . . The answer is because Psalm 22, the great passion psalm in the Old Testament, says: 'All who see me mock at me, they make mouths at me, they wag their heads'" (33/326).

The two "murderers" who had been crucified with Jesus, "one on his right and one on his left" (Mark 15 : 27), have in the earliest Gospel "their sole meaning in that through them the word of the prophet was fulfilled" (Bartsch 94a/453); (Isaiah 53 : 12: ". . . because he poured out his soul to death, and was numbered with the transgressors; yet he bore the sin of many, and made intercession for the transgressors.")

The last word of Jesus on the cross, in Mark 15 : 34 as well as in Matt. 27 : 46, "My God, my God, why hast thou forsaken me?", and also in Luke 23 : 46: "Father, into thy hands I commit my spirit!", correspond respectively to verses from Ps. 22 : 1 and 31 : 5. Occasionally a contrast is construed to exist between these two Psalm verses: the one expresses Jesus' doubt; the other, his trust in God. But

" 'My God, my God, why hast thou forsaken me?' . . . is not the outcry of one overwhelmed with despair, but is the beginning of Ps. 22; and the one who makes this his prayer is certainly not seized with rebellion against God, but is living and dying at peace with God" (35/131).

To the question whether this last word is historical, Dibelius answers: "Either Jesus did actually pray thus, in which case the purpose was not despair but faith that inspired him, or else these words were placed on his lips, in which case the purpose was not to describe his collapse —who among the Christians would have dared to offer such a description!—but to indicate his oneness with God's will" (35/131).

Conzelmann, who does not consider it to be historical, writes: "To object that one would not have placed this word in the mouth of Jesus if it had not really been spoken by him is to misunderstand the character of narrative. If one catches on to this saying, then one shows his death as fulfillment, and thus as victory over the scandal of the cross. One ought not to psychologically devalue the saying in order to reconstruct the feelings of the dying one" (32/647).

We complete this (not exhaustive) enumeration with a verse to which we have already hinted and which we shall have to consider further, that is, the word according to Matthew which became the doom of countless Jews, "His blood be upon us and upon our children!", which is constructed on an Old Testament foundation, "Your blood be upon your head; for your own mouth has testified against you, saying, 'I have slain the Lord's annointed' " (2 Sam. 1 : 16).

BIBLE PASSAGES HAVE PRODUCED HISTORY

Critical New Testament scholars are convinced that "entire motifs, even scenes . . . are spun out of the Old Testa-

ment" (32/646). A few "biblical passages have begotten
history," states Dibelius (34/188). To be sure, "we cannot
always, nor at once, reach a verdict about the historicity of
a motif by showing it had an Old Testament basis"
(34/189). On the whole, Dibelius thinks it appropriate to
speak of "the impression of a relative reliability of the
Passion narrative" (33/343). Occasionally, says Dibelius
again, one carries over "something scarcely believable"
(33/227) out of the Old Testament into the action of the
story of the passion of Jesus. So the author of Mark's
Gospel allows the members of the Jewish council to mishandle the judgment of Jesus: "And some began to spit on
him, and to cover his face, and to strike him. . . ." (Mark
14 : 55). The parallel in Isaiah reads: "I gave my back to
the smiters, and my cheeks to those who pulled out the
beard; I hid not my face from shame and spitting." (Isa.
50 : 6) The author of Luke's Gospel locates the scene
differently. It is no longer the reputable members of the
council, but the mockers, who mishandle Jesus (Luke
22 : 63f.).

The passage in Zechariah, ". . . when they look on him
whom they have pierced" (Zech. 12 : 10) corresponds to
the report in John's Gospel: ". . . But one of the soldiers
pierced his [Jesus'] side with a spear, and at once there
came out blood and water" (John 19 : 34). Dibelius comments: "The historicizing narrator . . . carries over the
conclusion out of the Old Testament—that the Jews had
pierced the Lord—into historical possibility, and transfers
the act to a soldier" (33/236).

According to numerous Protestant New Testament
scholars, the alleged transfer of the imprisoned Jesus from
the Jewish ruler Herod Antipas to Pilate for trial is artificially inserted into the passion narrative (Luke 23 : 6–12).
Herod has no role in the action but is said only, together
with Pilate, to fulfill the prophecy from Ps. 2 : 2: "The
kings of the earth set themselves, and the rulers to be

counsel together, against the Lord and his annointed."
Goguel wrote concerning this scene: "A flagrant improb-
ability." Dibelius says: "The case is symptomatic: the
proof from prophecy influences the cultic speech, this
produces events which, so long as the tradition is still
fluid, are absorbed into the Gospel" (33/292).

And concerning the thirty pieces of silver which Judas
allegedly received for his betrayal, Dibelius is of the
opinion that "the information was not given in, but read
out of, the scripture" (34/188).

The thought that the infamous reward to Judas could be
unhistorical continues to be foreign to Catholic readers
of the Bible. In almost every Catholic Bible, there is a
remark about how much the amount would be, converted
into current currency (about twenty dollars). And by no
means would Catholic and conservative Protestant theologians be prepared for such radical judgments as are
expressed by Protestant modern New Testament scholars.

The report of the prayer of Jesus in Gethsemane Dibelius attributes to the "compositions which insert known
words of Jesus into a situation prescribed by the Old
Testament" (33/255). The words of Jesus to his disciples
in Matt. 26 : 38, "My soul is very sorrowful, even to death;
remain here, and watch with me," is similar to Ps. 43 : 5:
"Why are you cast down, O my soul, and why are you dis-
quieted within me?" While his disciples sleep, Jesus prays:
"My Father, if it be possible, let this cup pass from me;
nevertheless, not as I will, but as thou wilt" (Matt.
26 : 39). This prayer is related to Ps. 39 : 12, "Hear my
prayer, O Lord, and give ear to my cry; hold not thy peace
at my tears! For I am thy passing guest, a sojourner, like
all my fathers."

Dibelius comments: "If the earliest church thought that
it knew Jesus' laments and prayers, then it inferred that
knowledge from the Old Testament" (33/226). And: "We
give back to the story its original flavor only when we

read it as it was first told, not as an interesting or stirring incident, not as a page of history from Jesus' last hours of life, but as the preaching of the message that this suffering corresponds to the will of God, that it corresponds to the preaching of suffering in the Old Testament" (33/271). Bornkamm has a similar opinion: "This story . . . should not be read simply as an historical record . . . [It is] . . . an historical document in a higher sense" (18/162).

New Testament scholars such as Dibelius and Bultmann and their students, who analyze with their form-critical method the reports of the last chapter in the life of Jesus, are convinced that the historical kernel of the passion narrative is buried in countless legends. Thus Dibelius considers as "historically certain [merely] the dating according to Mark (14 : 1: 'It was now two days before the Passover . . .'), the event of the last supper, the evening arrest with the help of Judas, the condemnation through Pilate to death on the cross, the procession to the cross and the event of the crucifixion" (33/256f.). That is scarcely more than the framework of the action as it is described with many details in the Gospels.

The Catholic dogmatician Geiselmann is of the opinion that "the exclusive use of the form-critical method runs the danger of turning the historical incident of the judgment and crucifixion of Jesus into a myth" (44/100). This statement may be true, if one looks only at the details. Yet if one's major concern is to lay bare the background of the events, then it appears rather to be the other way around.

WHY DID JESUS TURN TOWARD JERUSALEM?

If any light can really be shed on the dark background of the Jerusalem events, then it will be only through the methods of the modern theologians. They strive—as we have seen in the second chapter—to set free the historical kernel of the message of Jesus and to "interpret both his other activities and his destiny in the light of his preaching" (Käsemann 56/44). But "Jesus felt himself in a position to override, with an unparalleled and sovereign freedom, the words of the Torah and the authority of Moses. This sovereign freedom . . . shakes the very foundations of Judaism and causes his death" (56/40). The illumination of the events in Jerusalem lies in the opposition between the message of Jesus and the Jewish religion. Whoever does not proceed from the message of Jesus and his call to decision runs the risk of extreme interpretations. Jesus can, then, as is the case in Carmichael's interpretation, be the leader of a military rebellion or, as is the case in the interpretation of not a few conservative theologians, be the passive victim of the intrigue of his opponents.

"Anyone who sets out to maintain that Jesus planned an attack on the Roman forces of occupation or on the Jewish authorities is compelled to deny the whole tradition: not only the sayings about turning the other cheek or about service, but also the promises of the Kingdom which God will bestow upon the humble-minded, those who are detached from the world and, although in the world, are cut off from it" (35/99).

Generally, as an argument against the thesis that Jesus was a rebel, the reference to the tribute money (which even critical scholars such as Bultmann and Dibelius consider to be an authentic word of Jesus) is cited: ". . . and he said to them, 'Whose likeness and inscription is this?' They said to him, 'Caesar's.' Jesus said to them, 'Render to Caesar the things that are Caesar's, and to God the things that are God's!' " (Mark 12 : 16–17).

On the other hand, however, "the depth of Jesus' conflict with the Jewish tradition, the real profound ambiguity of the situation in which Jesus had involved himself, and thereby the depth of the meaning of his passion itself are obscured when, motivated by rash zeal for the image of Jesus' purity and sinlessness, we see only ill will on the side of his opponents" (73/254).

The distinctions in the picturing of the historical Jesus, as they exist between traditional Catholic and conservative Protestant exegesis on the one hand and modern Protestant exegesis on the other, may be most obvious when one considers the question of miracles; when one considers the question of the events in Jerusalem, however, they seem to be more important. Does the fact that there is discussion and controversy about miracles, but scarcely any concerning the more important question of whether Jesus acted actively or only passively at the end of his life, not point to the superficiality of present discussion in the Protestant churches?

In the books of conservative scholars, Jesus is pictured as the Messiah who is himself conscious of being sent but whose messiahship is kept secret from the people, who predicts his death in Jerusalem, and who becomes the victim of his opponents. Yet it is precisely in the evaluation of decisive events that conservative exegesis, which can or will give up scarcely a detail of the biblical report, winds up in difficulties and contradictions. This becomes most obvious when one considers the entry into Jerusalem and the cleansing of the temple—events which presuppose an active Jesus who confronts the people.

Jesus enters into Jerusalem, writes Catholic New Testament scholar Blinzler, "joyously acclaimed as Messiah by the masses"; on the other hand, "this event does not seem to have attracted particular notice on the part of his enemies" (17/50).

Also for the Catholic dogmatician Geiselmann of Tübingen, no picture seems possible which would be free of contradiction. There were good reasons for Jesus to forbid the disciples to speak of him as the Messiah, "For Israel, the Messiah was the national hero, who was to free his

people from Rome" (44/162). Jesus never identified himself openly to the Jewish people, prior to his passion, as
Messiah, "because he would be either rejected by the
people or would be misunderstood in a dangerous, namely
political, way." Concerning the related question of why
Jesus entered Jerusalem, Geiselmann answers (in my
opinion, not convincingly) that his entrance "affirmed the
Jewish messianic expectation and modified it at the same
time, in that the idea of the warlike messiah was rejected"
(44/118f.). But, in another place, Geiselmann writes that
when Jesus entered Jerusalem, he was "in fact celebrated
by the people as a political redeemer" (44/112).

The Roman Catholic scholar Ricciotti writes about the
entrance into Jerusalem: "Casually, as if by chance, the
messianic expectation of the masses and that Jesus met
one another in this event" (78/520). Yet what Ricciotti
considers to have happened "by chance" cannot have been
"by chance" for Jesus. Also, Jesus did not go for a "casual
meeting" with the people who expected a political (Geiselmann: "warlike") Messiah, but to force this people, in the
city ruled by his enemies, to a decision.

We have, above all, Rudolf Bultmann to thank for
radically questioning the justification of the traditional
picture. And it is also clear that when one considers the
events in Jerusalem, a statement of Bultmann's can be
valuable in the search for truth, even if one takes it only
as the asking of a radical question, as the demand for an
answer.

For Bultmann, as has already been mentioned, it is a
"fact that we cannot know how Jesus understood his
death." If he sought a decision, then "he scarcely reckoned
with execution by the Romans, but rather with the already
successful coming of God's rule" (21/16). The logic of
this argument is not to be denied. One cannot seek a
decision about something which one knows has already
failed. Specifically, if Jesus knew for certain that the

Romans would crucify him, then he may well have re-
solved to fulfill the will of God, but could not have attempted to force the people to a decision. If one may put
the question even more radically than does Bultmann,
would not a Jesus who was aware of God's plan rebel even
against the will of God if he had wanted something other
than the death decided upon by God? Would he not have
mistrusted God if he had considered even possible a different decision of the people, of the council, and of Pilate? It
seems that the certain knowledge of Jesus concerning his
nearing death (the conservative position) and the concern
for a decision (the modern position) exclude each other.

Bultmann is convinced that Jesus "demanded a decision
over against himself as the bearer of the Word of God, a
decision on which salvation or damnation depends"
(21/16). Yet Bultmann seems to be more reserved than
his students concerning the contrast between the message
of Jesus and the Jewish religion. "Naturally his [Jesus']
public activity," writes Conzelmann, "had to be understood by the leaders of the people as an attack on the basic
principles of religion and of the people" (32/647). One
may, says Bornkamm, "assume with certainty that the
Jewish authorities felt themselves compelled to intervene,
by the provocation of the scenes at the entry to Jerusalem
and at the temple" (18/159); and Jesus was, "on account
of political plots against Rome, placed under judgment by
Pilate and condemned to death. Even the inscription of
his cross announced his guilt to everyone and was said to
indicate that he was a dangerous messianic pretender.
Certainly, therefore, Pilate had taken him to be a leader
of the Jewish opposition which wanted to eliminate Roman
rule and to set up a theocratic–messianic kingdom in its
repressed land" (85/5f.).

The New Testament scholar Ernst Fuchs of Marburg is
of the opinion that "Jesus did go up to Jerusalem. The
sight of his followers could, in fact, make this appearance

look like an insurrection. Indeed, the attitude of the authorities suggests that they *did* regard the whole business as an uprising. Scenes like the cleansing of the temple could hardly be called anything else. Jesus was thus dependent on the degree to which he was understood. The partial defection of some of those who had understood him was bound to happen. For the politically minded do not take into account the transformation of an unknown heavenly figure, unless this figure were thereby to become calculable. But this possibility was excluded. It is inconceivable that Jesus could come to terms with the authorities of a religiously organized state. He certainly did not share the definitely political aims of the Zealots, but on the other hand he did not avoid a clash with the Temple authorities" (41/24). And in another place Fuchs writes: "That Jesus would have only made his claim in Jerusalem quietly contradicts his entire proclamation. Jesus' claim was radical, for he conceived the situation of man before God as being present. Only he who listened to Jesus could be certain with respect to the claim of Jesus, could find himself *within* the saving sphere of God. This preaching was an announcement of opposition to the Jewish cult and to the current usage of the law, because Jesus claimed to be bringing God himself decisively to speech in that he offered to every one of his hearers a new self-understanding before God" (42/243).

In this, that Jesus sought a genuine decision, even theologians of quite different leanings agree with the Bultmann school. Thus Dibelius writes concerning Jesus in Jerusalem: "He means to be either accepted or rejected by men there; and he means to confront the capital with the message of the Kingdom of God" (35/63). There was "a deliberate challenging of the leading circles of the Jewish religion. (35/92). Also, in the opinion of Pannenberg, "the deeper basis of the conflict that led to the indictment is certainly to be sought in the whole of Jesus' activity, especially in the way in which he placed himself above the law and claimed the authority of God himself for his activity" (73/252).

SHORT HEARING OR TRIAL WITH DEATH SENTENCE?

Catholic theologians and some Protestant New Testament scholars—and most Christians for nineteen centuries—have been convinced that Jesus was sentenced to death in a trial before the Jewish council on the charge of blasphemy. Protestant theologians who employ biblical criticism, on the other hand, consider it probable or even certain that Jesus came before Jewish courts, *not* on the charge of blasphemy, that he had only a short hearing before them, and that without trial and death sentence he was handed over to Pilate. The scholars come to this conclusion after the analysis of Jewish legal practice and the contradictory biblical texts which report this event.

"The most hotly contested historical problem" (32/647) is whether the Sanhedrin in Jesus' time still had the right to try criminal cases and could condemn Jesus to death, according to Jewish law, by stoning. Protestant scholar Hans Lietzmann (in 1931) decided that the Jewish council did have this right and therefore declared the trial as described in the Gospels to be unhistorical. According to Lietzmann, if Jesus had been condemned by the Sanhedrin, he would have been stoned and not crucified. This opinion is held today by numerous scholars, among them Professor Günther Bornkamm of Heidelberg. Bornkamm writes that "the Jewish council certainly had the right to execute legal judgments in its own domain, particularly in regard to religious affairs, and to carry out the death sentence by stoning" (87/3 : 7).

Other theologians reject the thesis that the right to try criminal cases was first taken away from the Sanhedrin after the death of Jesus, as is the opinion of Bornkamm and others. They think that this right was taken away before his death, and they see an indication of this in a passage in John's Gospel: ("Pilate said to them, 'Take him yourselves and judge him by your own law.' The Jews said to him, 'It is not lawful for us to put any man to death'" [John 18 : 31]). Therefore the Jewish council had to turn over the condemned Jesus to the Roman official Pilate, who alone made the decision to carry out the death sentence.

Yet, even if this opinion (which is held by a minority of Protestant theologians and by most Catholic theologians) were correct, there remain other considerations which stand against the biblical report of the trial. They contradict "our reasonably reliable knowledge of the Jewish procedure at court, though this knowledge is derived from later accounts of the scribes" (Bornkamm 18/163). It was forbidden that a capital crime—such as blasphemy— be handled at night or on the Sabbath or on a festival day, as it is described in the three Synoptic Gospels. A death sentence could not be pronounced on the first day, as it is in the trial of Jesus. The earliest that the death sentence could be pronounced is on the second day of the trial. It was blasphemy only when one spoke out the name of God. If Jesus simply said yes to the question of whether he was the Christ, the Messiah, as it stands in Mark's Gospel, then he could not be punished on the charge of blasphemy, as it also stands in Mark. There is "not one single instance of a person's ever being accused of blasphemy and sentenced to death by Jewish authorities because he claimed to be the Messiah" (Bornkamm 18/163). A trial beginning with the appearance of the witness for the prosecution, as is allegedly the case in the trial against Jesus, seems to be a bending of the law.

Many theologians are of the opinion that these definitions of the law had not yet been issued at the time of Jesus. Yet Protestant New Testament scholar Eduard Lohse of the University of Göttingen, for example, is convinced that there were also at the time of Jesus "strong prohibitions against legal action on the Sabbath or on a festival day." It remains at least "worthy of consideration that the report of the evangelists stands in irreconcilable opposition to the holy day commandment of the law" (62/34).

Many New Testament scholars do away with this difficulty by gathering from the first three Gospels the facts of the trial (which are not recorded in John's Gospel) and by deriving the date of the trial (the day before the Passover) from John's Gospel. The date appealed to, however, does not involve a trial against Jesus before the Sanhedrin, but only an examination of Jesus by the high priests Annas and Caiaphas. Yet here, as always, one may make certain judgments. The Bible itself furnishes proof against, rather than for, the genuineness of the reports of the Jewish trial against Jesus.

Only in Mark and Matthew is a death sentence given by the Jewish council, and only according to these two Gospels did Jesus foretell it: "Behold we are going up to Jerusalem; and the Son of man *will be delivered to the chief priests and the scribes, and they will condemn him to death*, and deliver him to the Gentiles" (Mark 10 : 33; almost *verbatim* in Matt. 20 : 18–19).

According to Luke, who probably knew this text and corrected it, Jesus foretold no death sentence by the council: "Behold, we are going up to Jerusalem, and everything that is written of the Son of man by the prophets will be accomplished. *For he will be delivered to the Gentiles*" (Luke 18 : 31f.). And according to this Gospel, Jesus is handed over without sentence to Pilate: "And they said, 'What further testimony do we need? We have heard it ourselves from his own lips.' Then the whole company of them arose, and brought him before Pilate" (Luke 22 : 71–23 : 1). "According to Luke," writes New Testament scholar Lohse, "a trial against Jesus took place only before Pilate and not before the Sanhedrin" (62/38).

And in the Gospel of John, as has already been mentioned, only the high priests Annas and Caiaphas hear the Nazarene. In the opinion of many Protestant New Testament scholars, a *sentence of death* against Jesus was *probably* not given by the Sanhedrin. And *certainly*, in their opinion, the hearing before the council did not take place as it is reported in the Bible. Bultmann writes: "I think the whole narrative in Mark is a secondary explanation of the brief statement in 15 : 1" (22/269f.). There it says: "And as soon as it was morning the chief priests, with the elders and scribes, and the whole council held a consultation; and they bound Jesus and led him away and delivered him to Pilate" (Mark 15 : 1).

The kernel of the report of the hearing is the question of Caiaphas, "Are you the Christ, the Son of the Blessed?" and the answer of Jesus, which—as we already have seen —has parallels in the Old Testament, "I am; and you will see the Son of man sitting at the right hand of Power, and coming with the clouds of heaven" (Mark 14 : 61–62).

But a question, as it was attributed to Caiaphas by the early Christians, is "unthinkable in the mouth of the Jewish high priest"; the Jews avoided "every expression regarding the divine sonship of the messiah in order to clearly separate themselves from the thought of the physical divine sonship which was foreign to them but widespread in the ancient world" (62/36).

Lohse comes to the conclusion that the description by Mark "is not an historical report, but is a report coined by the Christian confession and the polemic discussion of the Christian community with the synagogue." Historically, it is probable only that the Sanhedrin "allowed Jesus to be arrested, gave him a short hearing, and then handed him over to the governor to be executed as a political agitator" (62/38).

But even if it could be proved without any doubt that no death sentence was issued by the Jewish council, the guilt of the Jews—as it is pictured in the New Testament —is scarcely diminished. It is much more strongly set forth in the description of the trial before Pilate than in the sections on the hearing before the council.

PILATE IN THE TWILIGHT

Since the evangelists wrote their texts thirty to seventy years after the death of Jesus, that which was at stake was then no longer only the guilt of the Jews. Christianity had spread widely over Palestine and needed the good will of the Roman government. "Difficulties for the proclamation of the Gospel in the Roman world" prepared for the fact that "the one who was presented as one sent by God and as Savior . . . was judged by a Roman court"; the impression could have arisen "that conversion to the Gospel itself was allegiance to an insurgent who contested the power of the Emperor" (Goguel 49/313). It may be certain "that the Christian community expressed its loyalty to the Roman occupiers and therefore wanted to represent Pilate as a proper civil servant" (Lohse 62/25). Bornkamm agrees: "We have no reason to doubt this, even though the tendency of the Gospels is clearly to present the procurator as a witness of Jesus' innocence, and thereby to exculpate Pilate, the representative of Rome, and at the same time to make him into the involuntary instrument of public opinion aroused by the Jewish leaders" (18/164).

With the figure of Pilate, as the Catholic theologian Clemens Thoma has stated, "the official Roman world was described. . . . Christendom became legitimately the true concern of the Roman government. Out of this tendency the personality of Pilate—in which the Roman government could see itself mirrored—was described as positively as possible" (39/129f.).

In other words, the alliance between state and Church, which was consummated more than two centuries later by

the Emperor Constantine, was begun by the evangelists in
their reports of the last hours of Jesus' life before the
crucifixion.

Although the texts of the passion narratives in other
respects deviate only in details from one another, the
Pilate episode grows constantly stronger from one Gospel
to another by virtue of the anti-Jewish and pro-Roman
trend. Dibelius writes: "The report that Pilate made the
decision for execution on account of the kingly claim of
Jesus was the only certain information which a narrator,
who did not have eyewitness reports at his disposal, could
have of the sentencing of Jesus" (33/282).

In Mark's Gospel "the narrator has created a hearing
scene and yet has neither changed anything in the traditional report nor added anything of a really legendary
nature" (Dibelius 33/282). The evangelist has Pilate ask,
"Are you the King of the Jews?" (Mark 15 : 2). Jesus
remains silent, and the prosecutor says, "Have you no
answer to make? See how many charges they bring against
you" (Mark 15 : 4). And Jesus again remains silent.

According to Mark, then, the governor is still an almost
neutral interrogator (Pilate says to the Jews in Mark
15 : 14, "What evil has he done?"), but the legend grows
rapidly in Matthew's Gospel. The wife of Pilate dreams
that Jesus is a just man. Pilate washes his hands in innocence, but the Jews curse themselves: "His blood be on us
and on our children!" (Matt. 27 : 19, 24, 25).

In Luke's Gospel, which apparently was written in
Rome, the author has the Jews lie. They say that Jesus has
forbidden them "to give tribute to Caesar" (Luke 23 : 2).
He inserts the transfer of the prisoner to Herod Antipas
and allows Pilate to become totally a witness to the innocence of Jesus, which he asserts three times to the Romans
("I find no crime in this man" [Luke 23 : 4]; "I did not
find this man guilty of any of your charges against him"
[Luke 23 : 14]; "I have found in him no crime deserving

death" [Luke 23 : 22]). And finally, the evangelist is silent even concerning the fact that Pilate ordered the execution of the crucifixion. In the Gospel of Luke, Pilate hands over the Nazarene to the Jews: "So Pilate gave sentence that their demand should be granted. He released the man who had been thrown into prison for insurrection and murder, whom they asked for; but Jesus he delivered up to their will" (Luke 23 : 24–25).

And in the Gospel of John, finally, Jesus and Pilate have a conversation about the kingdom of God: "My kingship is not of this world" and "Everyone who is of the truth hears my voice." Pilate answers, "What is truth?" and utters the now-famous statement, "Here is the man" (John 18 : 36–38; 19 : 5).

This trend of sanctifying Pilate continues for centuries in the Church and produces increasing embellishments. Tertullian, around the year 200, called Pilate a "secret Christian." Four centuries later, Coptic Christians declared him officially to be a saint. For a long time, writings which were finally declared apocryphal by the Church were circulated among Christians. In one, it was reported that Pilate was crucified by the Jews, as was Jesus, but was taken away while still alive and handed over to Tiberius; the emperor then had him crucified again in Rome (111/506); in another, Pilate wrote to Herod that he had met the risen Jesus in Galilee (110/690).

Yet, it is not only this Pilate of the apocryphal writings, but even the Pilate of the Bible, who has little more than a name in common with the historical Pilate. King Herod Agrippa I, a contemporary of Jesus, wrote about the governor in a letter to the Emperor Caligula: " 'He was of an unbending and ruthlessly hard character.' In his time 'corruption, violence, robbery, oppression, humiliations, constant executions without trial, and unlimited, intolerable cruelty,' were the order of the day in Judea" (17/177).

There is, in fact, apart from the Bible, no positive witness to Pilate. He provoked the Jews to open rebellion when he allowed soldiers to enter into Jerusalem with images of the emperor who was hated by the Jews. He financed the building of an aqueduct out of the temple treasury and allowed the Jews who protested to be massacred. A few years later, when an armed group of Samaritans had gathered themselves around a prophet, he allowed a similar occurrence. This incident, in the year 36, led to the recalling of Pilate from his position as governor.

The difference between the historical and the biblical Pilate seems today to be self-evident to most theologians. Catholic professor of Judaism Kurt Schubert, of Vienna, sees Pilate differently from the way he is described in the Bible. The Sanhedrin "delivered Jesus to Pilate because he did not conform to their messianic ideas. But Pilate delivered him to death, either because he still perhaps could have been able to correspond to these expectations, or because Pilate wanted to ignore the religious enthusiasts who only bear 'witness to the truth'" (John 18 : 37) (39/109).

Yet for many this distinction is insignificant. And many declare even the historical Pilate to be unhistorical. Catholic New Testament scholar Blinzler states the problem fairly accurately: "If Pilate was a cruel and bloodthirsty monster . . . it is difficult to believe that he should have had scruples about crucifying an insignificant provincial like Jesus; and if he really was as inflexible as they say, it is difficult to understand how he should have allowed himself to be finally intimidated . . ." (17/182). With a sentence of his own, Blinzler attempts to save the biblical Pilate: "Although the gospels apologetically overemphasize his role as an innocent witness, they may prove to be essentially correct in their picture of Pilate" (101/505).

Blinzler pictures Pilate, whose behavior he interprets as coming from a deep "anti-Jewish bias" (17/183), not as

guiltless, to be sure, but yet as a more positive than negative hero.

It does not disturb Blinzler that even in the New Testament the true Pilate is mentioned "casually" (17/179). In
the Gospel of Luke there is a report of the Galileans
"whose blood Pilate had mingled with their sacrifices"
(Luke 13 : 1). Blinzler takes this to be a clue concerning
a clash between the Galileans and Pilate's troops in Jerusalem on the Passover festival of the year 29; it was,
according to Blinzler, the only one of the three Passover
feasts during the time of the public ministry of Jesus which
the Nazarene had not visited. (In the opinion of other
New Testament scholars, Jesus was only once, at the end
of his life, at a Passover festival in Jerusalem.) But "a few
days before" (17/179) these Galileans could have had
contact with their countryman Jesus; a few had apparently
"shared the experience of the feeding of the multitude and
through a clumsy misinterpretation of this event had ele-
vated it into a messianic–political sign" (17/179).

Blinzler considers the "momentous encounter between
Jesus and Pilate" (17/173) to be authentic in every detail.
On the other hand, concerning the frequent change of
scene which one must assume according to the Gospel of
John, Protestant New Testament scholar Haenchen of
Münster writes: "The evangelist finds nothing impossible
in this, that now Pilate himself as a fine citizen comes out
of his house and asks who it is that they bring to him.
. . . We know enough about Roman governors to be able
to say with certainty that it would not have occurred to
Pilate to appear in person and make inquiries himself. He
would certainly not have run back and forth between
Jesus and the Jews; he was no errand boy. But how little
this signifies, this quite correct observation! Here speaks a
narrator who reduces things to that which is for him
essential . . . , with this 'here' and 'there' . . . the evangelist makes clear how Pilate was torn between the two

parties: the mass of the Jews with the high priests here, and the lonely Jesus there" (104/96).

THE JEWISH FANATICISM

Whoever defends, as Blinzler does, the historicity must also attempt to explain all the legends. So Blinzer thinks Pilate washed his hands, according to the Jewish custom, as a sign of innocence in order to be perfectly understandable to "the Jews, who for the most part did not understand his words, which were spoken in Greek" (17/218). With the same Jews, of course, Pilate had to have been able to conduct extensive conversations—with the help of interpreters, as Blinzler explains in another place. These interpreters must have been present, "for only this way could the public follow the proceedings" (17/171).

Pilate, Blinzler reports, attempts repeatedly "to wrest from the grasp of the accusers the Victim whom they were demanding so stormily," although he knows "from experience how unpleasant Jewish fanatics could make matters, even for a man in his high position" (17/194). One may well ask whether there is a "German" or a "Catholic" fanaticism as well as a "Jewish" fanaticism.

The Jews, who, according to Blinzler, are fanatical and dangerous to Pilate, assume that Jesus is led out of "courtroom" and therefore out of their vicinity. The Roman governor hands him over to Herod Antipas "obviously in the hope of getting rid of an awkward case" (17/195); "it would seem that he reckoned on an acquittal" (17/196). Jesus is sent back to Pilate, however, by Herod Antipas, whom we must think of, Blinzler says, "not as a sinister inquisitor, but rather as a capricious, jovial and affable person" (17/198).

Now the Roman offers the Jews the release either of Jesus or of a certain Barabbas, who, according to the Bible, had taken part in an insurrection and therefore is

said to have committed a murder. The Jews decide for
Barabbas. He was "a popular figure despite his crime, a
kind of nationalist hero" (17/210). Josef Blinzler cites
approvingly Josef Schmid, another Catholic New Testament scholar: "The people do not place on their heroes any
high moralistic demands." One may well ask: Which
people is meant: the Jews at that time; Jews generally;
simply the people, therefore—for example—also the Ital-
ians, the Germans? And Blinzler's own commentary on the
selection between Jesus and Barabbas states: "Up till now
it was only the sanhedrists who had been seeking the
death of Jesus. Now His fate was placed for a time in the
hands of the masses. They let Him down and in so doing
placed themselves voluntarily, though not without being
influenced to do so, on the side of His deadly enemies"
(17/211).

Pilate, as Blinzler reconstructs the story, is "not only
surprised, but thoroughly upset by the vote for Barabbas."
His "lame and helpless question," what he ought now to
do with Jesus, is "promptly answered with a shrill yell:
'Crucify him!'" Blinzler writes: "What both leaders and
crowd demanded was death . . . , the most cruel and
shameful of deaths—the Roman death of the cross"
(17/212f.). The "inexcusable tactical blunder" to begin
dealings "with the people" brings Pilate into a "situation
which was already bordering upon open riot" (17/214f.).

Pilate now also discovers that his wife has dreamed that
Jesus is a just man. Blinzler writes: "Even a pagan woman
had recognized the innocence of Jesus and tried to save
Him from the fate which His own people had intended
for Him" (17/216). Pilate washes his hands and hears the
cry of the Jews: "His blood be on us and our children!"

For the Catholic theologian Thoma, it is certain "that
the crowd was not as determinative for the end of the trial
as it seems to follow from a superficial reading of the
gospel (39/133). According to Blinzler, on the other hand,

"we can understand why it was that this decisive phase in the trial of Jesus remained for so long a painful memory among Christians" (17/211). Blinzler comments: "And while Pilate, in the most emphatic manner possible, repudiated responsibility for the death of Jesus, the Jewish people, in frivolous and high spirits, took this responsibility upon themselves with equal emphasis" (17/216). Blinzler inserts, it must be admitted, that Matthew reproduces "the standpoint of the primitive Church on the question of guilt" (17/216), and in another place in his book he confesses in a footnote "unreserved adherence to the principle," formulated by another scholar, that " 'What Caiaphas and the other Jewish leaders of the time did is no reason for holding the whole Jewish people of that time and even later times responsible' " (17/8).

Yet what are these observations worth if Blinzler himself, in this place (as in others), speaks of the "Jewish people" and does not distinguish himself from "the standpoint of the primitive Church" by stating clearly that he accepts some other standpoint? Instead of this, he allows the Jewish people to assume the responsibility and argues, therefore, in the same manner as did "the primitive Church." Why is Blinzler's argumentation here a conflicting one, even self-contradicting? There are sufficient passages in his book which prove that he can formulate things precisely if he wishes to do so. . . .

Let us return to his report of the events. The "last possibility of saving Jesus" that Pilate sees, according to Blinzler, is in the scourging of Jesus, because the Roman official knows that he can "not get away with letting Jesus off completely unpunished." Yet he underestimates the Jews, who "insist on their demand more vehemently and obstinately than ever." (17/223f.).

Even when his soldiers mask Jesus as a king, Pilate hopes again. Perhaps now, "by showing Jesus to the mob in the regalia of mockery, he would convince them of His harmlessness" (17/228). His cry "Behold the man" ought to "have had a shattering or at least chastening effect on the spirits of the rioters, who were seething with hatred," but above all, it ought to have demonstrated "the harmlessness of the alleged pretendant to the throne" (17/228f.).

Yet as all attempts to save him miscarry, so also does this one. "Angry passion can reach a degree when it is proof against any sense of humor or feeling of compassion" (17/229).

DID PILATE HAVE POWER FROM GOD?

The cry of the Jews that Jesus has "made himself the Son of God" (John 19 : 7) makes upon the Roman heathen "a deep impression," and he thinks—about which Blinzler knows and reports: "Could this accused man really be a higher being?" (17/231). According to John's Gospel, he says only: "Where are you from?" (John 19 : 9).

When Jesus does not answer him, Pilate asks: "Do you know that I have power to release you, and power to crucify you?" Jesus answers: "You would have no power over me unless it had been given you from above; therefore he who delivered me to you has the greater sin" (John 19 : 10f.). The commentary of Blinzler states: "These words do not mean to say, as is so often asserted, that the authority of the state rests upon God, the source of all authority. . . . But in God's plan of Redemption, the Roman official is the instrument chosen to bring Jesus to the Cross, and however he strives against it, he will have to do it, because he cannot escape either the plans of God or the force of earthly combinations, in this case primarily the demand of the Jews, and his own personal inadequacy to cope with the situation. . . . Because Pilate is acting, not on his own free volition but in the execution of the special authority against Jesus given him by God, his guilt is less than that of the Jews, who are striving for the

death of the Messiah purely out of hate and wickedness"
(17/232).

One may well ask whether it can also be said of the Jews
(to use Blinzler's term) that they acted "not out of free
volition but in the execution of the special authority given
to them by God"? Or to put it differently, is it not God who
allows them to strive "for the death of the Messiah
purely out of hate and wickedness"? But if it is God who
allows the one (Pilate) as also the other (the Jews) to act
in such a way against Jesus, has then the one less guilt
than the other? No theologian ought to answer that
question too quickly.

Back to the report. "The Jews," Blinzler continues, now
play "their last and most important trump card" (17/236).
They threaten a report to the emperor in Rome. That is
naturally an "infamous Jewish threat" and with it "Pilate's
resistance . . . breaks down" (17/237). Pilate takes
revenge for "the shameful role forced upon him." He
succeeds in hammering "into the consciousness and memory of the masses the fact that the death sentence about
to be pronounced was at their own express demand and
consequently their own responsibility" (17/238). Blinzler
reads that out of the text, "Shall I crucify your King?"
(John 19 : 15).

Blinzler finds his picture of Pilate, as well as the guilt
of the Jews, confirmed in other passages in the Bible.
Commenting on the report that Pilate handed over the
body of Jesus to Joseph of Arimathea on his request,
Blinzler writes: "Only if it is true that Pilate had seen in
Jesus no real insurrectionist and had spoken the sentence
of death only under duress, is it understandable that he
agreed to the proposal of the handing over of the body
without condition or official orders" (17/89 [German ed.]).

And as for the guilt of the Jews, we may look to the
parable of the vinegrower (Mark 12 : 1–12). Jesus himself
points to the "coming punishment of the Jewish leaders."

The parable is to be understood as indicating that God will " 'destroy' them, that is, let them fall into eternal damnation." And the parable "recognizes not alone the guilt of the sanhedrists but also the complicity of the people, who as a whole were solidly on the side of their leaders" (17/279).

In a quite different manner, Cardinal Bea comments on this passage: "Who would not, in fact, arrive at the opinion, if he listened to the text of the parable of the vinegrower, that God, after the Jewish leadership had finally rejected Jesus, rejected summarily his chosen people and gave the benefits of the kingdom of God to other peoples. But in reality nothing of the sort happened. The apostles continue to teach for decades among the Jews of Palestine, and only gradually do they spread out, but even then they turn first to the Jews in the synagogue. Saint Paul would not disagree with this" (97/652).

Through other passages in the New Testament, in Blinzler's opinion, could the Jews in no way be exonerated. The Apostle Peter, with the statement: "And now, brethren, I know that you acted in ignorance, as did also your rulers" (Acts 3 : 17), definitely had in mind "a culpable ignorance" and not only a subjective guilt (17/284).

And if, in the New Testament, the author of the crucifixion seems "at one time to be the sanhedrists and the inhabitants of Jerusalem, at yet another, Judas or Pilate, or the devil and his wicked hosts; or again God, or Jesus Himself," it is at any rate not intended "to dispute or even to minimize the guilt of those historically responsible" (17/288f.).

On the next to the last page of his book, Blinzler nevertheless remarks "how anti-Christian it would be on the part of Christians today to harbor feelings of dislike and enmity toward the descendents of those who incurred guilt through what happened on Good Friday on Golgatha" (17/294). One may simply wish to ask: Even if the Christians wanted to (and were permitted to), could they then do it? If the witnesses to the trial before Pilate, according to Blinzler, "consisted only of inhabitants of Jerusalem" (17/292), how could then someone *today* decide whether, after nineteen centuries, he is dealing with a descendent of that allegedly or actually guilty Jerusalem mob or with the descendent of a Galilean?

CONSCIENCELESS INSTIGATORS

Near the end of his book, Blinzler expresses himself on the problem of the murder of God: "Much has been spoken of deicide. It should be noted that the New Testament makes no such reproach either to the Sanhedrin or to the procurator. Since the enemies of Jesus lacked any deep insight into the mystery of His being, their act was not actually the crime of deicide. The Christian who, because of his belief in the divinity of Jesus, cannot regard His death on Golgotha otherwise than as a *deicidium*, would also do well to avoid this term when discussing the human guilt involved" (17/293).

One may well ask: Is it only "better," therefore, so to speak, tactically more clever, to avoid such a term? Or is it simply necessary to strike this word out of the vocabulary of Christians because it has so often been used and has brought so much blood upon the Jews?

In the so-called *Understanding of the Jews* of the Second Vatican Council, this word does not appear. To be sure, that has a negative rather than a positive ground. A minority prevented the inclusion of a phrase saying that the reproach of "God murderers" was no longer to be raised against the Jews.

How widespread in the Catholic church is the opinion of Blinzler that the Jewish people have taken upon themselves the guilt of the death of Jesus? What do Catholics read in their Bibles (all of which appear with imprimatur and with notes) about the Pilate-scene and, above all, about the blood curse? Are they pointed to the fact that "the Jews" and "the people" are not meant here? Or is it Catholic practice, as with the commentators of Protestant Bibles, to give information about coins, dimensions, and weight details, but to be silent about such questions?

In a New Testament published in 1959, the Catholic theologian Otto Karrer explained the curse of the Jews in this way: "Regular phraseology of the Old Testament with the meaning: 'the responsibility and the consequences for the death sentence we shall bear ourselves.'"

In the New Testament published in 1962 by Kösel-Verlag (Munich), "new edition" of the 1951 New Testament edited by Student Pastor Werner Becker, there is reference to the "untruthfulness and the malice of the Jewish representatives."

And in 1964, there appeared, with "episcopal approval and recommendation" and with the imprimatur of the bishop of Rothenburg, Karl Joseph Leiprecht, in the Keppler publishing house of Stuttgart, a million copies of a Bible in which theological professor Peter Ketter writes concerning the curse of the Jews under the cross of Jesus: "The inserted self-curse shows to what a people can come if it gives ear to conscienceless instigators."

One can also say it in another way, to be sure, without "episcopal approval and recommendation": The history of the Church shows that well into the late Middle Ages countless Jews met their death because Christians gave ear to "conscienceless" instigators—the quotation marks may show that the author chooses not to maintain that they had been conscienceless—among their pastors and saints.

Only a few are cited here. Saint John Chrysostom preached: "I know that very many believers feel a certain attraction for the Jews and hold their ceremonies in honor. I see myself therefore compelled to root out completely such a fatal opinion. I have already mentioned that the synagogue is not worth any more than the theater . . . Therefore the synagogue is not only a theater but also a brothel; It is a den of thieves and a hiding-place for wild animals . . . and not simply for animals, but for unclean beasts" (12, 16).

Sixteen centuries later, Gregory Baum, a priest of Jewish descent, has written: "If one were convinced that the New Testament contained an inspiration of contempt and hatred for the Jewish people, or for any people, one could not believe that it embodies divine revelation and the source of salvation for mankind" (11/17).

"A CORPSE," theologian Rudolf Bultmann repeated and confirmed in a discussion with philosopher Karl Jaspers, "cannot come back to life or rise from the grave." That this is also true for the crucified and dead Jesus is clear from the context: "But how am I," Bultmann asks without answering, "in my capacity as pastor, to explain, in my sermons and classes, texts dealing with the Resurrection of Jesus in the flesh?" (55/60).

Jesus indeed rose and appeared to his disciples, says Hans Grass, professor of systematic theology in the University of Marburg, but "in such a way that a camera or a tape recorder would have noted nothing" (51/225).

Whether the resurrection of Jesus was "an event that violates the laws of nature," Wolfhart Pannenberg, professor of systematic theology at the University of Munich, would not be able to say. That here "judgments must be made more carefully" than in relation to general occurrences is clear from modern physics (73/98).

And Willi Marxsen, professor of New Testament at the University of Münster, responds to the question "Is Jesus risen?" by saying, "The answer cannot be ascertained" (66/19f.). According to Marxsen, "the question is with what right one *may* speak of the resurrection of Jesus at all *in a Christian way?*" (66/34).

These Protestant theological scholars, who are counted among the leading figures of German Protestant theology, repeat the confession of faith as do other Christians in the worship service: "I believe in Jesus Christ . . . on the third day he rose again from the dead . . ." Yet they do not believe that which most Christians believe who sit on Sundays in the pews of Protestant or Catholic churches.

For simple believers, the risen Jesus met two disciples on the road to Emmaus, ate fried fish, showed to his disciples the wounds which had remained from the nails on the cross and from the spear of the soldier, engaged in conversation, and explained to his disciples the scriptures "beginning with Moses and all the prophets" (Luke 24 : 27). And for many believing Christians, the risen Jesus also ascended into heaven before the eyes of the disciples. Indeed, it says this in the Holy Scriptures.

This confidence in the literal meaning of the resurrection reports is encouraged by conservative Protestant and Catholic theologians and historians who—so Grass criticizes—"take the reports naïvely as stenographic records and recommend obedient acceptance" (51/13).

Conservative authors of books about Jesus often talk about the risen Christ in about the same way that they talk about any other earth-dweller. Thus one Catholic scholar, Joseph Ricciotti, transfers to a natural setting the biblical report about a meeting at the lake of Tiberius of the disciples with the one who was believed to be dead:

"They steered again to the shore, in order to tie up. When they were still about 100 yards out, they noticed in the darkness a figure on the shore, who was not clearly distinguishable, but who apparently waited for them. Perhaps it was a retailer who wanted to buy their fish. When they had come within shouting distance, the man asked: 'Lads, do you have anything to eat?' After a night of fruitless effort, the question sounded like a sneer. So out of the boat there came a dry 'No,' which cut off any further inquiry. Yet a rejoinder succeeded. The man called through the morning fog: 'Throw the net out on the right side of the boat, and you will catch something.' A bit later, Peter covered the 100 yards with powerful strokes and was surprised to see the risen Jesus. Those remaining in the boat came slowly, for they had a huge catch to take care of. . . . The awe did not decrease their hunger. All enjoyed the bread and the fish, which Jesus distributed to them. After they had been strengthened physically, there came spiritual nourishment." And Ricciotti writes concerning the ascension: "At the time of the final meeting with the risen master, the apostles sensed that something extraordinary was in the air. . . . The risen one gave his final instructions. . . . And it happened, while he blessed them, that he departed from them and was carried away into heaven. . . . The ascension took place near Jerusalem, on the Mount of Olives, close to Bethany, forty days after the resurrection" (78/662ff.).

Nothing of that which Ricciotti relates actually happened, according to modern Protestant theologians, for the risen Christ did not have "flesh and bone," as Jesus himself maintains. ("See my hands and my feet, that it is I myself; handle me, and see; for a spirit has not flesh and bones as you see that I have" [Luke 24 : 39]). And he neither rose "on the third day" nor ascended into heaven forty days after the resurrection, according to theologian Grass of Marburg in his very important book, published in 1956, *Ostergeschehen und Osterberichte.*

The ascension, for almost two thousand years a festival for Christians, described and portrayed countless times, never took place.

Protestant theologians are united on what happened after his death as little as they are on every other problem having to do with the life of Jesus. And there are also differing notions about what the resurrection means for Christians.

WITHOUT EASTER THE CHURCH WOULD SIMPLY BE A JESUS SOCIETY

When one speaks of these differences and contradictions, the fact cannot be denied that almost every theologian emphasizes the meaning of the resurrection. It is said *that* the resurrection means a great deal, but theologians are not able to agree on *what* it means. Heinz Zahrnt, who is fought as a neorationalist by the Confession Movement, writes: "Without Easter the crucifixion would mean the ruin of Jesus, and the Church would simply be a Jesus Association or a Jesus Society, in the same way as we have Goethe, Luther, Ranke or Bach Associations or Societies. Christianity stands or falls by the resurrection of Jesus from the dead" (93/120). And Günther Bornkamm insists that "there would be no gospel, not one account, no letter in the New Testament, no faith, no Church, no worship, no prayer in Christendom . . . without the message of the resurrection of Christ" (18/181).

And according to Eberhard Müller, without the resurrection "our whole faith is 'moonshine.' Moonshine is perhaps better than total darkness. It illuminates the way, but it conceals the goal. It indicates outlines and forms, but it also begets specters. It produces comforting moods, but it pales in the sober light of day" (69/121).

Modern and conservative theologians seem also to be agreed that there is a "historical kernel" of the Easter events. Often in this connection reference is made to the fact that the disciples forsook their Lord after the arrest of Jesus and fled, and that, nevertheless, there is no doubt that after the death of Jesus a community of Christians was formed. The argument of New Testament scholar Martin Dibelius has become popular: "Something must have happened in between, which in a short time not only produced a complete reversal of their attitude but also enabled them to engage in renewed activity and to found the primitive Christian community. This 'something' is the historical kernel of the Easter faith" (35/141). Willi Marxsen (we shall return later to his position) and Ernst Fuchs seem to be the only ones with different opinions. Fuchs writes: "It is curious that the Easter events are often understood as having had to heal a despair originating in the crucifixion of Jesus. That seems as though the 'first' faith of the disciples in the cross of Jesus was shattered. Later, then, the true faith would have been grounded in a 'countermove' to that, precisely on the cross of Jesus. With what right does one psychologize *suddenly* at *this* point? The flight of the disciples, as also of the betrayer, is simply a literary motif. . . . What were they supposed to have done when the police came?" (42/18).

Yet what good is the agreement of the great majority of theologians if there is disagreement about this "something"? Actually, the differences of opinion with regard to the Easter event and the Easter faith are at least as great as they are about other problems of the historical Jesus and the kerygmatic Christ.

Although on many other questions the borders between theological positions are as hazy as are the theological concepts used to describe them, one needs only to be able to count to three regarding the resurrection to be able to distinguish an entirely conservative from a modern theologian.

For the former, three men walked from Jerusalem to Emmaus, as it stands in the Bible, two disciples and the risen Jesus ("While they were talking and discussing together, Jesus himself drew near and went with them" [Luke 24 : 15]). For the latter, the modern theologian, it was either two (one of the two disciples had a vision) or it was no one (if the entire scene is taken to be a legend).

The parties divide also at the tomb of Jesus. "There is no Easter message without the report of the empty tomb," said Walter Künneth of Erlangen in the Westfalenhalle (12/38). "God did not have to make the tomb empty in order to perform the Easter miracle," wrote Althaus, who also taught at Erlangen (4/32) and, in practically identical words, Grass of Marburg concurred (51/185). There is, regarding the tomb, still a third party: those theologians who contend, as does Bultmann, that the tomb *can* have been empty (cf. the Bultmann interview in the last chapter).

On the question of Easter event and Easter faith we find a few theologians who are sometimes conservative and sometimes modern. Yet even these fence sitters cannot— or have not been able to—forge a unity.

Protestant theologians themselves are not united about the central issue of the Christian faith: "If Christ has not been raised, then our preaching is in vain and your faith is in vain" (1 Cor. 15 : 14). There is only a residual agreement remaining, namely, that (perhaps with the exception of Marxsen, whom we must still investigate) a report of Paul concerning the witnesses of the resurrection is taken to be the most valuable document.

Paul says: "For I delivered to you as of first importance what I also received, that Christ died for our sins in accordance with the scriptures, that he was buried, that he was raised on the third day in accordance with the scriptures" (1 Cor. 15 : 3–4). And the Apostle counts off the witnesses of the resurrection: ". . . and that he appeared to Cephas (Peter), then to the twelve. Then he appeared to more than five hundred brethren at one time, most of whom are still alive, though some have fallen asleep. Then he appeared to James, then to all the apostles. Last of all, as to one untimely born, he appeared also to me" (1 Cor. 15 : 5–8).

Paul probably wrote this letter to the Corinthians in the

year 56 or 57—a quarter century after the death of Jesus, about ten years before the first Gospel (Mark) and about forty years before the last Gospel (John) were written. For many Protestant theologians, Paul is the only one of the New Testament authors who himself had seen the risen Jesus or had had a vision of Jesus. The Gospels according to Matthew and John, these theologians say, were not composed by disciples of Jesus (contrary to earlier Protestant opinion and, even today, the usual Catholic view).

Paul himself traces his conversion back to Christ alone, that Christ appeared to him—in the year 33, three years after the death of Jesus as theologians have figured it.

Hans von Campenhausen of Heidelberg writes concerning Paul's list of witnesses: "Whoever wants to doubt their reliability, must, to be consistent, doubt everything which has been handed down in the New Testament—and more than that!" (30/10f.). But Paul lists only witnesses. There are neither places nor any other kind of details given for the appearances, and there is no mention of the empty tomb. In the four Gospels, on the other hand, not all the witnesses whom Paul names are mentioned. For example, nothing is said about an appearance before "five hundred brethren," and that Christ appeared alone to Peter (Cephas, Simon) is mentioned only in the Gospel according to Luke (. . . who said, "The Lord has risen indeed, and has appeared to Simon!" [Luke 24 : 34]).

DANCING SPARKS AND COLORED CIRCLES

The Gospels are distinguishable from the letter to the Corinthians also in that they speak of the empty tomb and the manner of the appearances. That "appearances of the resurrected Lord were really experienced by a number of members of the primitive Christian community and not perhaps freely invented in the course of the later legendary development," Pannenberg thinks ". . . has good historical foundation" (73/91). But when one starts to speak about the manner of the appearances, "the greatest difficulties begin to arise" (73/92). "Of all the received reports," says Campenhausen, "not two agree" (30/21).

According to Matthew's Gospel, Jesus appears to the disciples in Galilee; according to Luke and John, in Jerusalem and its surroundings. Whereas, according to Mark's Gospel, the risen Christ ascended into heaven on the first day, he lets himself, according to Acts, be seen among them "during forty days" (Acts 1 : 3). Whereas, according to Matthew, he appears only once to his disciples, according to John, he appears three times.

Distinguishable also are almost all the details. According to Mark, three women hurry to the tomb; according to Matthew, two, "Mary Magdalene and the other Mary" (Matt. 28 : 1). According to Mark 16 : 9 and John, only Mary Magdalene of the women sees the one believed to be dead; according to Matthew, "the other Mary" also catches sight of him ("And behold, Jesus met them and said, 'Hail!' " [Matt. 28 : 9]); according to Luke, he appears to none of the women. According to Mark and John, the tomb is already opened when the women enter it ("And looking up, they saw that the stone was rolled back; for it was very large" [Mark 16 : 4]); according to Matthew, an angel "came and rolled back the stone, and sat upon it" (Matt. 28 : 2)—with the strange result "that Jesus must have gone out of the still-sealed tomb through the stone block," Campenhausen has commented (30/30). That which seems strange to this church historian was once considered to be self-evident by Luther; namely, that Jesus was raised through the stone (51/26). According to John, the corpse of Jesus was annointed immediately after death; according to Luke, the women still wanted to do it on the third day after the crucifixion, which is "impossible in the East where the body decays very rapidly" (Grass 51/20).

These and numerous other contradictions are evaluated in various ways by the theologians. For Barth the difficulties are few; the reports speak "to us in freedom, in fantasy-making and poetic forms and in the shadows of historical saga. They do describe, in fact, an event that is inaccessible to historical comprehension and description" (63/203).

On the other hand, Künneth writes: "Whoever turns the primitive Christian 'physical' realism of the Easter reports into legends has, by doing so, proved that the decisive center of the Easter kerygma, the witness of the new imperishable existence–reality, remains closed to him" (63/207). The Easter reports are; "in contrast to myth and legend, an apostolic–prophetic witness concerning the new Christ-world, which is ununderstandable by the immanent and inexpressible by the profane" (63/205).

For many theologians the contradictions are an index for the genuineness of the reports. Cardinal Bea remembers "the well-known psychological principle that the more we have to do with moving events which excite the onlooker, the more difficult it is to preserve accuracy of observations." But, at the same time, Bea says that there is "obviously no question here of cases of diseased or abnormal excitement, as is supposed in some theories which consider the apparitions of the risen Christ as hallucinations of the witnesses, including the apostles. What we are supposing is the excitement which is understandable and quite normal in the face of such an extraordinary event" (13/53). Helmut Thielicke, professor of systematic theology at the University of Hamburg, argues in a similar way. "If someone, for example, receives a blow in the face, his ears will rumble and his eyes will see colored circles. He therefore has optical and acoustical impressions, although that which happened to him had nothing to do with optics and acoustics, with seeing and hearing. . . . The one perceives a rushing noise, the other the ringing of bells; the one sees dancing sparks and the other a rainbow. Even if a blow on the head is not exactly a perfect example with which to illustrate the resurrection, yet the main point of this comparison is important. The eyes, the ears, the mind and also the phantasy of those who experienced the secret of the resurrection morning were suddenly confronted with a reality, which simply overstepped their capacity, which placed too great demands on their normal functions. . . . It would be necessary to be able to synchronize and to harmonize a bit so that the various impressions could be put together into an exact, agreed-upon statement, if witness were to be made more believable. But that is not done; the 'dancing sparks' and the 'rainbow' are allowed to stand next to one another" (91/211f. [German ed.]).

As do Thielicke and other theologians, Catholic dogmatician Karl Adam praises the "character of the primitiveness and believableness" of the reports. They cause "every artificial working-over of the accounts, every attempt at harmonization, to fail." The purpose of the reports is to transmit "simply and truly the direct impression of the eyewitnesses."

However, numerous Protestant theologians have been convinced for a long time that such statements about legends only spread legends. The "accounts" of the resurrection are, in the opinion of these theologians, not only artificially worked-over but, for the most part, are not accounts at all, but legends. And most of the "sparks" began to dance for the first time several years and even decades after the event.

Such interpretations are not limited to Bultmann and his school. The Erlangen theologian Althaus, for example, wrote that we could not always "handle the resurrection narratives as the primitive Easter witness of the disciples," for the "struggle against hellenistic spiritualizing of the appearances led to the dogmatic emphasis on the bodily character of the resurrection" (3/274).

Recently this opinion, which Rudolf Bultmann and Martin Dibelius laid out in great detail, is carefully defended also in Catholic theological literature. The Jesuit Günther Schiwy went a bit farther than have other Catholic authors when he wrote a review of Grass's book *Ostergeschehen und Osterberichte* in the April 1966 issue of *Stimmen der Zeit*. Grass stated that the evangelists "put together their reports, in that they collected, compared, cut out, and worked over the local traditions about how it had really been; in that they transcribed from one another and elaborated on certain vague hints where they had no doubts, they were free to change details and to form a not entirely reliable history which demonstrated, nevertheless, its theological, pedagogical, or apologetic intent" (112/285).

LEGENDS WITH CONTRADICTIONS AND IMPOSSIBILITIES

Protestant theologians employing biblical criticism have analyzed the resurrection narratives with the same methods that they have used on the other parts of the New Testament. Accordingly, they have stated that a few passages seem to merely serve the purpose of defending the resurrection of Jesus against doubt and the attack of the Jews.

According to Mark, the Roman governor Pilate "wondered if he [Jesus] were already dead; and summoning the centurion, he asked him whether he was already dead." (Mark 15 : 44). Church historian Campenhausen considers it to be "somewhat noteworthy with what emphasis the fact of the death of Jesus is here stated and, as it were, officially confirmed" (30/35). The reason behind this is possibly to verify that "Jesus was really dead, that is, that he was not taken down from the cross before dying, when he only appeared to be dead. Therefore the later disappearance of his body cannot be explained away" (30/36).

The narrative of the tomb, according to Matthew, "is packed full of contradictions and impossibilities" (Campenhausen 30/20), because a legend about a Roman guard at the tomb of Jesus has been inserted into the story; it is supposed to do away with the notion that the disciples had succeeded in taking away the corpse of Jesus. This motif recurs even in the Gospel itself: "The chief priests and the Pharisees" ask Pilate about making the sepulchre secure, so that his disciples may not "go and steal him away, and tell the people, 'He has risen from the dead'" (Matt. 29 : 62, 64). The Jews make reference, therefore, to the announcement of Jesus that he would rise again after three days (Matt. 27 : 63). Campenhausen comments: "The resurrection-announcement by Jesus must be presupposed as generally known, so that the 'chief priests and Pharisees' can also refer to it, and they do this with precision. The guard is necessary only until the third day, and the request to the governor is made with the limitation" (30/29).

Therefore the pagan guards do not become ear-witnesses of the conversation between an angel and the women at the tomb. The author of the Gospel has them so frightened by the appearance of the angel that they, "became like dead men" (Matt. 28 : 4). Nevertheless, after this the soldiers report "all that had taken place" (Matt. 28 : 11), to be sure—a further contradiction—not to their chief superior Pilate, who had ordered them to the tomb, but to the Jewish chief priests. "And although these villains thereby only spread their own lies [that the body of Jesus has been stolen] the Christians, as the record shows, have very precise information concerning everything that has happened" (Campenhausen 30/29).

Campenhausen traces back to "apologetic design" also the difference between the Gospel according to Mark and that according to Matthew. In Mark the women come upon the tomb already opened; it had been opened first by an angel. According to Matthew, "the tomb was not only sealed and guarded. It remained so even to the last moment, since the witnesses are at the place entirely undisturbed, and no robber or thief can have set foot in it" (30/30).

Several theologians also suspect apologetic motifs in the report that Peter found in the empty tomb the "linen cloths" of Jesus and his napkin "not lying with the linen cloths but rolled up in a place by itself" (John 20 : 5, 7). Campenhausen takes this to be a scenic presentation of the thesis that the dead one can not have been stolen. "No one who wants to get rid of a corpse first unpacks it carefully and then drags it out 'naked' " (30/31f.).

And even the scene in which Mary Magdalene sees the risen Jesus and imagines that he is a gardener (also in John 20 : 14–18) is, according to Campenhausen, "the direct answer to Jewish accusations and doubts" (30/30). The women consider the risen Jesus to be the thief of the dead Jesus: "Sir, if you have carried him away, tell me where you have laid him, and I will take him away" (John 20 : 15). With these legends the Christians responded to a legend of the Jews, that "Juda the gardener" had foreseen the threatening fraud and had managed to remove the body of Jesus. When the disciples then claimed that Jesus had risen, the corpse was displayed and carried through the streets (30/32).

Tertullian alluded to these anti-Christian legends when he wrote about how Jesus would come forward as judge in the last judgment: "There he is, whom his disciples secretly removed so that they could say that he was risen, whom the gardener had set aside so that the many visitors would not injure his vegetables!" (30/33).

Critical theologians state, in addition to that, that many tendencies grow from one Gospel to the next. An obvious

example is that in the oldest Gospel, Mark, there is talk
only of the "tomb" of Jesus (Mark 15 : 46); in Matthew,
it is a "new tomb" (Matt. 27 : 60); in Luke, it is a tomb
"where no one had ever yet been laid" (Luke 19 : 41).

Even more important is it that the reports of the tomb
and of the women were at first independent of the reports
concerning the appearances—the Christophanies—to the
disciples. According to Mark, the women find the tomb
empty and are commanded by an angel to inform the
disciples and to tell them to go to Galilee. But the women
"said nothing to anyone, for they are afraid" (Mark 16 : 8).
Campenhausen comments: "The clear and forcefully
formulated order, one must conclude, is not carried out
at all, and it remains unclear how the disciples nevertheless arrived in Galilee where Christ was to appear to
them" (30/26).

In the subsequently written Gospel of Matthew, the
women do bring to the disciples the message of the angel
"with fear and great joy" (Matt. 28 : 8), yet it still
"remains unclear how the report of the women reached
the disciples at all, and how they have received it" (Campenhausen 30/39) since there is nothing reported about a
visit of the disciples to the grave. The reader only knows
that they meet Jesus in Galilee. In the Gospel of Luke, the
disciples do not believe the women's report of the empty
tomb: "But these words seemed to them an idle tale, and
they did not believe them" (Luke 24 : 11). Nevertheless,
"several" disciples go to the tomb and find it "just as the
women had said" (Luke 24 : 24). In the last Gospel
(John), the two best-known disciples, Peter and John,
hurry, on the basis of the news, to the grave: "They both
ran, but the other disciple [John] outran Peter and reached
the tomb first" (John 20 : 4). Grass comments: "John runs
faster, not because he is younger, but because he is the
beloved disciple" (51/55). Ernst Fuchs is of the opinion
that the statement about the empty tomb contained in

John's Gospel is, perhaps, even made light of by the race of the two disciples (42/467).

As are the disciples, so also is Jesus, brought into an increasingly close relationship to the tomb. Luke states explicitly that Jesus does not appear at the tomb (". . . but him they did not see" [Luke 24 : 24]); also in Mark it is reported that only the angel announces his resurrection. In Matthew's Gospel, Jesus appears to the women when they have left the tomb, and in John, he stands directly at the tomb. The angels sit only "as an honor guard at the empty tomb. They are no longer messengers of the resurrection-miracle" (Grass 51/58).

NOT TO SEE AND YET TO BELIEVE!

The physical character of the risen Christ is also pictured with increasing emphasis. In Mark's Gospel, it is neglected. The last twelve verses (9–20) of the last chapter, which talk about the physical resurrection, are, in the opinion of almost all New Testament scholars, an extension of the original text which ends with the eighth verse or, at any rate, is preserved only up to this point.

In Matthew the risen Jesus only speaks. In Luke he walks about with two disciples, with whom he also sits down and eats. When he appears also to the other disciples, he emphasizes his body: "See my hands and my feet, that it is I myself; handle me, and see; for a spirit has not flesh and bones as you see that I have" (Matt. 24 : 39). He asks: "Have you anything here to eat?", and "before them" (before their eyes) he eats a piece of broiled fish (Matt. 24 : 41–43). According to John's Gospel, Jesus enters a room even though the doors are closed (John 20 : 19), shows to the disciples "his hands and his side" (John 20 : 20), and asks "eight days later" (John 20 : 26) the unbelieving disciple Thomas to touch him: "Put your fingers here, and see my hands; and put out your hand,

and place it in my side; do not be faithless, but believing"
(John 20 : 27). Only in John's Gospel is it also reported
that there was a meeting by the Sea of Tiberius where the
risen Christ helps the unsuccessful and hungry disciples to
get a huge catch of fish ("Jesus said to them, 'Children
have you any fish?' They answered him, 'No'" [John
21 : 5]; and he says to them: "Come and have breakfast!"
[John 21 : 12]).

The Thomas episode, which ends with the words of
Jesus "Blessed are those who have not seen and yet believe" (John 20 : 29), is interpreted differently by theologians everywhere. Conservatives value it mostly as an
impressive proof for the physical resurrection. In the
opinion of others, however, it is "told exclusively for the
purpose of emphasizing that one ought to have Easter
faith even without the Easter message" (Harnack 63/53).

In various ways theologians also evaluate the genuineness of the Gospel presentation of the Easter events in
general. Grass writes: "Even if one could successfully
eliminate all legendary pictures and proliferations, there
would still be no kernel obtainable, through this peeling
process, of which it could be said that it clearly reflects the
original events in their proper sequence." (51/11). With
regard to the appearances of Jesus, Professor Pannenberg
of Munich comes to the same conclusion: "The appearances reported in the Gospels, which are not mentioned by
Paul, have such a strongly legendary character that one can
scarcely find a historical kernel of their own in them. Even
the Gospels' reports that correspond to Paul's statements
are heavily colored by legendary elements, particularly by
the tendency toward underlining the corporeality of the
appearances" (73/89).

Conservative Protestants and, certainly, most Catholic
theologians do not wish to draw up the balance sheet in
that way. Yet they do admit that one or another of the
scenes—for instance, the scene of the Roman guard at the

tomb of Jesus—is legendary. The discussions are most difficult when it gets down to two key questions: whether the tomb of Jesus was empty, and whether (and in what sense) the risen Jesus walked about in a physical body.

A CORPSE CANNOT COME BACK TO LIFE

In the controversy concerning the empty tomb, three groups—as has already been pointed out—have arisen among Protestant theologians. For the first group, the empty tomb is "an objective and testable fact." As Ethelbert Stauffer has formulated it: The Christophanies lose "their objective support and concrete meaning apart from the empty tomb" (89/24). Künneth writes: "The empty tomb signifies the objectivity of the Easter event" (63/200). Karl Barth and Paul Althaus may serve as representatives for the second group. According to Barth, "this tomb may be proved finally to be closed or open; it really makes no difference" (63/199). And according to Althaus, "Jesus' tomb must not have been empty, so that . . . we can be certain of the eschatological corporeality of his appearance. And our, that is the Christians', tombs will not be empty when God calls us on his day to new bodily existence. Our old body will long since have decomposed in the earth" (4/31). And in a third group may be included all those who, as Bultmann, are of the conviction that "a corpse cannot come back to life or rise from the grave" (55/60).

There is also a contradiction between the views of the theologians and those of the Christians in the congregations. Eberhard Müller errs in his thinking that only in previous centuries was an external facet of the resurrection account made characteristic of the orthodox faith of genuine Christians, namely "the empty tomb" (8/138). The empty tomb is still a criterion for correct faith even today (or again today). For a few leaders of the Confession

Movement, the conviction that the tomb was empty is the criterion for faith in the resurrection of Jesus.

Taking part in the controversy about the empty tomb are also scholars who think about the account of the appearances from the conservative side; for instance, church historian Campenhausen and systematic theologian Pannenberg. Pannenberg uses as his basis: "Jesus' empty tomb, if it should be a historical fact, belongs to the singularity of Jesus' fate. He precisely had not lain many years in his grave or decayed as the other dead had, but after a short time he was 'transformed' to another life, whatever such an expression may mean" (73/100).

On almost every single problem the theses of the proponents of the empty tomb and those of their opponents stands against one another. Campenhausen: "The decisive impulse which brought everything into play was the discovery of the empty tomb" (30/50). Grass: "Not the empty tomb, but the appearances [were] the decisive impulse which brought everything into play" (51/119). Grass: "If one allows the proof for the empty tomb to be pursued into every detail, then one could almost prove historically the fact of the resurrection. But this is obviously not possible according to God's will. It ought to remain an 'unheard-of-thing' which is not possible to arrive at by means of human proof" (51/184f.). Pannenberg: "Where does Grass obtain his information about what is possible by God's will and what is not?" (73/102).

"From the beginning on," the fact of the empty tomb had been preached in the primitive Christian community, according to Gerhard Gloege, systematic theologian at Bonn. He appeals to the fact that it is stated in 1 Corinthians "that he was buried, that he was raised" (1 Cor. 15 : 4). Gloege says: "The empty tomb is not discussed in detail but assumed and taken for granted" (46/283). But even according to Campenhausen, who is troubled about positive proof for the empty tomb, it is "certainly too much" to deduce from that Pauline sentence a knowledge of the empty tomb (30/20). And even for Pannenberg it is "probably doubtful" that Paul "should have known the Jerusalem tradition of the discovery of Jesus' grave" (73/100).

After the death of Jesus, there was agreement between Jews and Christians that the tomb of Jesus was empty. Künneth argued this way in the Westfalenhalle: "Even the enemies cannot deny the fact of the empty tomb" (12/38): the Jews maintained that someone stole the body; the Christians believed in the resurrection. To Künneth, however, one might say: The Jewish polemic could just as well have been a reaction to the Christian affirmation that the tomb was empty as to the empty tomb itself.

According to Althaus, the message of the resurrection "could not have been maintained in Jerusalem for a day, not even an hour, if the emptiness of the tomb had not been established as a fact for all those concerned" (4/22). Such views, replies Emanuel Hirsch of Göttingen, are based on the inability "to think oneself into a situation in which the grave and the corpse are surrounded by taboo-like fear, in which, therefore, no one can think about opening grave chambers in order to take bodies out and to identify them through scientific examination" (73/100).

In the opinion of most Protestant theologians, the attempt to ascertain the identity of the tomb found in the time of Emperor Constantine, in the year 326, through the comparison of Bible verses with the measurements of that tomb is fruitless. A few researchers have indicated, for instance, that the fact that there is in this tomb only one place on the right side agrees with the account given in the Gospel of Mark that the angel sat "on the right side" (Mark 16 : 5) in the open tomb. Grass writes that "the right side is simply the side of honor. . . . If even the sitting place of the angel must be confirmed by archaeological findings, then one can as well ask whether the three women sat together with the angel (Mark 16 : 1, 5) in the narrow tomb of three by six feet, whether there would have been room" (51/141f.).

In more recent times, Grass and Campenhausen have attempted to determine from the tomb accounts in the Bible whether the report of the empty tomb is historical.

Campenhausen, concerned about the evidence, supports his thesis in part on the basis of the report in Mark's Gospel that the women had "said nothing to anyone" (Mark 16 : 8) about the empty tomb. This tendency, "which at first glance is somewhat mysterious," (Campenhausen 30/26) is explained by countless theologians—for example, Günther Bornkamm—by saying that, on the one hand, the fact of the open tomb had to be reported, and on the other hand, at the same time, it had to be indicated why it had not been known immediately after the death of Jesus (cf. 18/182f.). Campenhausen thinks that this thesis cannot be maintained. "The unhistorical intent with which the questionable sentence was formulated may be comparable to some products of medieval fabricators of legends, but is completely without example within the old Protestant tradition" (30/27). Campenhausen's meaning is this: "The disciples, the evangelist wants to say, had nothing at all to do with the empty tomb. . . . The empty tomb is an event for itself, whose witness is only subsequently joined to the experiences which the disciples later had in Galilee; it therefore deserves both faith and consideration, but the disciples themselves had nothing to do with it. . . . [But in the] endeavor to avert a determined threatening distrust, . . . [the evangelist has] not at all noticed to what strange consequences his presentation must lead, as soon as one pursues it in another direction than he had in mind" (30/37f.). The "solution chosen by Mark"—the women had not informed the disciples—is therefore not preserved by any other evangelist (30/39).

The central biblical figure in the discussion concerning

the empty tomb is neither the risen Jesus, nor a disciple, nor one of the women who were, according to the reports of the evangelist, at the tomb. It is much more Joseph of Arimathea, whose person is described differently in each of the four Gospels but about whose behavior after the death of Jesus the four Gospels agree. He "went to Pilate, and asked for the body of Jesus," received it, "wrapped him in the linen shroud, and laid him in a tomb." (Mark 15 : 43, 46).

Campenhausen thinks that "the name of Joseph of Arimathea, and therefore also the report of the burial of Jesus, must be historical; they can not simply be set aside. . . . One found and indicated, in all probability, actually an empty tomb, and if we do not wish to explain everything as the Jews, as a swindle and as subsequently manufactured ideas, then there is no reason why we should not receive it as it comes to us from the earliest tradition" (30/42). Grass disagrees with Campenhausen and considers it possible that the body of Jesus was not buried by Joseph of Arimathea, but was taken away by his enemies. "If the enemies of Jesus really succeeded in removing his body, then the tradition would have developed in this way. Jesus was laid in a common tomb because he had been executed as a criminal. One endured that, but knew that no one of his own had rendered to him the final service of love. A stranger must have done it, and his corpse was thus saved from final disgrace. It could of course be no unimportant stranger, but one who could risk approaching the authorities. It must have been a member of the Sanhedrin. The name, as many other names in the gospel tradition, was simply selected and gradually there developed out of a pious stranger a secret disciple of Jesus (John 19 : 38), or even an open disciple (Matthew 27 : 57), one who had not consented to the purpose and deed of the Sanhedrin (Luke 23 : 51). . . . The narrative of Joseph of Arimathea, therefore, is not a complete mystery" (51/180). The residue of the tradition, according to which the corpse of Jesus was buried by his opponents, Grasz finds in a passage in Acts: ("And when they had fulfilled all that was written of him, they took him down from the tree, and laid him in a tomb" [Acts 13 : 29]) and in a passage in John's Gospel ("Since it was the day of Preparation, in order to prevent the bodies from remaining on the cross on the Sabbath for that Sabbath was a high day, the Jews asked Pilate that their legs might be broken, and that they might be taken away" [John 19 : 31]).

Campenhausen resumes his investigation of the account of the empty tomb: "There is much which speaks for it, and nothing which speaks thoroughly and definitely against it; it is therefore probably historical" (30/42). On the other hand, Grass says: "The critical examination of all arguments for the historicity of the empty tomb" have the result "that nothing of this argument has proved itself to be unconditionally convincing." It is "acknowledged that the gaps in the historical proof for the empty tomb are very narrow. But they are present. . . . The fact that the historicity of the empty tomb can not be convincingly proved brings to the theologians, but above all to the dogmaticians, the task of thinking through the problem of the resurrection also under the presupposition that the tomb possibly was not empty. . . . The speed with which those interested in apologetics on behalf of the resurrection have hurled themselves into attempts to prove the historicity of the empty tomb must be rejected. In a word, we do not believe in the empty tomb, but in the risen Lord" (51/183ff.).

THE EMPTY TOMB—FACT OR LEGEND?

The historian Campenhausen and the systematician Grass have not been satisfied simply to collect and to test the arguments for and against the empty tomb. "Using conjecture cautiously," Campenhausen has instead attempted "a reconstruction of the Easter history" (30/43), and Grass has set himself to a similar task.

Campenhausen's conclusion is that the disciples remained in the city of Jerusalem after the arrest and crucifixion of Jesus. "Not only Luke, but also Mark and in general all of the evangelists agree to this, that the disciples remained first in Jerusalem and found themselves still in the city at the time that the empty tomb was discovered. There is not the slightest reason to doubt the correctness of that statement" (30/44). Peter understood the report that the tomb was empty "as a pledge of the success of the resurrection" (30/51). He made a decision, which later "was placed into the mouth of an angel" (30/50), to go to Galilee. For "where would one find Jesus now? Jerusalem, the godless capital of his enemies, the city where he was persecuted and nailed to the cross, was certainly not the place for his appearing again. He must have proceeded into his home surroundings, to Galilee where he had worked, where his supporters were, where he and all the disciples were at home, the holy land of their remembrance and henceforth also of their hope" (30/49f.). The disciples proceeded, as Campenhausen reconstructs it, "under the leadership of Peter toward Galilee . . . in the hope that they would there meet Jesus" (30/51).

Grass thinks that the presentation of Campenhausen is "more unbelievable than the most massive Easter legends of the New Testament. It is unbelievable to speak of a Jesus who has left Jerusalem, whom his disciples follow, full of misgivings, in the hope that they will see him again in Galilee—even though Galilee is very large. . . . If descriptions of the being and behavior of the risen one were fashioned in the heads of the disciples at all before meeting with him, ought they really to have been thought out in such a primitive, clumsy, mythological way?"

(51/119). Campenhausen softened his thesis in a footnote in a new edition of his book *Der Ablauf der Osterereignisse und das leere Grab*. Campenhausen now says that even if one—as Grass—does not wish to investigate the motivation of the movement of the disciples to Galilee, one does not need to revert to the usual claim of a flight of the disciples. "Some time or other the pilgrims to Jerusalem had to depart for home" (73/100).

Grass admits that the disciples, conversely, went from Galilee (where Jesus appeared to them) to Jerusalem and that, there, "no certain information was to be had concerning the whereabouts of the body, that an investigation by friend and foe was fruitless. The investigation was not conducted with particular haste by the disciples, because they were certain of the risen Lord through the appearances" (51/184). To that, or rather against that, Pannenberg writes: "The possibility that Jesus' body and his tomb had not been heard of again after such a short time is worth considering only under the presupposition that Jesus was buried as a criminal in just any tomb that happened to be empty or even in a mass grave without anyone having taken the trouble to inform Jesus' followers of its location" (73/103). Grass also, as we have seen, does not, in fact, exclude that possibility.

Grass considers the accounts of the appearance of the women at the tomb to be a fabricated solution to the problem. "The disciples were no longer in Jerusalem when the story of the finding of the tomb developed. They therefore cannot be brought into connection with it. On the contrary, one knew it from the women. One has to thank them for the valuable reports concerning the crucifixion of Jesus. What then would be more obvious than to make them witnesses and bearers of the events which later would be told about the crucifixion and the final events of the story of Jesus" (51/182).

DOUBT CONCERNING THE DATE OF THE THIRD DAY

If the Grass thesis is correct, then the date of the resurrection—on the third day—is also more than doubtful. It is then this "third day" on which the women are supposed to have found the tomb empty. Gerhard Koch of Berlin states positively: "The experience of the empty tomb by the women created this time assertion. . . . The fact of the empty tomb has its meaning for the kerygma in this, that the kerygmatic expression of the third day originated from it" (61/33). This connection also means, if negatively stated: Without the fact of the empty tomb, there is no fact of the third day.

Grass is convinced on several other grounds also that this date is a "theological setting" (51/136). The prophecy of Jesus that he would rise "on the third day," according to countless New Testament scholars, was first attributed to him by the early Christian community after his death. Even if one had, in fact, come upon the empty tomb on the third day, the time of the resurrection would still be uncertain. No one knew when the miracle happened, and "the notion that the risen Christ had advised his disciples about it" is certainly odd (51/129).

The hint of the Apostle Paul that Jesus was raised on the third day "according to the scriptures" (1 Cor. 15 : 3f.) means—according to Grass—that the source of the date is to be found in the Old Testament. In fact, there are three places which could possibly be the source of the resurrection date: Jon. 1 : 17—"Jonah was in the belly of the fish three days and three nights"; 2 Kings 20 : 5—"Behold, I will heal you; on the third day you shall go up to the house of the Lord"; Hos. 6 : 2—"After two days he will revive us; on the third day he will raise us up."

Grass is of the opinion that the resurrection of Jesus was dated according to the Hosea passage: "The phrases 're-vive' and 'raise up' made it obvious to relate the passage to the resurrection. And since Hosea 6 : 1 speaks of the Lord who was 'torn' and 'stricken' for us, the relation is also clear to the cardinal passage of the early Christian proof-text for the persecuted and martyred servant of God —Isaiah 53 : 4f. ('Surely he has borne our griefs and carried our sorrows')—and therefore to the christological interpretation of Hosea 6 : 1f." (51/136). For Campenhausen, also, the origin of the date of the third day is "doubtful," but it "could have been, with some difficulty, developed out of the scripture alone." One would have to "presuppose as probable that 'the third day' somehow had already been suggested before it was discovered in the Old Testament, and could be accepted into the Church's confession" (30/11f.). Campenhausen also knows that the number "three" plays a role in other religions and, for instance, that three days is accepted as the space of time "that the soul lingers near the corpse before it decomposes." But if one traces back the date of the resurrection, it is "richly indefinite, in no way obviously derived. So one will have to at least leave open the possibility that the assertion of 'the third day' was historically given" (30/12).

However differently New Testament scholars, historians, and systematic theologians make judgments about the historicity of the empty tomb, it seems to be certain that the present emphasis on the empty tomb is objected to by the majority of theologians. Eberhard Müller, years ago, formulated a view which has since been dominant at the universities and evangelical academies: "This old controversy concerning the empty grave ought . . . to be put aside. Nobody can ever prove or disprove that the grave of Jesus was empty. . . . Likewise, faith in the risen Christ is not decided by the question of what happened to the material substance of his physical body, but rather by the question of what God did with Jesus himself—whether he let him drop or whether he raised him up to new, eternal life" (69/127).

We close this section with the criticism which Ernst Fuchs makes of the defenders of the empty tomb: "The empty tomb apparently has only logical significance. One will postulate that the tomb of Jesus was empty as a result of his resurrection as soon as one wants to emphasize that Jesus Christ is risen in as material a way as possible. But precisely this interest shows, contrary to one's intent, that, when one deals with the evidence, he is much more convinced by our bodily reality than by our relationship to God. God is not a stopgap for an unquestioned loss of reality in traditional faith!" (42/467).

DID THE DISCIPLES ONLY HAVE VISIONS?

Many consider the account contained in Acts that Jesus appeared on earth for forty days between his resurrection and ascension to be unhistorical. According to Grass, Jesus was not transformed at all in some "quasi-human way while he was with his disciples in Galilee or in Jerusalem" (51/110). It is much more likely that the disciples only had visions of him. At the present time, among students of Protestant theology in the universities and seminaries, this thesis is more popular than any other resurrection theory. It is even defended by Pannenberg, whom Bergmann presumably has placed in the company of the Confession Movement. Bergmann writes concerning Pannenberg that "he throws Bultmann and his students out of the saddle by using their own methods of research" (14/47); and, "I have worked considerably with Professor Pannenberg, and believe that in him and especially in Professor Künneth, Bultmann finds his master" (14/58).

The bodily resurrection, which most Christians hold to be a special Christian teaching, is, according to both Grass and Pannenberg, a Jewish notion which was still shared by Jesus and his desciples. Pannenberg writes: "In all probability the earthly Jesus' expectation was not directed to-

ward, so to speak, a privately experienced resurrection
from the dead but toward the imminent universal resurrection of the dead which would, of course, include himself should his death precede it" (73/66); the appearance
of Jesus as "an encounter with one who had been raised
from the dead can only be explained from the presupposition of a particular form of the apocalyptic expectation
of the resurrection of the dead" (73/93).

Jews and Christians thought at that time that the end
of the world was near, which would mean, then, the resurrection of the dead. When the disciples of Jesus "were
confronted by the resurrected one, they no doubt understood this as the beginning of the universal resurrection of
the dead, as the beginning of the events of the end of
history." First "for the second generation of New Testament witnesses, for Mark, Matthew, Luke, John, . . . did
it become clear that the resurrection of Jesus was not yet
the beginning of the immediately continuous sequence of
the eschatological events, but was a special event that
happened to Jesus alone" (73/66). "But," asks Pannenberg, "can the apocalyptic conceptual world still be binding for us? In any case, one cannot deny this question
without being clear about its importance. Although the
apocalyptic concept of the end of the world may be untenable in many details, its fundamental elements, the
expectation of a resurrection of the dead in connection
with the end of the world and the Final Judgment, can
still remain true even for us. At any rate the primitive
Christian motivation for faith in Jesus as the Christ of
God, in his exaltation, in his identification with the Son of
Man, is essentially bound to the apocalyptic expectation
for the end of history to such an extent that one must say
that if the apocalyptic expectation should be totally excluded from the realm of possibility for us, then the early
Christian faith in Christ is also excluded; then, however,
the continuity would be broken between that which might

still remain as Christianity after such a reduction and Jesus himself, together with the primitive Christian proclamation through Paul's time. One must be clear about the fact that when one discusses the truth of the apocalyptic expectation of a future judgment and a resurrection of the dead, one is dealing directly with the basis of the Christian faith" (73/82f.).

How much the first Christians were men of their own time is emphasized by Grass even more strongly than by Pannenberg. Grass writes that characteristic of those times was an atmosphere in which "visions, revelations, heavenly prophecies, ecstatic behavior and the like were experienced"; it could "scarcely be contested from a sober historical point of view" that the appearances of the risen one, in spite of their "special position, should be considered together with these phenomena" (51/206f.). The disciples were "men to whom ecstatic raptures, ecstatic speaking in tongues, appearances in the night of heavenly messengers, prophecies, and assorted bits of information came and were experienced from the exalted lord" (51/196). Grass is convinced that "from the beginning on what the disciples experienced at Easter was interpreted by them with the intellectual tools of Jewish belief in the resurrection" (51/266). And if "in the Easter texts of the gospels the style of the appearances is perceived as a return into worldly fellowship with the disciples, then, along with all kinds of apologetic and polemic motifs, the intellectual tools of Jewish belief in the resurrection were more highly valued than had originally been the case" (51/266). Grass finds his views confirmed in the New Testament, in whose earliest sections "resurrection and exaltation fall together. Here there is no intermediate state, a quasi-earthly existence of Jesus between death and exaltation" (51/229).

It is scarcely noticed in the present controversy that Bultmann made this observation before Grass did, and after Bultmann, there were other theologians also who can in no way be counted as belonging to his school in a narrow or even a wider sense. Thus Peter Brunner is convinced "that in the earliest materials of the kerygma Easter and Ascension (resurrection and exaltation) are still identical. Over against that stands the present interpretation of the Easter history, that Jesus first came back to earth from the tomb, and from here then entered a second stage" (79/197). In a similar vein Gloege writes that "possibly even in the pre-Pauline period, there was a belief that Jesus was exalted directly from the cross of God" (46/277f.).

This opinion is based primarily on the following passages in the New Testament: "He humbled himself and became obedient unto death, even death on a cross. Therefore God has highly exalted him and bestowed on him the name which is above every name" (Phil. 2 : 8–9); "And I, when I am lifted up from the earth, will draw all men to myself. He said this to show by what death he was to die." (John 12 : 32–33); "He entered once for all into the Holy Place, taking not the blood of goats and calves but his own blood, thus securing an eternal salvation" (Hebrews 9 : 12).

In addition to that, Grass and Pannenberg base their vision thesis on the fact that the only appearance which is described by an eyewitness—Paul—obviously involved a vision. Paul saw, according to Acts, on the road to Damascus, "at midday . . . a light from heaven, brighter than the sun," . . . and . . . "heard a voice" (Acts 26 : 13–14). Pannenberg comments: "A spiritual body . . . not a person with an earthly body" appeared to Paul. It "did not involve an encounter taking place on earth, but an appearance from on high from 'heaven,'" and it could "have happened as light phenomena." (73/92). It could also be inferred from the biblical accounts that the appearances were participated in only by him and not by his associates. Acts states (if indeed in a contradictory way): "Now those who were with me saw the light but did not

hear the voice of the one who was speaking to me" (Acts
22 : 9). In another place, one reads the opposite: "The
men who were travelling with him stood speechless, hearing the voice but seeing no one" (Acts 9 : 7). Pannenberg
is of the opinion that "an event of this sort must be designated as a vision. If someone sees something that others
present are not able to see, then it involves a vision"
(73/93).

Both theologians, Pannenberg and Grass, consider it
probable that all other appearances of the risen Jesus were
also visions. The characteristics of Paul's vision "with the
possible exception of . . . the light phenomenon, may also
be presupposed for the other appearances of the resurrected Lord" (73/93).

The most important argument of the two scholars is
that Paul lists the appearances without giving any hint
whatsoever about any distinction among them. He obviously presupposed "that the appearance that happened to
him had been of the same kind as those imparted to the
other apostles" (73/92). That Paul equates all these appearances is noteworthy because he carefully distinguishes
them from other visions.

If the appearances have to do with visions, with "extraordinary sights" (Pannenberg 73/93), then it means
that "the eating and drinking and also the manner of
speaking of the risen Lord, as it is portrayed by the evangelists, must be given up" (Grass 51/253). It is conceivable that "the Christophany as such said to the disciples
what they had to do, that the event itself was 'Word'
without the hearing of words, without auditions being
necessary." But probably the visions did not lack some
"auditionary elements," and the risen Christ did confer
some commission (Grass 51/254). But if there were
auditions, then they did not have to do with "a voice
shouting down from heaven . . . and certainly not with

words of a physical Lord present with the disciples. [A] neutral disinterested observer and hearer would have perceived nothing. The words of the risen Lord cannot be objectively verified" (Grass 51/255).

With their vision-thesis Grass and Pannenberg separate themselves from the conservative theologians who described the corporeality of the risen Lord. Althaus, for instance, writes that "it is not possible for us to determine exactly the character of the appearances." Althaus would agree neither with Pannenberg nor with Ricciotti. He would insist that the appearances "were clearly distinguishable both from visions and from the manner of the encounter which the disciples had had with the historical Jesus." It had to do, at the same time, with "the unvisionary bodily reality and with the secret supernatural reality" (4/22). The appearances are to be understood "not spiritualistically, but also not naturalistic-realistically, but eschatological-realistically" (3/273).

Künneth makes a similar distinction. On the one hand, he knows of a "bodily similarity to other men" and emphasizes that "the risen Lord represents himself as a conscious, splendidly acting and planning, active and effective personality, whose speech communicates clarity, insight and wisdom." One the other hand, "his existence may not be compared to the continuation of earthly life; his reality is of a transcendent dimension" (64 [German ed.] /207).

Are these theologians able to refer to the Bible as do Pannenberg and Grass? Often, in this connection, they refer to the story of the road to Emmaus: "But their eyes were kept from recognizing him" (Luke 24 : 16). That happened only later: "When he was at table with them, he took the bread and blessed, and broke it, and gave it to them. And their eyes were opened and they recognized him" (Luke 24 : 30f.). And even at the Sea of Tiberius the disciples did not at first recognize Jesus: "Just as day was breaking, Jesus stood on the beach; yet the disciples did not know that it was Jesus" (John 21 : 4).

The farther one separates himself, as do Grass and Pannenberg, from the naturalistic way of thinking (for instance, Ricciotti) and also from the arguments of theologians such as Althaus and Künneth of Erlangen, the more one moves in the direction of the vision theories which were earlier very widespread and even today are still defended by many theologians. Emanuel Hirsch of Göttingen, for instance, in 1940 (in *Die Auferstehungsgeschichten und der christliche Glaube*), proposed the view that the ecstatically talented Peter had had a vision which caused a kind of chain reaction among the others, who were also prone to visions. Yet Grass and Pannenberg make a distinction between the position represented by Hirsch, which they call "subjective," and their own "objective" vision theory. It is not faith that gave rise to the vision, as Hirsch would have it, but the vision which gave rise to faith in the resurrection (Grass 51/234). Therefore the argument that the appearances came into being "by the enthusiastically excited imagination of the disciples . . . does not hold, at least for the first and most fundamental appearances" (Pannenberg 73/96). That the Easter visions of the disciples may not be regarded merely as "subjective projections," Pannenberg concludes (among other reasons) from the experiments by American parapsychologists at Duke University, who investigate clairvoyance and telepathy, along with "prophetic intuition" (precognition). Pannenberg writes: "One should be on guard against drawing direct conclusions for our question about the reality of the Easter appearances from such investigations. Up to now they show nothing more than the possibility of visionary experiences that are not merely to be judged as subjective projections but—in statistically demonstrable numbers—involve something to which they coincide, that is, they lay hold of extra-subjective reality" (73/95).

As he does for the visions, Pannenberg also expects arguments for the bodily resurrection of Jesus from the natural scientists. He expects support for saying that the resurrection at least does not set aside natural laws (73/98). Yet Pannenberg thinks that "only a part of the laws of nature are ever known." Natural science expresses "the general validity of the laws of nature but must at the same time declare its own inability to make definitive judgments about the possibility or impossibility of any individual event, regardless of how certainly it is able, at least in principle, to measure the probability of an event's occurance." . . . Pannenberg continues: "The judgment about whether an event, however unfamiliar, has happened or not is in the final analysis a matter for the historian and cannot be prejudged by the knowledge of natural science" (73/98).

Other theologians think much more critically about the meaning of physics for theology and faith. Manfred Mezger, for instance, professor of practical theology, writes: "As if it were a victory if the physicists, who today have one opinion and tomorrow another, declare that there are irregularities in nature or a breaking down of strict causality! What benefit can theologians or defenders of the faith derive from that? Has the Christian faith its own thing to say, or must it inquire elsewhere to find out whether anyone will buy it?" (72/232).

ASCENDED INTO HEAVEN

We have, to this point, scarcely mentioned "demythologization." This seems to be the right place to investigate this concept, its content and its meaning. What is the meaning of "descended into hell" and "ascended into heaven" for

the conservative and for the modern demythologizing theologian?

Bultmann coined the word "demythologization" in 1941
(9*/1–44). He has often been accused of wanting to
rob the creedal confession of its contents, and, on the other
hand, the impression has arisen that Bultmann's opponents
want to hold on to everything which is said about Jesus
Christ in the Apostle's Creed.

Yet is the line drawn that clearly? Are the ascent into
heaven and the descent into hell simply "finished" (9*/4)
for Bultmann and the other modern theologians? Do the
conservative theologians, who (as we have seen) affirm the
virgin birth, the empty tomb, and the bodily resurrection
on a more or less broad and consistent front, also insist
that Jesus after his death descended into hell and ascended
into heaven? Or, one may ask whether it is true that a
theologian is conservative or modern depending on whether
he is against or for demythologization.

Bultmann has stated clearly what demythologization is
or ought to be. It is "the radical application of the doctrine
of justification through faith to the area of knowing and
thinking. As does the doctrine of justification, so also demythologization destroys every longing for security. There
is no difference between security on the basis of good
works and security which rests on objective knowledge"
(27 [German ed.] /100).

Bultmann sees in demythologization the only way to
prevent two things: One, that the Christian must bring
with him a *sacrificium intellectus*—a sacrifice of the understanding, a "renunciation of intellect"—if he takes over
conceptions which he "cannot honestly hold to be true"
(27 [German ed.] /15); and the other, that Christians
simply "pass over those places in the New Testament which
contain such mythological conceptions" (27 [German ed.]
/15). Bultmann is not interested "in throwing out the
Christian message as a whole, but rather the world-view of

the Bible, which is the world-view of a past age, which only too often is retained in Christian dogmatics and in the preaching of the church. Demythologization means to deny that the message of scripture and of the church is bound to an old and obsolete world-view" (27 [German ed.] / 37).

And the same Bultmann, who criticizes so severely his students who attempt to approach the historical Jesus with historical–critical methods and to make differentiations in the tradition, carries out a similar program on another level with demythologization—at least, so it seems. He explains numerous expressions about Jesus as being time-conditioned and wants to be careful that (as Ernst Fuchs formulated it) the "particularity of Jesus be not confused with the particularities of the world-view of that age." The demythologizers want "to point to Jesus in such a way that no one can say: I don't have anything to do with Jesus because I no longer have anything to do with ghosts" (41a/176f.).

Bultmann puts an end, as it were, to the development which, in his opinion, began after the death of Jesus. He sees a "development of Christology in primitive Christianity whose traces are clearly discernable in the New Testament, a development the result of which is that from the man Jesus, who knew himself to be the eschatological King chosen by God (or at least was thought by others to be that), was made a heavenly divine being to whom pre-existence was attributed, that his cosmic power participated in the creation of the world, that he became man, died, and rose, ascended into heaven, and there as divine essence is enthroned next to God, is worshipped by the community of believers as divine, hears prayers, dispenses miraculous powers, and will come again in order to judge and to conquer the evil cosmic powers, death, and the devil. This development came to pass so quickly because both in Judaism and in heathenism there were available

mythological ideas about a divine being who is the redeemer of men, and these ideas were transferred to Jesus"
(23/246). Bultmann is convinced that "the Christology of
the New Testament exhibits *nothing specifically Christian.*"
The historical figure of Jesus, "by virtue of the strong impression" it made, "became the occasion to take old wishes
and fantastic dreams for reality. If it was first thought that
these pictures were modified, enriched, and deepened on
the basis of the historical events, the earthly work and
passion, the cross of Jesus, that the deep thoughts of the
condescension of the deity, of the suffering of the redeemer, and his self-sacrifice for sinful humanity were
taken up into the old myth, this view has proved itself
false. The heathen mysteries knew not only the figure of the
dying redeemer-God, but above all the heathen–gnostic
mythology knew that figure of the pre-existent being of
God that, obedient to the will of the father, clothed himself
in the garment of this world and accepted misery and need,
hate and pesecution, in order to prepare the way for his
own into the heavenly world" (23/247).

That which now specifically applies to the descent into
hell and the ascent into heaven presents a problem completely different from the other problems of the resurrection. Bultmann can formulate it as sharply as he wishes—
he only says that which most theologians have for a long
time insisted on. Bultmann writes: "No one who is old
enough to think for himself supposes that God lives in a
local heaven. There is no longer any heaven in the traditional sense of the word. The same applies to hell in the
sense of a mythical underworld beneath our feet. And if
this is so, we can no longer accept the story of Christ's
descent into hell or his ascension into heaven as literally
true. We can no longer look for the return of the Son of
Man on the clouds of heaven or hope that the faithful will
meet him in the air" (9*/4).

Is there now, in fact, Protestant agreement that, as Professor Kreck of Bonn writes, "it is absolutely worthless when we painstakingly attempt to present in old pictures a descent of Jesus into hell, a descent into the underworld, instead of recognizing that here the sovereign lordship of Jesus Christ over all things, even the dead, is proclaimed? Or what does the message of the ascension of Jesus and the sitting at the right hand of God say to us if we understand it as a spatial rising into a high cosmic place, instead of grasping that this has to do with the still hidden, to be sure, but already real lordship of Jesus Christ over the world?" (60/54). One can also read similar things in works whose authors are not exactly considered to be modern. "Apart from primitive communism, no one thinks that the ascension of Jesus is to be understood in a spatial way," writes Hans Schomerus (45/26). Yet, according to another of the six authors who express themselves in a little book, entitled *Himmelfahrt-Hindernis oder Hilfe für den Glauben?*, it is not only communists who think in this way, but also "those who with the fundamentalists will not allow one jot or tittle of the words of the Bible to be shaken"; they make themselves "at best laughable when they want to consider as true that there was a trip through the air by the risen Lord in the direction of a localized dwelling of God the Father" (45/7). "What ought we to do today with these Biblical pictures?" the modern theologian Manfred Mezger asks, in the same volume, and answers: "with *one* word: nothing. The event itself, whether it happened or did not happen, is for us meaningless because it makes no impression on us. Certainly we can find it quite beautiful; but that is about all. . . . To be sure, many men protest that everything is overthrown if the ascension did not literally happen. It does not overthrow anything at all; everything goes on smoothly" (45/28).

Yet no one may be certain that this agreement exists at the present time, and certainly no one ought to have made the attempt to maintain such an agreement for the past.

For Luther, on whom many claim to base their views, hell was not a place. He was of the opinion that Jesus suffered hell in Gethsemane and on the cross, and that he conquered. Yet "the authority of the creed, in which the 'descent into hell' comes first after the 'dead and buried,' and a few Bible passages convinced him also to teach a descent into hell after the death of Jesus. That contradicted his own thoughts and brought Luther into such difficulties that he finally had to give up any theological explanation of the descent into hell after the death." (Althaus 3/265f.).

Many Christians today seem to be involved in similar difficulties. Thus in the *Braunschweig Theses* it is stressed, on the one hand, that the Gospel bears witness to "the real ascent into heaven, the place of God" (which, to be sure, "cannot be understood with the categories of this world") but on the other hand, it is demanded that "any interpretation which labels the report of the ascension of Jesus as a legend and as a mythological expression for the confession of Christ as the lord must be rejected" (113/5).

The question remains, why is the ascension celebrated if it never happened? Among those few who ask this question and seek an answer to it, one could name Althaus. He was of the opinion that one must distinguish "the *transpiring* of the exaltation from its 'objective' meaning for Jesus Christ and our salvation. The first is considered by the church more in relation to Easter, the second more in relation to the Ascension. Thus, if not historically at least dogmatically, the close relationship and the sequence of Easter and the Ascension make good sense in the church year. Even though two separate 'salvation events' are not celebrated, but rather two sides of one and the same event, yet each of the two days has its special theme" (3/275).

We conclude this section with an indication of the contradiction in the argument of Althaus, which presumably has been taken over by not a few theologians. Althaus says that "the narrative of the ascension of Jesus forty days after

Easter, as it is found in Acts 1 : 9ff., is a late development. The original kerygma knows nothing of it. It knows no 'exaltation' of Jesus which followed in chronological sequence after his resurrection. Rather, the resurrection is itself, at the same time, the exaltation through which Jesus is seated 'at the right hand of God' " (3/274). May one— in relation to the ascension—appeal to the original kerygma and in another place—in relation to the resurrection— ignore it? Must not those who attribute such meaning to the primitive kerygma also explain the appearances of the risen Lord as legends?

NOT INTERESTED IN THE HISTORICAL QUESTION

In the opinion of Grass, theological reflection must hold fast to the fact that, when we deal with the experiences of the disciples, we have to do with God's action toward them and not merely with the products of their own fantasies or reflection. Every purely immanental explanation is theologically intolerable (51/243). "It is impossible to affirm the Easter faith of the disciples, and the Easter proclamation which originated from it, as an act of God, and at the same time to leave open the question whether the *what* in which this faith believes and which it proclaims corresponds to a reality. If one leaves it as an open question, or if one answers it negatively, then God's action is placed in an intolerable twilight. God would then appear as one who would have deceived the disciples in that he would have brought about faith in the risen Lord and the sight of the risen Lord without Christ actually having been raised and living" (51/245).

For Grass "everything which is reported in the New Testament Easter witness boils down to the simple fact that God has not abandoned Christ in death, but has awakened him to new life and exalted him. And he has in a series of visions revealed Christ to a chosen circle of disciples as living and exalted Lord, so that they could say with certainty, 'He lives.' More cannot be said, and even that only faith can say and know. . . . Everything else which is contained in the New Testament Easter witness, the finding of the empty tomb, the bodily moving about of the risen Lord with the disciples, is clearly a later interpretation of the original happening or even, as the empty tomb, so uncertain that it cannot be referred to when speaking of the Act of God in Christ" (51/246). Grass sees this "objective vision hypothesis" as "the only possible procedure for modern scientific theology." He believes that it satisfies two claims: on the one hand, it takes seriously historical criticism—so seriously, in fact, that the empty tomb and the appearances of the risen one in the "space/time world" are no longer taken to be provable; on the other hand, it does not give up the fact "that Christ lives as the exalted Lord, because faith and the church would no more have any right to exist without a living exalted Lord" (51/248).

Whatever may be the case according to the scholars who pursue historical truth, for the theologians it has different meanings. For Pannenberg the events are essential. "If we would forego the concept of a historical event here, then it is no longer possible at all to affirm that the resurrection of Jesus or that the appearances of the resurrected Jesus really happened at a definite time in our world" (73/99). . . . "If, however, historical study declares itself unable to establish what 'really' happened on Easter, then all the more, faith is not able to do so; for faith cannot ascertain anything certain about the events of the past that would perhaps be inaccessible to the historian" (73/99, 109).

With Althaus it is somewhat the opposite. "What really happened at Easter, history as such cannot say. That is a matter of religious judgment, of faith, which originates in the total witness to Jesus. Certainty concerning Easter is not an historical knowledge, which could precede faith; it dawns on us first in and with faith" (4/26). Gerhard Gloege says that "no one else can answer for us as to whether we see Jesus and God himself at work in their Easter experiences or not. We must answer this ourselves. One thing is certain: just as historical research cannot give us Easter faith, neither can it take it away" (46/281). And for Bultmann the results of historical research are completely beside the point: "The historical problem is scarcely relevant to Christian belief in the resurrection" (9*/42).

RESURRECTION ONLY AN INTERPRETATION?

A number of theologians and pastors are of the opinion that Willi Marxsen, the New Testament scholar at Münster, has brought new insight to theological research through his work *Die Auferstehung Jesu als historisches und als theologisches Problem.* We shall attempt first to sketch the basic outlines of Marxsen's position before we try to see whether he does in fact come up with anything new.

Marxsen proceeds in this way: "If a witness reports to me a fact, then the facticity of this fact is constantly maintained for me by witnesses; it is never a direct facticity" (66/10). Paul, again, is for Marxsen no witness of the resurrection; he understands only "something, which never happened to himself, as event" (66/14). The Apostle merely heard, argues Marxsen, the assertion of Christians that Jesus has been raised. "That which he then experienced on the Damascus road brought him to the conviction that that which the Christians asserted must be correct. The conviction of the eventfulness of the resurrection of Jesus Paul grounds, therefore, *not* in the happening of that which he considers to be an event; It is much more the result of a final-process. One may therefore in no way appeal to Paul if one wants to designate the resurrection of Jesus (directly) as an event which took place, but one must first ask whether this final-process is legitimate. We therefore ought not to short-circuit the conviction of Paul into a—for us useful—historical judgment" (66/14).

Marxsen reaches the conclusion that even the so-called objective vision hypothesis is subjective. He argues that even if Paul maintains the "historical happening of the resurrection as event, he speaks *merely* out of conviction without mentioning witnesses, still more without being able to mention witnesses at all" (66/14). Consequently, it is an interpretation. That the appearance has "to do with an event brought about by *God* was not gathered from the event itself; it is therefore interpretation" (66/17). Consequently, "the so-called objective vision hypothesis is therefore on closer examination *also* a subjective one, in that it requires a basis of proper faith" (66/19). Marxsen calls it "the unfortunate feature of Grass' way of thinking" that he "begins by dealing with faith, but on the way proceeds to the confirmation of events" (66/18). If "no one today was a witness of these visions, how can then a believer *today* 'see God at work in the visions of the disciples?'" (66/18). Here faith becomes "once again an organ for receiving knowledge about a happening which would otherwise remain inaccessible" (66/19).

With such ideas, Marxsen prepares the way for his key sentence. "If one looks more closely, he discovers where the error lies. If according to the subjective vision hypothesis it is the disciples who, through their faith, so to speak, create the visions, then according to the objective vision hypothesis it is the *present* faith which deals with objective visions" (66/19).

What can be said, according to Marxsen, "with greater certainty? . . . Witnesses maintain, after the death of Jesus, to have seen *him*, . . . [and they came] then through reflective interpretation to the formula that Jesus was raised by God, or, that he is risen" (66/19). But today one could no longer speak "so directly of the resurrection of Jesus as of an *event*," but must "simply say that it has to do with an *interpretation"* of the Apostle. "If one today, therefore, puts the question historically (!) whether Christ has been raised, then we can only answer that it cannot be established that he did" (66/19f.).

That the resurrection interpretation is not to be regarded as the only possibility (66/21), Marxsen illustrates by pointing to the Greek-Hellenistic notion that the body is the prison of the self (the soul), which leaves the body at death and enters the future. Marxsen ponders, "obviously hypothetically," how the "experience of seeing Jesus" by witnesses with this Greek-Hellenistic thought would be reflected: "One would then have said, 'To the soul of Jesus (= to Jesus) the hope of the future has already become reality.' . . . One would have spoken of the fact that Jesus had *really* vacated his body and that the presupposition for that was that one could then see him— There would have been not a word said about 'resurrection.' " (66/29).

Since interpretations are "assumptions through reflections," Marxsen replies negatively to the question, What could one later do with these assumptions? He says: "Basically nothing at all; for these assumptions can at best inform about a *conviction* of those who worked through this reflection (with the help of *their* thought-forms)." It does not have to do with a *matter of fact*, but with a *conviction*. The "reflection at that time" is "misunderstood, if one says that faith must hold on to the formula of the resurrection. It holds on in that case only to a set of ideas out of religion which, however, may not be identified as such with the matter with which we are here concerned" (66/27). That one "interprets the experience of 'seeing' as resurrection consequently fits together with the peculiarities of *Jewish* anthropology" (66/29).

Marxsen distinguishes between two interpretations. The one is "functional" and has the "sending-motif" as its content. It says that "the mission of Jesus continues"

(66/25). The other is "personal." In this, one sets "a date through reflective interpretation: God raised Jesus on the third day. So then one qualifies the crucified one, in that one calls him the risen one" (66/26).

Marxsen characterizes it as a "further reflection on the reflection 'he has been raised'" when at that time, in the light of the Jews' and the Christians' common expectation of the resurrection of the dead, something is expressed by Jesus "which for other men is still a hope. But then in the resurrection of Jesus the end has already broken in, the end-time *has* with his resurrection already begun, and in this way, then, the 'resurrection' of Jesus *becomes* the central datum of 'holy history'" (66/28).

For Marxsen it is not the resurrection, but the person of Jesus himself, that is "the decisive datum" (66/33) . . . "Jesus has experienced in his earthly work as an anticipation of the Eschaton, as an event of God" (66/33). The "experience of seeing" is "historically constitutive for the church" (66/33). "But the actual happening of the resurrection is not constitutive of the fact that the community knows 'Jesus present,' for the speaking about the actual happening of the resurrection is a (at that time quite understandable and perhaps even necessary) for us forbidden historicizing of an interpretation" (66/34).

Marxsen's argumentation ends with a negative and—in his opinion—with a positive statement. The negative: "Christian theology can and may, therefore, proceed in no way from the resurrection of Jesus. It cannot argue from it as its alleged focal-point, but exactly the opposite. It rather must be asked whether theology has any actual right at all to speak *Christianly* about the resurrection of Jesus" (66/34). The positive: Marxsen himself would like to decide for the formula "He lives." But the Christian could also, "in older terminology," the "distinct limitations" of which must be recognized, confess also today the formula,

"He lives. He has not remained in death. He is risen" (66/35).

So much for the statement of Marxsen's resurrection theology. One could make it easier for himself by refusing to accept it. He could summon a rally, cite Paul ("If Christ has not been raised, then our preaching is in vain and your faith is in vain" [1 Cor. 15 : 14]), and, finally condemn Marxsen by saying: He does not believe in the resurrection; therefore, he is no longer a Christian. The dialogue would be finished before it had begun.

But one could also make it easier for himself by realizing that Marxsen, nevertheless allows the sentence "He is risen" to remain valid, even though it is assigned limitations, and that he himself confesses "He lives." One does not even have to begin the dialogue because he knows beforehand that there is friendly agreement.

One can make Marxsen's theology both easy and difficult by considering it to be dangerous, abstruse, or superfluous but, at the same time, stating that the Church can and ought to do nothing against it. Or one may well begin the dialogue knowing that it can never be concluded, in which case it is not, of course, begun seriously. That approach is also characteristic of the modern Protestant style of life, to live with conflicts.

Yet there is still another way. One could undertake a true conversation, which is neither hotheaded heresy-hunting nor endless talk, and demonstrate in this way that the Protestant church, a community of believers in Christ, does not need to be incapable of action when the issue is faith. An open and basic disputation with Marxsen, in which his arguments are taken seriously and understood and—so far as possible—refuted, would expose the fact that there is no fundamentally new understanding hidden behind the many new words.

Such a dialogue could begin with the simple statement

that one must believe *something* if one does not want to be faithless—whether this something is much, including the empty tomb, or little, as Marxsen's "He lives." And something else is common to each and every faith, the idea of interpretation. What is Marxsen saying here that is new? Is it not self-evident that Paul and those whom he lists as witnesses have interpreted on the basis of faith? That they were not witnesses of the resurrection "on the third day" is known to every Bible reader. And is it not also self-evident that one can come to a statement of *objective* visions (as with Grass and Pannenberg) only as a Christian, therefore on the basis of faith, therefore through interpretation? It is granted that Marxsen has formulated these self-evident items better than many others. Does that fact deserve such a swelling up of protest? Marxsen has said, only a little differently, exactly that which other modern theologians have been saying for a long time.

RISEN IN THE PROCLAMATION

What does the resurrection mean for Christians today? Even conservative scholars, above all, the theologians of the Bultmann school, have a great deal to say about this. In the opinion of Künneth, the teachers of the Bultmann school, and its masters, hold that the resurrection as "foundation and criterion of faith in Jesus has more or less radically been demolished" (63/159). At the very least, it is certain that for modern theologians "the resurrection of Jesus is not the central datum of the Christian faith" (Marxsen 66/33). For Bultmann, Jesus is raised in the kerygma, in proclamation: "Christ meets us in the preaching as one crucified and risen. He meets us in the word of preaching and nowhere else. The faith of Easter is just this—faith in the word of preaching" (9*/41).

Therefore Jesus is not, as it is attributed to Bultmann by some of his opponents, "risen as Goethe" (Bergmann

14/45). "For in the proclamation Christ is not in the same
way present as a great historical person is present in his
work and its historical after-effects. For what is here involved is not an influence that takes effect in the history of
the human mind; what does take place is that a historical
person and his fate are raised to the rank of the eschatological event" (29/305f.). "One lives now, obviously, not
among the 'effects' of Jesus as one can live among the
effects of the Thirty-Year War, of the Enlightenment, of
the French Revolution, or of Goethe. Otherwise the coming
of Jesus would not be the *eschatological* fact" (23/145).
Bultmann can say that Jesus is, thanks to his "eschatological setting," the "turning of the ages," and that through
him "our history has achieved the possibility of being
characterized by love instead of by hate, a fact which as
such is neither establishable nor experienceable, but can
only be believed" (23/106).

For Bultmann the word of proclamation itself belongs
"to this event and meets the hearer as personal address.
He hears it as the word which is spoken to him, the word
granting to him death and life, and so he believes the
risen Lord. . . . [And the] word of grace is embodied in
Jesus Christ, who is present as the word of God in the
preaching of the church" (25/73). The kerygma, the
proclamation, is "neither the bearer of a timeless idea nor
the communicator of historical knowledge, but its 'here
and now,' in which that 'here and now' is made present
in the address, confronts the hearer with decision"
(23/208).

Bultmann defends his sentence "Jesus is risen in the
kerygma" against attacks by saying that "Jesus is really
present in the kerygma; it is *his* word that meets the
hearer in the kerygma. If that is the case, then all specula-
tions concerning the mode-of-being of the risen Lord, all
narratives of the empty tomb, and all Easter legends
(which may include some moments of historical fact and

so may be true in their symbolical form) become a matter of indifference. To those who believe in the Christ present in the kerygma, this is the meaning of Easter faith" (21/27).

With his kerygmatic theology Bultmann drives his life-work, it seems, to absurdity. Certainly it is to his credit that he developed the form-critical method, deepened the understanding of the proclamation-character of the New Testament, and freed the historical kernel of the biblical accounts of Jesus from the ballast of legends. It is also to his credit that he announced the program of demytholo-gizing, eliminating angels, demons, and the three-deckered (heaven, earth, and hell) world view from the vocabulary of many people. But insofar as he, with only a minimum of overlapping, separates the historical Jesus from the Christ of faith and sets the kerygma in the place of the resurrection, he—the historical–critical researcher, the demythologizer—makes Christ into a myth. If those who hear the word of proclamation already believe in the risen one, then they are, in truth, spared the decision for or against faith in the resurrection.

The same holds true for the resurrection theses of a few Bultmann students. Gerhard Ebeling stresses constantly "that the Resurrection of Jesus is not to be regarded as one object of faith alongside others, as though Easter only added the Resurrection of Jesus as something to be be-lieved along with everything else. Rather, faith in the Resurrected One simply expresses faith in Jesus. This is not something additional to the Person of Jesus, but Jesus himself" (37/62). "It was not a case of a single additional *credendum* (the fact of the resurrection), but of faith itself—and that, too, in relation to Jesus as the source of faith. Hence what is so confusingly called Easter faith is really a case of nothing else but faith in Jesus. The faith of the days after Easter knows itself to be nothing else but the right understanding of the Jesus of the days before

Easter" (38/302). "To have faith in Jesus and to have faith in him as the Risen One are one and the same" (37/71).

The concept of Easter faith is also openly given up by Ernst Fuchs. "Even Bultmann still speaks about 'Easter faith.' This concept makes discussion particularly difficult. . . . In truth it must be maintained that Jesus' execution as well as the confession of his exaltation, or his resurrection, have really nothing at all to do with faith, except that these concrete events (Jesus' cross and the confession of his exaltation, or his resurrection) have compelled faith to reflect on what it really is" (41a/99). If this "kernel sentence" of Fuchs has a Christian kernel at all, then it is to be seen in its appendix ("except that these concrete events . . ."). And how Christian is the faith in Jesus which theologian Herbert Braun of Mainz describes is for Christians as well as for non-Christians difficult to determine. Braun says: "To believe in Jesus as the exalted Christ does not mean to have a definite opinion concerning immanental and therefore testable events, which make understandable the movement from the Jesus of history to the Christ of faith. It also does not mean to reckon with the fact that Jesus remains influential in a *general* way. I can only believe in Jesus as in the exalted Christ in that I, myself, as an *individual*, admit immediately and responsibly the 'God does thus,' in whatever form this 'thus' meets me" (79/148). But is it not then possible in this case to easily exchange Socrates or any other great name for Jesus?

8. Crisis of Faith
Without Any Remedy?

THE REDUCED PICTURE of Jesus of the modern theologians, argues conservative theologian Walter Künneth, does not "challenge to true decision, does not correspond finally to faith, but to general religiosity and the faithlessness of modern men." Faith has become, through "restrictive manipulations, conflictless and free of every annoyance; it has become devoid of every excitement and personal engagement of modern existence; it has become sensible and understandable" (63/67).

At least equally true is that which Professor Ernst Barnikol directs, with a rhetorical question, to the conservatives: "How long does one think that all of us, particularly the youth, may ignore pressing spiritual questions and problems which all too many church convents, 'Kirchentags,' and Bible courses can dispense with by using antiquated concepts of a stubborn and sterile dogmatics? How long does one think that all of us can put up with a smug anti-historical religiosity which neither Jesus nor the apostles ever proclaimed as their faith?" (79/581).

MUST THE CHURCH BE SILENT ABOUT THE FAITH?

The Protestant church has fallen into a crisis of faith which is without parallel in its history. Of course, there were always individuals, often even many theologians, who went their own ways. But never has the predominant direction of Protestant theology stood so much in opposition to the faith of many Christians in the congregations. And never have both groups, the Christians behind the lecterns and those in the pews, been as strange and as distant to the faithless majority of their fellow-men as they are today.

It does not involve only the theology of the scholars. It involves the understanding of the Bible—whether it can remain for the congregations a "book fallen from heaven" when, for the theologians, it is a book whose decades-long history of development is readily discernible in its verses; when it is for many theologians only a book which *contains* God's Word but no longer *is* God's Word. And it involves the faith, which is not only on all sides differently defined, but which also at any given time has a different content from that which the other side assigns to it.

It is a conflict which would be unthinkable in the Catholic church. In a church which has fixed its truth in dogmas and punishes every blunder with excommunication, there can be no oppositions concerning the grounds of faith. One may welcome this or deplore it, but it must be said. There have been, of course, individual Catholic theologians who have come into deep conflict with their church. The history of modernism and its opposition by the Church, names and works which have stood on the now-abolished *Index*, tell the story. On the other hand, there may be much in the style of the struggle as pursued by the Confession Movement which is reminiscent of the former inner-Catholic struggle with modernism. Nevertheless, that which is happening at the present time in the Protestant church is a typical Protestant crisis.

The conflict is so bitter that most Protestants seem to agree that the Church cannot solve it. There ought not to be, may not be, and cannot be a teaching office. It is not only, and not even chiefly, an anti-Roman phobia which lurks in the members of Protestant churches. It is a thoroughly positive and much-valued confidence in the Bible which is at work in bringing about this attitude.

Here lies the opportunity and also the risk of the struggle which involves the faith. The Protestant principle of "the Scriptures alone" can prove itself to be life-giving in the present crisis. Then the Protestant church, in which theologians and congregation members have become hostile toward one another concerning the Bible, can be filled with new power and radiate in a world which is no longer Christian. The principle, however, can also be destroyed and can become an empty watchword, a phrase, so that "the Scriptures alone" may no longer be able to unite Protestant Christians. Then the Protestant church would be pressing to absurdity (whether it participates in or merely observes the struggle) the principle by which it lives—or thinks that it lives.

But why, really, is the Church unable to say something about the faith to its Christians if it still thinks that it can and must say a "word" about almost everything that happens in the world? "It is not quiet at all," I hear the leaders in the church offices answering indignantly. But is not everything which the Church has said to date concerning modern theology literally meaningless? This is true of all the resolutions and helps which have been discharged and distributed for a decade and a half. These papers have not lessened the conflicts, have not influenced modern theology, have not settled down the congregations.

The Church can decide how high its tax proceeds should be, how modern its church buildings, how old its songs. It can take care that preaching is heard everywhere. But *what* is preached, the Church simply puts up with, as the farmer does with sunshine and hailstorm. Just where, one may well ask, does the Church distinguish itself from the state which also provides room and teacher for religious instruction in the schools?

Has the freedom of its Christians become a dogma in the Protestant church? If so (and many would say that it has), must it not necessarily lead to unfairness and in-accuracy?

It is unfair when a young pastoral candidate is chased out of a congregation because he, perhaps due to incompetence or dilettantism, yet nevertheless honestly and candidly, repeats that which he has heard in the university. And is not the temptation great to hinder through administrative channels the professional progress of an instructor or professor whose teaching one cannot condemn, but would like to? And may—a much more important question—the dogma of freedom be more important than a common confession? Would there ever have been Protestants, would there ever have been Reformed, Lutheran, and Free Church Christians, if it had been impossible all along for Protestants to mark out the boundary lines of their faith? Many Protestants seem to have forgotten the early history of their church, which long ago had to do with a struggle over confession.

It is an illusion to think that the Church can evade a decision. It decides *de facto* even if it does not decide *de jure*. If it is incapable of declaring an atheistic sentence of a theologian (Braun) to be atheistic, then it legalizes, then it "Christianizes," this sentence. If the Protestant church cannot say no, then it says yes to literally everything which, for example, has been collected in this book, to all the contrasts and contradictions. It acts, then, through "determined conduct," as the lawyers would say. It would be, to put it bluntly, a decision *for* modern theology with all its abuses and a decision *against* the goals of the Confession Movement. The Church does not "want" that at all. The only thing that it, in any case, can "want" is the preservation of the *status quo*. It corresponds to its inability to act. . . .

PROTESTANT STRUGGLE WITH CATHOLIC METHOD

Yet is there, in fact, no action? There is such intense storming against a teaching office that one is secretly tempted to bring the typically Protestant struggle about faith to a conclusion by employing a "Catholic"—or, as one may say after Vatican II,—a pseudo-Catholic method.

If there is no teaching office for church bishops and synods, there is at the lowest levels. Do congregational executive committees, which hold examinations for pastoral candidates (testing knowledge of the virgin birth, bodily resurrection), act any differently from the pope and the Holy Office? Certainly the Protestant congregation has a right to select its pastor. But is this right as limitless as is the freedom of Protestant Christians? And if the Confession Movement ever did become as powerful as it, at times to-day, already pretends to be, would there be a partition of the clergy? Would this partition not result in the conservatives being in the pulpits and the others working in television, radio, the military chaplaincy, student pastorates, prison chaplaincies, journalism, marriage counseling, evangelical academies, public relations, etc.?

It is not only in this area that one can detect a "Catholic" tendency. It was, and it is, Catholic to say truths loudly as well as softly. Has not the Protestant church become much too accustomed to say loudly only that which does not disturb the other "brethren?" It was, and it is, Catholic to call open conflict between theologians, or even between bishops, an annoyance and to prevent it. Did the Westphalia President Wilm (to mention here only one name) act in a Protestant or a Catholic way when he wanted the dispute settled in a conference room rather than out in the open field?

In all openness, could and ought Protestant Christians to show that they take the discussion about Jesus, about Christ, at least as seriously as the planning of buildings, the state treasury, sex, and criminality, to mention only four of the half-worldly or totally-worldly topics of discussion which are so loved in the evangelical academies.

In case there are still not enough questions listed that would be worth discussing, here are a few more:

On which side does the intellectual of today belong, the man whom Karl Rahner has described as "the spiritual child of historicism and the natural sciences—a terribly sober, careful and disillusioned man—a man who suffers from God's remoteness and silence (as he does in fact experience this)" (75/87)? Does he not remain in the no man's land between the fronts?

"They [the minister and theologian] must make it quite clear what their hearers are expected to accept and what they are not" (Bultmann 102/9). Which pastor can say in the pulpit what is true if there are two truths? Or is there only one truth, and the Confession Movement as well as the modern theologians err in like manner if they choose against the (at any given time) other "truth"?

How does a pastor preach a Bible verse as the Word of God if he does not consider it to be a Word of God; how on a miracle if he does not consider it to be a miracle?

Does not the question of Calvin (in which I have substituted the word "Bible" for the word "church") hold good for those Protestants who consider every word in the Bible to be God's Word: "Does one call that faith if one has no kind of knowledge but merely subjects his reason in obedience to the Bible?" And is not the sentence with which Calvin follows this question also timely? "No, faith rests not on ignorance, but on knowledge. . . . We attain salvation not by being ready to accept everything which the Bible orders us to believe as true . . . but only when we recognize that God, for the sake of the reconciliation which has happened through Christ, is our gracious Father, and that Christ is given to us for righteousness, for holiness, and for life. Through this knowledge, I say, and not through an abdication of our reason, we attain entrance into the kingdom of heaven" (82/31).

Is not faith in the words and letters and punctuation as

blind as that faith of many Catholics, of whom Catholic theologian Thomas Sartory writes: "The dogma at any given time could even say the exact opposite of that which is defined by it, and it would be accepted just as readily, on the basis of the infallible authority of the teaching office" (82/29)?

Is it then true, as Hans-Dieter Bastian of Bonn writes in a brochure recommended by several Church leaders, that "many pastors" at the Kirchentag in Köln in 1965 would have demonstrated "a total unawareness of the language of modern Biblical science"? And "the protestant church Christian (in the widest sense) is estranged from the Bible even, and precisely, if he (still) allows himself to be preached at (!) each Sunday" (60/9f.)?

If all of that is *not* true, then why do none of these pastors rise up and rebel, these pastors who are here scolded for being ignorant of a discipline, their own discipline, pastors of whom it is said that the more they preach, the more they alienate the "Church Christians" from the Bible? But if all of that *is* true, then how great must be the "wailing wall" to which the Christians must go?

Many console themselves by saying that at the present time two extreme directions—the completely conservative and the completely modern—are prominent and that the truth is to be sought and found in the middle along with the majority of Protestant Christians. But must that not first be demonstrated? Is it true for the majority of professors of theology? And how could one find the correct mixture in the middle and still avoid mediocrity?

"The church has no right to appeal to Jesus, to Luther, or to Calvin, if it values faith less than statistics" (Rudolf Augstein 94). This if-sentence is aimed at the Protestant church. Is there anyone who hesitates to express a truth, or even a truth of faith, because he fears the departure and the (statistically measurable) forfeiture of biblical literalists, or the loss of prestige by the departure of the modern theologians? One ought not to answer that question too quickly.

May one in the Protestant church deny the existence of God from a professor's chair, but not from a bishop's chair? One is inclined to ask this question after reading Gollwitzer's comment: "If Mr. Braun, if the Braun party, would grasp the leadership of the church, as it happened in the time of the German Christians [during the Nazi years—Translator], this could only result in a schism. But there is no danger of that. The danger lies in the other direction. The church is run by other parties, in whose criticism I am very much united with Herbert Braun" (90/40).

And ought Gollwitzer to sign a resolution that protests the interdiction of the congregations when he himself can write a sentence such as the following: "Our congregation members must receive information about that [historical research] but we must consider the measure of their receptivity, how it is set for them through the limitations of time, their training, and their intellectual grasp?*

Professor Grass says, very simply, that it is a question of veracity and states that "the preaching on the great church festivals of Christmas, Good Friday, Easter, Ascension, and Pentecost fills a special need for our churchly proclamation, and, to be sure, for the preacher as well as for the congregations. There is no compulsion to preach on an Easter text" (51/281). But there is this compulsion. How great, then, is the veracity?

CONFESSION—AN AWKWARD WEAPON

Does what Gerhard Ebeling writes about every confession still apply to the Apostles' Creed: It has "a separatist

---

* Proposal No. 2b "Wort Gottes und Heilige Schrift" from meeting of the Synods of the Evangelical Churches in Germany (EKD) in Frankfurt and Magdeburg, March, 1965, worked up by Professor Gollwitzer, mimeographed, p. 7.

function. It draws the line between true and false doctrine. A uniting confession in the sense of one that refrained from drawing any distinctions from false doctrine would be a contradiction in terms. For a confession always presupposes a *casus confessionis*. It is the pronouncement of a decision" (38/187). And if this no longer applies to the Apostles' Creed, how otherwise will the "line between true and false doctrine" be drawn?

In the Apostles' Creed there is much which many can no longer believe or will no longer believe. Modern theologians teach that a man must not, or perhaps only ought not, believe it. Why not another confession of faith which every believer can speak without qualification? Professor Barnikol has asked this question and has wanted to know whether "the congregations and the servants of the Word today must not have the evangelical courage to do it" (79/561). He received no answer.

A church is not credible in which literally everything is, and remains, questionable. But a church is credible in which one may, to be sure, ask everything, but in which one cannot answer everything.

Luther once wrote: "It is not we who preserve the proclamation of the Church; it was not our forefathers; it will not be our descendants. But it was, is still, and will be him who says 'I am with you always, to the close of the age'" (6/Chap. 6). "It is not we," Hans Grass also consoles the reader at the end of his book on the resurrection, "who preserve the church in the storms of the time and in the often still more dangerous times of calm when everything seems to go so well and smoothly, when Christianity has become again a self-evident presupposition of the middle-class and when we are in danger of becoming sluggish in the faith and of falling asleep. But it is he who preserves the church" (51/286f.).

He = Jesus.
Which Jesus?

9. Without Facts of History
No Act of Faith

Interview with Pastor Gerhard Bergmann, Ph.D.,
of the "Confession Movement 'No Other Gospel.'"*

H.: Are rallies the most appropriate means to conduct a
discussion on matters of faith?

BERGMANN: Before we moved to rallies, we had long
conversations with modern theologians. Because they
are determined to penetrate into the congregations with
their "new interpretations," we have the right and the
obligation to enlighten the congregations about it. That
has happened in the Westfalenhalle in Dortmund and in
later rallies. I am of the opinion that conversation with
individual theologians and the rallies for the enlightenment of the congregations are not mutually exclusive.

H.: I am of the opinion that most of those who sat in the
Westfalenhalle were not enlightened and did not become enlightened. The level of their information is
shockingly low.

BERGMANN: It depends a great deal on what you understand by "enlightenment." If our congregations are not
generally informed about modern theology as its repre-

---

* These texts were scrutinized and approved prior to publica-
tion by the persons interviewed. All statements in parentheses
were added to the interview texts.

sentatives would like them to be, we can only be thankful for that. For the penetration of modern theology would simply bring confusion to our congregations because no genuinely biblical enlightenment results from modern theology.

H.: You speak and write a great deal about the decision which must be made. But can anyone in the congregation decide, can he make judgments at all, if he only experiences your prior judgment, regardless of whether it is correct or false?

BERGMANN: We constantly enlighten the congregations, even at the rally in Dortmund, about what has happened in modern theology. And that this enlightenment is conducted in more correct and appropriate ways is, for us, a very earnest desire.

H.: The modern theologians do not sit somewhere in a far distant land, but in the university cities. One could and should let them speak for themselves.

BERGMANN: Yes, that also happens. But as a Confession Movement, we have the task in open rallies, not of theological discussion, but of equipping the congregations and of preserving in them faithfulness to the Gospel. But that does not exclude, on another basis, discussion and conversation.

H.: Is it not unreasonable to expect that modern theologians will allow themselves to be damned in the rallies and, at the same time, respond to invitations for small group discussions?

BERGMANN: We do not condemn them. But we have the right and the obligation to raise a symbol with a great rally and to make it clear to all the world that we do not come to terms with it, that a process of alienation from the Gospel is taking place. It really has to do with the center of the faith, whether Jesus is dead or whether Jesus is bodily risen and lives. The congregations know that this is what the current discussion is all about. And since our rallies have the purpose of keeping faith with the confession of our fathers, they are not only allowed but bitterly necessary.

H.: You have protested in your *Tagebuch eines Evangelisten* against the tendency of the Evangelical *Kirchentags*, which bring modern theology to the people. Is there an opposition between the Confession Movement and the *Kirchentag?*

BERGMANN: That depends on the leadership of the *Kirchentag* itself. We would in any case be very happy if the pressing desire of the Confession Movement would be taken into consideration by the *Kirchentag*. We have brought to the *Kirchentag* the urgent request not to pursue the so-called line from Cologne.

H.: What is it that disturbed you in Cologne in 1965?

BERGMANN: That representatives of the modern direction, for example, Professor Willi Marxsen, Günter Kline, and especially Frau Dr. Sölle, were entrusted with Bible studies and lectures: Frau Dr. Sölle, with her "Theology after the death of God," is absolutely unbearable. Or, when it was said there that the incarnation of Jesus is only a title which was later attributed to Jesus Christ, then we are not willing to put up with that. John the Baptist already designates Jesus as the Son of God. For us, as a Confession Movement, the incarnation is an expression of the being of Jesus Christ, and not some kind of expression of respect, as it is said in modern theology. We cannot wish that the parishes of Jesus Christ no longer believe in the real incarnation. At the Cologne *Kirchentag* there was a shaking of and an undermining of the person of Jesus Christ, and to that we say no!

H.: Also to that which Kline in Cologne said about the fishers-of-men saying and about the—as he said—legend of the wonderful draught of fish?

BERGMANN: Also that ought absolutely to have no place in the *Kirchentag*, because these speculative expressions of

Professor Kline have no support in the New Testament. We cannot make speculative views of a professor the object of Bible studies to which members of congregations come in great numbers.

H.: But Kline attempted, precisely on the basis of the New Testament itself, to explain that the report of the miracle of the draught of fish has a history of development.

BERGMANN: Kline is not the only one who makes this attempt. That cannot change anything in the fact that other New Testament scholars think quite differently about these questions. That makes clear that we cannot go behind the canon when formulating binding expressions. To grant this and to recognize it is decisive.

H.: The process of the origin of the Gospels, which lasted seven decades, and the establishment of the canon itself, which was first closed in the fourth century after Christ—that does not interest you?

BERGMANN: It does interest me! But we cannot so illuminate the prehistory that we would know exactly how it was in detail. Therefore we are directed to the statements of the New Testament as they lie before us. And we have also every reason to present these statements to others with confidence.

H.: What would happen if at the next *Kirchentag* Professor Marxsen and Professor Kline or other "neorationalists," as you call them, were to speak?

BERGMANN: Then we would recognize in that fact that the leadership of the *Kirchentag* is ignoring our earnest request. Then no one could blame us if we should carry out our responsibility by calling our own rally.

H.: During the *Kirchentag*?

BERGMANN: Yes, of course, and precisely out of responsibility to the congregations. The *Kirchentag* has the task of strengthening faith, of calling men to Jesus Christ, and of making men courageous in discipleship. I am not able to see how that is going to be possible through modern theology, which denies the great salvation events of God.

H.: It would not suffice for you if, in Room three, Marxsen and Kline would speak, and, in Room four, Künneth and Bergmann?

BERGMANN: Then the *Kirchentag* would become a playground of theological argumentation, and that is not its purpose. We cannot experiment with confession; confession has for us an obligatory value.

H.: Do you suppose that we could discuss a few examples of where you would draw the limits of biblical criticism? It is disputed whether Jesus really preached the Sermon on the Mount or whether that which we read in the New Testament as the Sermon on the Mount is only a collection of sayings. Very many theologians, even Catholic, believe that it is possible to say the latter with unanimous certainty.

BERGMANN: With unanimous certainty! You see, there lies the problem. It cannot be said absolutely that the Sermon on the Mount did not take place. I am convinced, on the contrary, that the living remembrance of the Sermon on the Mount maintained itself in the primitive Christian community. I am really convinced of this, that Jesus did preach the Sermon on the Mount. Of course, that does not mean precisely as it is reported to us word for word in the Gospel. I am convinced that Jesus Christ said a great deal more than is preserved for us in the New Testament.

H.: Now the Sermon on the Mount is recorded differently in the Gospels, in Matthew differently and more extensively than in Luke. Which rendering do you consider to be historical?

BERGMANN: That is not an either–or between which I must choose.

H.: Could I summarize your opinion in this way: One ought not to deny *that* the Sermon on the Mount took place, but one may have a number of interpretations about *how* it took place, what Jesus preached?

BERGMANN: Yes, but with some caution. No one would maintain that Jesus said nothing which does not appear in the Sermon on the Mount. On the other hand, much in the Sermon on the Mount may be an insertion of what he perhaps said in other places. That is possible. We take the Sermon on the Mount simply as it is passed on to us, even in the differing reports.

H.: Another question. There are two feedings of the multitude reported, one of five thousand (Matt. 4 : 13–21; Mark 6 : 30–44; Luke 9 : 10–17; John 6 : 1–8) and one of four thousand (Mark 8 : 1–9; Matt. 15 : 32–39). Do you consider it allowable to decide for only one feeding of the multitude, or ought it to be maintained that there were two?

BERGMANN: If the neorationalistic theologians would say that one feeding of the multitude did take place, then the other question of whether a second took place would no longer be so relevant, although I personally trust the Holy Scriptures, that there were two. The problem lies in the fact that the neorationalists deny the one as well as the other.

H.: But what now is the criterion? Apparently the present situation. Because *both* feedings are contested, would you be content if at least *one* were believed?

BERGMANN: It is a question of authority, not so much a question of numbers. If we could agree on the fact that Jesus had the power to multiply bread, then this dispute about whether there were one or two feedings would be insignificant. But the real issue concerns the central question of whether Jesus Christ had this power. And because for me Jesus Christ as the Son of God is not only man, he was perfectly able to allow his incarnation to be clearly signified.

H.: If one, therefore, responds affirmatively to the question of whether Jesus had this power, then may one—if I have understood you correctly—be of a different mind concerning the particular miracle of the feeding of the multitude? Does that also go for the miracle of the changing of water into wine at the wedding of Cana? May one say, as Dibelius says: "It makes no sense to me; it was not necessary for Jesus to supply a lack at a celebration which only began because they had already drunk too much." Would you give the freedom not to believe in this miracle?

BERGMANN: No. We do not have this freedom from the Holy Scriptures. For in the Holy Scriptures stands the basis of the miracle, namely John 2 : 11: He "manifested his glory; and his disciples believed in him." With that it is said unequivocally that this miracle is to be seen in the service of the manifestation of his incarnation. Why then do modern theologians always attempt to de-historicize? Because they want to bring about a de-objectivization. We speak against that because we stand directly on the Scriptures and on the confession: Without facts of history, no act of faith. Report and kerygma build in the New Testament an unbreakable unity.

H.: How would you conduct yourself as a counselor with a man who says the following to you: I believe that Jesus is risen and lives and that I cannot live without him. But I cannot grasp why I ought to believe that this Jesus, in the year 28 or 30, walked on the water. If I must believe that, I should rather no longer be a Christian.

BERGMANN: We must distinguish between not being able to believe and not wanting to believe. I would by no means demand from this man that he believe that Jesus walked on the water. For him other questions are important. I should want to lead him to Jesus Christ as to the mouth of God, as to one in whom God has broken the silence of eternity and who has come to be the lamb of God which takes away the sin of the world. If we understand this Jesus Christ in his center—crucifixion, resurrection—then we can come from there, moving in ever-widening circles, to the knowledge of Jesus. That is what I would say to him.

H.: Modern theologians would also say that, namely, that it does not depend on a walk on the water at that time, but on the living Christ today.

BERGMANN: The difference between the modern theologians and the doubter of whom you spoke consists in this: that the doubter cannot believe that. The modern theologians can also not believe it, certainly. But they make of that fact a world-view and maintain that therefore it cannot have happened. And against that, we raise our energetic opposition.

H.: How was the knowledge of Jesus different from the knowledge of other men at that time?

BERGMANN: It says about Jesus: ". . . for he himself knew what was in man." (John 2 : 25). That means that Jesus Christ cannot be measured with the criteria of the merely human.

H.: Did Jesus share with the man of his time the world-view which we today consider to be antiquated and false? Did the earth consist for him, as for his contemporaries, of a disk and the world, of three layers—hell, earth, and heaven?

BERGMANN: Jesus didn't say very much about this. He was not concerned about some world-view question or another, but came in order to make the sinner holy. That has nothing to do with world-view.

H.: But it is still no doubt possible that the world-view of a man of that time was something other than the world-view of men today.

BERGMANN: If you mean by that the Ptolemaic world-view in distinction to the Copernican world-view, you are no doubt correct. But in the present theological conversation about world-view, there is more involved than that.

H.: The men at that time did not know that the earth revolved about the sun. Did Jesus know it?

BERGMANN: He never expressed himself on that point.

H.: Jesus did not know it and, as all men of his time, "erred" on that point. May a theologian say that?

BERGMANN: Then he would have to be able to demonstrate it out of Holy Scripture. And that he can't do.

H.: Then this question must remain open?

BERGMANN: Yes, I should say that. But I should also think that the question about world-view is not so terribly important. It is the soteriological question that is decisive.

H.: That God is all-knowing—is that something that without doubt every Christian accepts?

BERGMANN: Certainly. Whether Professor Herbert Braun of the University of Mainz accepts that God is all-knowing, I must doubt. Because for Braun, God does not exist as person.

H.: And we men are not all-knowing. On that, for Christians as for non-Christians, no doubt is possible?

BERGMANN: No.

H.: And Jesus was, if I have understood you correctly, neither only a man as other men, nor simply a god walking upon the earth.

BERGMANN: Yes, that's right.

H.: Which intermediate stage of his knowledge have we then accepted, if he was not as all-knowing as God and not as unknowing as we men?

BERGMANN: That we cannot say. Today the tendency seems to be to always draw Jesus Christ into the human. And precisely for that reason, we who stand on Scripture and confession have the other task, namely to see Jesus Christ in his uniqueness and in his preexistence, to testify to him in his deity, so that we can believe in him.

H.: You would, therefore, rather be inclined to accept the omniscience of the earthly Jesus?

BERGMANN: Yes, I should be inclined to do that.

H.: Then can Jesus not have erred?

BERGMANN: I impute no errors to Jesus Christ! Jesus Christ has not erred!

H.: Modern theologians, far beyond limits of the Bultmann school, are agreed that Jesus supposed the in-breaking of the kingdom of God to be very near and that he erred—if we want to say it—at this point.

BERGMANN: A distinction must be made between the proper expectation of the end and the immanent in-breaking of judgment which came to Jerusalem. Think of the mission command which the risen Christ gave! With that command Jesus Christ looks far beyond the generation living at that time.

H.: Even the Catholic theologian Vögtle, who is certainly not modern, is convinced that the mission command was not given by Jesus Christ, but was attributed to him by the early Christians.

BERGMANN: Does one think that that can be confirmed on the Holy Scriptures?

H.: Yes, one refers to the history of the primitive community as it is witnessed to in the New Testament. It excludes—so says Vögtle—the possibility that the mission command was given by the risen Lord. But we perhaps do not want to go into that here. It is clear that one cannot discuss even the smallest detail without raising concomitant questions, without taking the Bible in hand.

Perhaps one more. Much will have to be discussed in a simpler way. What does the so-called man in the street ask himself if the talk is about the knowledge and the infallibility of Jesus? He asks for instance: Why did Jesus call as one of his twelve disciples Judas, who turned out to be a traitor?

BERGMANN: I am convinced that the calling of Judas is not traceable to a mistaken blunder of Jesus, but that the calling of Judas lay in God's plan of salvation. Jesus himself says: "The Son of man goes as it is written of him, but woe to that man by whom the Son of man is betrayed!" (Matt. 26 : 24). That Jesus was more than only a man is shown by the fact that he already knew about the betrayer before the betrayal was carried out.

H.: A few more questions about world-view. You have protested against Bultmann's demythologization.

BERGMANN: No, I should like in no way to be counted among those who demythologize. Demythologization abandons that which is most important. The "Confession Movement 'No other Gospel' " never abandons that which is most important.

H.: Then I should like to know from you, entirely concretely, whether it really happened as it is written in Luke 24 : 51, or not: "While he blessed them, he parted from them?" [The German text quoted here includes "and was carried up into heaven," which is given as a textual variant in the RSV—Translator]

BERGMANN: Yes, of course that happened. It has to do with a fact, with the ascension.

H.: Hans Schomerus, certainly no modern theologian, has written: "Apart from primitive communism, no one thinks that the ascension of Christ is to be understood spatially." But apparently you do?

BERGMANN: No! What is the ascension? The ascension is the ending of the earthly life of Jesus. The ascension is the return out of space–time into the invisible reality, into the dimension from which he came. So one must know, to be sure, that the invisible reality lies not next to, not under, not over the visible reality, but it lies in the visible reality so that they are intertwined with one another.

H.: If I understand you correctly, then Jesus disappeared before the eyes of his disciples, but he did not "ascend into heaven," as it stands in the Apostles' Creed and as all Christians for many centuries believed and as it is, even today, taught to countless confirmands?

BERGMANN: The question concerning the ascension is not a question about so many centimeters but, as I emphasized, the change from the visible into the invisible reality. I should like to believe that Jesus Christ came to meet his disciples halfway in their understanding when he disappeared from them. The ascension was an act of observation. But whether he needed three yards in order to disappear or whether he vanished immediately, in a moment, that is not decisive. It is decisive that this event did take place.

10. Anxiety about the Bible Mixed with Ignorance about the Bible

Interview with Professor D. Hans Conzelmann of the University of Göttingen

H.: How would you characterize the task of theology?

CONZELMANN: The notion is widespread that theology consists of a collection of unchangeable sentences and that faith is that which holds these sentences to be true. Faith is, therefore, essentially learning. But it is not the task of theology to formulate, somewhat like mathematics, timeless sentences to be taught. Theological thinking and formulating must happen anew day by day, for it is reflection on the Word of God which desires to be said and heard anew each day. Theology is systematic deliberation on that which is preached and how it is preached, what the preacher is and what the hearer is.

H.: How are professors of theology and pastors to be related to one another? Is the professor superior to the pastor?

CONZELMANN: No, on the contrary! Faith comes from preaching, so in that sense the professor is subordinate to the pastor. The professor of theology is neither a representative of *the* Christian position or of "Christendom," nor is he a faith-specialist. He is simply a specialist in a few areas of faith-*teaching*, or doctrine.

At the same time, he is a member of the Church, a hearer of preaching, and therefore in no other position than every member of a congregation; namely, a hearer who through the preaching wants to be taught about that which has to do with God's relationship to him, to the entire Church, and to the world. I want, therefore, to experience what I have expected from God and what God demands of me; that is, I want to experience God. This dimension "God" I should like to so understand that I understand (through "him") myself, my past, my present, and my future, my church and my world, the rules of human relationships. As a hearer, I am invited to test that which is heard and the tool with which to do that is the Bible.

H.: It ought to be. Is it in fact that today for Christians?

CONZELMANN: Concerning the average popular ideas of Christianity, the knowledge of doctrine, I should like to emphasize two symptoms: anxiety about the Bible and the widespread ignorance about the Bible, even about the elementary things of doctrine. How many Christians can give any clear information about the Christian hope? About the question when the dead are raised? About what the Holy Ghost is? Yet this knowledge is the presupposition of confirmatoin. Are even ten percent of pastors well informed about the Church's teaching of the Trinity, of the person of Christ, about Luther's doctrine of the Lord's Supper? How many pastors really represent in their preaching Luther's teaching of the bondage of the will, of justification alone through faith without appended conditions?

H.: We are agreed that the lack of information of many Christians about what faith is, what confession is, is shocking. Yet you also mention anxiety about the Bible. It is not new. . . .

CONZELMANN: It has its history. In the nineteenth century, the world-view of the Bible was defended against modern science, against the teaching of the origin of the world and the development of man. So theology was maneuvered out of one position after another until it finally noticed—to its salvation—that it had been working in vain, that in reality it had not fought for the faith but for an outdated world-view.

H.: People are not even, at this point, entirely united on that.

CONZELMANN: In any case, one can say that the world-view of the Old Testament is no longer an object of battle. However, a secret anxiety of believers has remained about science, about information concerning the historicity of the Bible. It is significant that the Old Testament is, so to speak, passed over silently. If one is serious about the entire Bible, this means that one must make distinctions within the Bible, between Israel and Church, Old and New Testament, sacrificial cult and "reasonable worship," between law and gospel, world-view and meaning. Without this distinction, the Bible is not the record of revelation and of faith, but a collection of early items from Oriental religious history, or a "paper" pope.

H.: Many see a danger that the Bible may be lost in the Church.

CONZELMANN: I should go farther than that and say that it *is* lost and that the task is to find it again. That is only possible if it is referred to rigorously in preaching as the preeminent Word of God. The same goes for the Apostles' Creed. This also one does not have by mere recitation. One has it only if it is constantly clarified through preaching about what faith is today. The world-view of the Apostles' Creed is that of the old world; heaven is above and hell below. That is not our way of reading the world. It is also not required that we adopt that world-view. To do that is impossible anyway. We do not believe in a world-view. The Apostles' Creed can only be credible if it is understood as the confession to the one God, the creator, who reconciled the world to himself in Christ.

H.: May I now ask you a few questions which are currently asked by the leaders of the Confession Movement? Is the Bible the Word of God?

CONZELMANN: This sentence is only correct if it is explained how the Bible is the Word of God—as word of men, as historical document. The notion that there is a, so to speak, pure, distilled Word of God, free of all human traces, pure from every earthly residue, is not Protestant but Fundamentalistic.

H.: Many theologians and pastors say and write that criticism of the Bible is criticism of God's Word and, therefore, not allowed.

CONZELMANN: Biblical criticism is not only allowed but necessary. The objection sketched by them, that one may not subject the Word of God to the criticism of unbelieving reason, I consider to be senseless. The Bible is a historical document. Therefore the task is to investigate its history of development, the world-view at that time, the language; what one understood at that time by spirit, flesh, soul, and so on. What do the pictures of the transcendence mean? Neither the world-view nor the pictures of transcendence are in themselves Christian. They become Christian only by interpretation. The pictures originate out of Judaism, the ancient Orient, and the Greek world. The point at which it matters is this: whether and how through these pictures and concepts God's acts of salvation in Christ are expounded.

H.: Must one therefore be "educated" in order to be an especially "good" Christian?

CONZELMANN: Not at all. To understand Christianity is something other than faith. But we need theology and the theological explanation of the Bible in somewhat the same way that one needs studies in grammar in order not to subjectively misunderstand a work of poetry. Theology is a trade, a craft, and wants to be judged as such. And if the Bible is a historical document, it must be tested. The statement, "I certainly believe whatever stands in the Bible," would not be a Protestant statement. It corresponds to the Catholic way of thinking— believe whatever the Church teaches. In the Protestant church, one cannot believe for someone else or allow faith to be amputated. And a Christian man must be able to give the particulars of his faith.

H.: What is correct faith?

CONZELMANN: Faith is not imitation or repetition but application of the Word. The "Faust rule" is valid for faith: One must be able to proffer his head for a truth of faith. One cannot do that for a well-established fact because it would be senseless. I cannot rationally offer my head for the fact that the Second World War broke out in the year 1939, for the tendering of the head would change nothing in regard to the fact. I cannot proffer my head for the fact that an Apostle James wrote the Epistle of James. And I cannot tender it for the historicity of a miracle story. Whoever says "You must hold this and this to be true" must also show *how* one can do that. Otherwise, he is a preacher of the law.

H.: Is there nothing which the Christian *must* believe if he really wants to be a Christian?

CONZELMANN: What we must believe, not on the basis of a demand of a man, but on the basis of the announcement of God, is this one thing: that God accepts us exclusively out of grace and that this grace is called Christ.

H.: Does it disturb you that the present debate revolves about entirely different things?

CONZELMANN: It revolves around the virgin birth, the empty tomb, the nature miracles. It is significant that these themes rule the conflict and not justification, the validity of the Sermon on the Mount, even in politics, legislation, and jurisdiction. It excites no one if the Church is offered protection by atom bombs. The points of conflict today are points without risk, on the side of the preachers as well as that of the hearers. One can "believe" in the virgin birth fully without obligation and one can teach it without obligation, namely, without crisis of existence in the world, without risking conflict. No preacher may enjoin the virgin birth as a requirement of faith, because he cannot establish the *ability* to believe that. Otherwise he has overstepped himself and must be called to task.

H.: It is demanded, on the other hand, by the leaders of the Confession Movement that the theologians who do not consider the virgin birth to be a historical fact "must be called to task." What can, what ought, the preacher "to enjoin as a requirement of faith"; what can and ought he to preach in a binding way?

CONZELMANN: That God's grace is new every morning and *why* it is new, namely, because God in Christ grants reconciliation and, to that end, the word of reconciliation; and *how* it is new, *what* grace is: not indulgence but eradication of guilt, therefore release, the gift of hope against appearances, against itself. If that is proclaimed, then I know who I am and where I am. More the preacher cannot offer, and more he cannot require.

H.: That does not satisfy the Confession Movement, and it does not satisfy most pastors either. Do the spirits divide on the question whether and in what sense it must be preached that Jesus is the Son of God?

CONZELMANN: "God's son" means nothing other than that God is visible in the crucified Jesus. Then one can no longer ask so stupidly whether Jesus is God's son or not. One can force into that question whatever he wants, every arbitrary fantasy. Jesus is simply the crucified, "God's being" in the world. The incarnation, so understood, means that faith is not an inner flight to a distant god, but that it orients itself on this, that God is encountered in the world.

H.: What is your answer to the question whether Jesus is risen or not?

CONZELMANN: Whoever asks that is really not asking at all, but already knows what the resurrection is. The question is completely senseless, whether the resurrection is a historical fact, whether it is an event in space and time. Of any real significance is only this: that the crucified was not destroyed, that he is there, and to be sure in such a way as it is expressed at the conclusion of the Gospel according to Matthew: "I am with you always, to the close of the age" (Matt. 28 : 20). It is important that he is the Lord, that therefore the world stands under the sign of the cross. For the risen one is the crucified one. Only as such is he to be seen for us. Mark 16 : 6 is valid: "He has risen, he is not here" and so is John 20 : 29: "Blessed are those who have not seen and yet believe." That is the miracle. And all other miracles are to be judged by it. If that is clear, then one can say in fact: He is risen, and specifically independent of my faith. Even faith, which I have not bestowed upon myself, says to me that the risen one is at work before me. And faith also says to me that no man can show or see the risen one except through witness to him.

11. Are There Heresies in Protestant Theology?

Interview with Professor Walter Künneth of the University of Erlangen

H.: Professor, you have thrown the catchword "heresy" into the debate. What could, what must, in your opinion, be declared as heresy?

KÜNNETH: Knowledge about a revelation of God which has taken place includes the necessity of very definite and clear proclamation. With that is also given the necessity of a doctrine which expresses the central content of the proclamation. The doctrine must therefore struggle to remove all alien elements and all fuzziness, so that the message of revelation may be expressed as unambiguously as possible.

H.: It is often said that there would be no precedent in the Protestant church to declare anything as heresy, that it would be plainly unevangelical, un-Protestant, to speak of heresy.

KÜNNETH: I consider that to be an extraordinarily strange, indeed a plainly impossible, assertion. One could, at best, say it about neo-Protestantism, which is already a quite decadent phenomenon. But one can never say it about the foundation of the Protestant church, the Reformation, for in the Reformation doctrine was a central, fundamental concern.

H.: Who ought to decide what is correct doctrine and what is false doctrine?

KÜNNETH: If I speak from the Lutheran understanding, I should say that, in the first line, it is the preachers and the bishops, the proper theological exponents, who have the task of watching over and judging the Church's doctrine. I should consider that the typically Lutheran position. The Reformed position is much more inclined to make judgments according to democratic procedure in the synods.

H.: The problem of the courts is for you secondary?

KÜNNETH: I turn to all those who are responsible in the Church in a special way. Here in Bavaria, for instance, I have turned to the Church leaders. It is important to me that we be no longer silent, that the endless toleration of every, literally every, opinion, must stop. And it will stop.

H.: One may regret it or welcome it. If the Church leaders and the synods do not decide, they decide *de facto* for modern theology and against the demands of the Confession Movement.

KÜNNETH: That's entirely correct.

H.: I should like to hear from you more concretely what, in your opinion, ought to be declared as heresy.

KÜNNETH: There are central statements with which the message stands or falls. According to the common view of the New Testament, it is the salvation-reality of the of the crucified and risen Christ. Therein is grounded what the Reformation called justification. Today it is to be condemned as heresy when one thinks it possible to hold fast to justification, in that one says God is gracious and the sinner experiences forgiveness through God's grace, and at the same time to be silent about, to re-interpret, or to deny the presupposition, the basis which makes this justifying act of God possible.

H.: As the basis which makes this possible you under-stand . . .

KÜNNETH: . . . the salvation-reality or the salvation-facts or the facticity of the crucifixion and the resurrection—call it what you will. It does not have to do with these expressions, but with an event taking place outside of man which wants to be brought to expression. That is doctrine. This doctrine can have infinitely many variations and interpretations. There isn't any uniformity here. But if the central content is disputed, then heresy begins.

H.: The impression has arisen that the Confession Movement and you have declared as heresy an entire direction of theology—the "existentialist" theology.

KÜNNETH: No, that would be theologically quite inaccurate. That would be somewhat too simple, not stated with sufficient care.

H.: But then you must have corrected those in the Confession Movement who do say that the entire starting point of existentialist theology is false and that, therefore, its doctrine is false.

KÜNNETH: I should say that the beginning is basically false. And it is evident that, step by step, out of this does come forth heresy.

H.: Are you not afraid that in the Protestant church something is imminent which the Catholic church has with great effort put behind it, and on which many Catholic theologians think back only with unhappiness? I mean the battle, the careless battle against an entire direction of theology, which at that time was called "modernism".

KÜNNETH: I do not want, as I said, any general condemnation. I have, for example, made no objection at all to the case of the historical–critical method. Why not? Because it depends entirely upon the presuppositions, the spirit, and the goal. I have also made no objection at all to existential interpretation. We all do that. But if that is done absolutely, then out of it is sure to come heresy.

H.: Ought, then, as in the Catholic church, particular conclusions and individual sentences of modern theologians to be declared as heresy?

KÜNNETH: Yes, that's what I mean. The Church must be able to say: Whoever today maintains or teaches this or that contradicts correct doctrine. And whoever wants to be a preacher of the Church can and ought not to preach it.

H.: Are you not afraid that that would be entirely too Catholic and not up to date? Many Catholic theologians are happy that at the Second Vatican Council no heresy was condemned.

KÜNNETH: I do not believe that the identification of heresy is no longer up to date. It is precisely the opposite. The most up-to-date thing today is the laying out of a clear proclamation. That is just what the contemporary man needs. Precisely that! Vagueness and "this as well as that" and liberalism and the lowest common denominator—of that he has had his fill.

H.: What ought the criterion to be by which true doctrine and false doctrine are distinguished?

KÜNNETH: The criterion seems to me to be given with the central expression of the New Testament proclamation, in the intention of the Reformation confessional statements. I mean not in details, not formally, not according to citations, but according to the primary intention.

H.: Theoretically there may perhaps be agreement that this is where the criterion is to be found. But in practice one can't be sure.

KÜNNETH: It does not depend on whether one defends this or that view, but on how the view being considered identifies and grounds itself. And I am thoroughly convinced that the view which I represent is identified by New Testament and confessional intention and substance. And that which one hears from the other side is not identified in that way and often stands even in

opposition to it. It does not have to do with theological
directions at all, but with the question whether we as
Church, as Christians, still have the courage to say that
we believe something, that we have a doctrine, a teaching, that we have something to give to the world, or
whether we simply turn over everything to subjectivism.

H.: The theologians of the other direction can say almost
all of that word for word. And they do say it, and in a
very similar way.

KÜNNETH: But they have no right to say it. If someone
says that Jesus was only a man and nothing but a man,
that may be a personal conviction which I can respect.
But he cannot claim to be appealing to the New Testament if he omits half of the statements.

H.: In your opinion he cannot; in his own opinion he can.
How ought the Church to decide?

KÜNNETH: It is clearest at the point of the central problem, the resurrection. If someone says: "Naturally, I
also speak about the resurrection, but the resurrection
does not have to do with the person of the crucified, but
only with the idea, with the kerygma, with the testimony
to Christ in the Christian community," then one cannot
appeal for that to the New Testament. And the Church
is quite able to see that.

H.: To what extent have heresies been accepted? In the
Braunschweig Theses there is reference to over sixty
points.

KÜNNETH: Heresy, I should say, is not a quantitative affair.
It is not a matter of whether there are ten, twenty, or
fifty points, but . . .

H.: But if you want to condemn heresies, then it surely is
a matter of separating out a greater or lesser *amount* of
correct doctrine.

KÜNNETH: Quite right. Only I want to say that the limits
are flexible. Let us take the problem of the virgin birth.
In and of itself one can say correctly that whoever does

not accept it advocates a heresy. But I should say that certain statements, not fully corresponding to the New Testament, can be tolerated on various grounds.

H.: On what basis are you justified in being so generous at this point?

KÜNNETH: These interpretations do not concern the center. They lie somewhere out on the periphery. I should therefore not shoot there with the big "true doctrine and false doctrine" canon. I should say one must talk about it, one must converse, but one can tolerate an opposing opinion.

H.: And it concerns the center when it concerns God, the cross, the resurrection?

KÜNNETH: I should like to include the person of Jesus, because I think that in him God, in a special way, has become transparent. And I should also include the Parousia.

H.: Such statements as, for example, Martin Dibelius and Ernst Käsemann have made about miracles, you would not want to declare as heresy?

KÜNNETH: Such opinions are a curtailment, a finally forbidden curtailment for which I can easily recognize the source. When the question concerns miracles, then the struggle ought not to be stated in terms of one being obligated to believe this and that or all miracles. I always have the suspicion, when the miracles of Jesus are contested, that something is not in order in the background of the contesting theology; namely, its philosophical starting point. For that reason they come to their conclusions in the interpretation of the miracles; for that reason also their Christology is out of kilter. The discussion about the miracles is therefore Christologically conditioned.

H.: If we assume that heresy would be officially declared and condemned in and by the Protestant church, what consequences ought that to have (a) for the theologians who defend these doctrines, and (b) for the congregations?

KÜNNETH: For the theologians it would have existentially no results at all. They are government employees. No one can take away their positions. They can continue to teach and write more books. I happen also to think that this is the way it should be, for it would be fatal if somehow a personal hardship were connected with it.

H.: They do fear, it seems to me, the consequences . . .

KÜNNETH: It is important what consequences the Church draws out of such a declaration of heresy for the training of future preachers, pastors, teachers, etc. One can forbid nothing in the present situation. Everyone can hear and teach whatever he wishes. The Church leaders ought also to thoroughly affirm the importance of future pastors becoming acquainted with various opinions and doctrines. Yet the Church must take care that its future preachers can competently represent the doctrine of the Church. Therefore the Church leadership will have to provide, if necessary, preparation time and to give other helps before the various examinations.

H.: I should consider that to be a fatal development. I consider—if you would allow me this criticism—that your attitude in this point is inconsistent. *If* something is declared to be heresy, then it ought no longer to be advocated in the Church. And *if* theologians belong to the Church, then they also ought not to advocate these heresies. Perhaps we ought to discuss concretely an example. If anything can be declared heresy at all, then it would certainly be Herbert Braun's concept of God. Let us assume that student of theology *x* has heard Braun's lectures for six semesters in Mainz.

KÜNNETH: I should not accept him. I should not forbid him to hear Braun. But I should say: You can study there six semesters, but I do not recognize Braun's lectures because training in the New Testament with

Braun is not training in the New Testament according to the mind of the Church. Very simple.

H.: But isn't it really quite complicated? Let us assume that Braun's concept of God would be condemned. Why ought his entire instruction to be condemned at the same time? What about his course of lectures on the Dead Sea Scrolls or the Epistle to the Romans, or his lectures on introduction to the New Testament.

KÜNNETH: Of course, if Braun holds such lectures, he can say some very worthwhile things. I certainly recognize that. But he cannot say, on the basis of suppositions, that which *also* must be said. That he can't do at all. Therefore, I still insist that it is a serious question whether a theology student who spends his time at Mainz with Braun in New Testament or with Mezger in practical theology is properly prepared for admission to the office of preacher. And I should answer it negatively. If and how I can recognize it must be decided from case to case.

H.: The schizophrenia, which I am convinced makes the Protestant church even today largely incredible, would —if the Church would proceed in the way you suggest—not be eliminated but would rather proliferate. Braun would become a comic figure. He would have a chair of heretical theology, which no one could officially dispute. One could only secretly drive away the students. I should think that theology as a discipline, and the Church, would then become even more incredible. And perhaps in the course of a year the Confession Movement would succeed in the pulpit, and modern theology, in the world of the lectern. Then there would be theology without Church, and faith without scholarship.

KÜNNETH: Theology without Church, even without faith, we have already. We stand, in fact, before a very threatening situation. I am thoroughly convinced that it would be more inconsistent if something which was declared to be heresy were no longer allowed to be taught.

H.: But?

KÜNNETH: The difficulty is that the Church has no authority over the faculties in the university.

H.: Then it is precisely the Church, if it wants to ascertain heresy and to remain credible, which must alter the state/Church arrangements and secure for itself the necessary influence.

KÜNNETH: That it could do. But why take the third step before the first and second? It is first important that it be made clear in the Church that not everything may be taught and preached. What consequences that ought to have and will have for state/Church regulations, that cannot be thought through today.

H.: Are you—as other members and associates of the Confession Movement—of the opinion that it is separated less from the Catholic church than from modern Protestant theology?

KÜNNETH: That is also my conviction. The Catholic church has upheld doctrinal substance also in the sense understood by the Protestant church and rests on it even today. That which is offered today by modernistic Protestant theology is precisely a total abandonment of this doctrinal substance.

H.: Now I should like to ask a few questions which arise from your book *Theologie der Auferstehung.* You have written that the Biblical expression about Christ's preexistence has "a strangeness about it, and in a strict sense is not necessary for salvation" (64/120). Is it legitimate to come to the conclusion that there can be no heresy concerning the preexistence of Christ?

KÜNNETH: Yes. To be sure, the preexistence of Christ is a legitimate and meaningful conclusion growing out of the kernel of the Gospel. But I should not say that a theologian who thinks otherwise on this point is a teacher of heresy.

H.: You have written that the resurrection of Jesus is "an event which is veiled" and that the Church must "reject every attempt to conceive that resurrection as a visible happening in which the Crucified reveals himself in divine majesty" (64/258). Does that mean that you consider a historical argumentation partially questionable?

KÜNNETH: Yes. I should be of the opinion, for example, that many argumentations by Pannenberg are not theologically valid. I believe that Pannenberg wants to do too much.

H.: If one pursues the discussion about the empty tomb, one has the impression that an attempt is made with logic and pure historical research to make this thing a matter of a certain degree of probability. Seventy to eighty percent of the way is left to the historian, twenty to thirty percent are then a matter for the theologian and faith. Does not faith in this case—if one wants to state it sharply—become a stopgap?

KÜNNETH: I should say so. Faith in the risen Lord is not dependent upon whether this or that historian makes the empty tomb or some other event probable or not. But I should say that if the theological–historical researcher is active to a certain fixed limit, then it is legitimate. But the "more," the event which is veiled, comes out of an entirely different sphere.

H.: You indicate in your book, concerning the empty tomb, that "on theological principles it would be conceivable to dispense with the discussion of this question, if it could be done without prejudice to the reality of the resurrection and the witness of it" (64/91). Would you still say that today?

KÜNNETH: In and of itself the empty tomb does not stand in the center, but on the periphery. In the present situation it has, to be sure, taken on significant importance because here a sign is erected for the concrete reality of an event. The modernistic theologians come with general figures of speech about the resurrection. But in this point it is concrete. In this way, that which in and of itself lies on the periphery again becomes meaningful.

H.: May the empty tomb be made into a criterion for proper faith?

KÜNNETH: Yes, now, a criterion . . .

H.: If one wants to distinguish you and your opponents, then would the different conception of the empty tomb be a line of demarcation?

KÜNNETH: In the present situation I should thoroughly agree to that. But I could imagine that twenty years ago it would by no means be the case, or that at a later date it will be.

H.: Is it heresy according to your view when Bultmann states that the corpse of Jesus could not again become alive?

KÜNNETH: Yes. That is total heresy. It stands in contradiction to the New Testament report.

H.: Where does the meaning of the empty tomb lie for the future hope of Christians, if the tombs of Christians some day will be empty because—as Althaus once wrote—the bodies will long ago have decomposed?

KÜNNETH: We must begin again from the true center; the bodily resurrection of Jesus. The sign for the bodily resurrection of Jesus is the empty tomb. What does the bodily resurrection of Jesus mean for the congregation? I should summarize it in the following sentences: Preservation of personal individuality in a new corporeality. It will not somehow affirm the identity of a soul-kernel because man is body, body now in the immanent, and body then in the resurrection of the dead. That happens here proleptically.

H.: But for the new corporeality of Christians, the emptiness of some tomb will not be necessary. Why must then the tomb of Jesus have had to be empty?

KÜNNETH: The graves of Christians do not necessarily have to be empty, precisely as the tomb of Jesus did not have to be empty in order to make possible his resurrection in new corporeality.

H.: Aren't you coming here very close to the modern theologians?

KÜNNETH: God could have also done it in another way, but he did not do it in another way! And so I can say that here a particularity of Jesus is under discussion which has meaning, deep meaning. But it is really the concrete corporeality which is decisive here, on which an eternal promise rests.

H.: Pannenberg has brought natural science into play on the question of the empty tomb and has sought help from it.

KÜNNETH: That is completely impossible. That is an attempt at proof which is out of order.

H.: May one with regard to other miracles hope for assistance from the natural scientists which would make faith easier? And if so, then certainly not for the walking on the water, for the raising of the dead, and for the resurrection.

KÜNNETH: A natural scientist can only determine in a purely statistical way the profusion of experiences. He can say that on the ground of certain factors there will be certain causal results. But if the presuppositions change, if some potential enters into the situation which up till this time was specifically not findable in the immanent dimension, then there results, precisely from this potential, other consequences. If, therefore, in that Jesus of Nazareth there really was a concentration of potentiality present, then must the consequence be a fully other one than if this potentiality were not present. And out of that come different results. The natural scientists can say after the event: "Yes, of course, here we have definitely unprecedented effects. We must therefore inquire about a new potential. What kind of power it is, we don't know. But we cannot deny the new data."

H.: But natural scientists must see themselves as incompetent when it is a question of a walking on the water, a raising of the dead, a resurrection.

KÜNNETH: It is often said that such things contradict natural laws. I can only say that they contradict prior experiences. Natural laws are only a representation. . . .

H.: Would you really think it possible that sometime walking on water and raising the dead will be explained as fitting in with natural law?

KÜNNETH: We've already experienced that. Think of the example of Indian fakirs! I would not exclude them from consideration. But it doesn't depend on that for me. That something extraordinary happens doesn't make it a miracle of God. A miracle can only be Christologically interpreted and understood. Not the particularly spectacular is important. That does not interest me at all. But it is important only that this Jesus Christ, this one finally identical with God, works here in an extraordinary way.

H.: Professor, in the interpretation of the appearances, there are two extremes. On the one hand, they are painted—as Ricciotti does it—so naturally that one would think there was almost no difference between the life of Jesus before and after his death. On the other hand, Hirsch has written that the apostles had only subjective visions. In your opinion, how narrowly must the limits be drawn?

KÜNNETH: Concerning the appearances, we can only speak in the form of antinomies and, specifically, on the basis of the consequences of the events themselves. Because the revelation event was a veiled event, transcendent and immanent at the same time, historical fact and at the same time metaphysical reality, therefore, I can make only paradoxical statements about the point of intersection, I can speak only in the form of antinomies. On the one hand, the identity with the historical Jesus of Nazareth: stigmata, speaking, eating. On the other hand, the "totally other" which I cannot photograph, which evades my categories. Both belong together if one wants to transcribe in an appropriate way the phenomenon of the appearances.

H.: Are there—unless we're completely mistaken—also naturalistic interpretations represented within the Confession Movement? Do you think that's possible?

KÜNNETH: No. There are certain naïve, pictorial conceptions. What naïve people think does not disturb the faith. They mean the right thing, but express it perhaps only in an awkward and childish way. As a theologian I must naturally use ideas in a quite different way.

H.: And what is your opinion now about heresy on the other side—the vision side?

KÜNNETH: The subjective vision theory is heresy without question. The decisive thing is the objective reality.

H.: But not in the sense of camera or tape recorder?

KÜNNETH: That would be a false understanding of objectivity, which has been rejected by us again and again. One simply does not grasp—or will not grasp—that objective can mean not only "graphic," but can also mean reality existing outside of me, which confronts me. That is what I mean when I speak about objective reality.

H.: But may I ask very simply: How does one reconcile to say, on the one hand, that camera and tape recorder would have captured nothing and to argue, on the other hand, that the risen one ate and drank?

KÜNNETH: I should say that the concepts eating and drinking are clues to the objectivity of the resurrection event. With that ought to be excluded precisely the idea that men only imagined something.

H.: But are you then not related to the objective vision

theory as Grass has developed it? Under "objective," he understands that it had to do with a happening set by God, while he explains the eating and the drinking of the risen one as legends.

KÜNNETH: Where do the legends stop? Where do they begin? Who guarantees me that the other will not also be explained as legend?

H.: No one.

KÜNNETH: Quite right. I consider the concepts "legend" and "myth" to be theologically illegitimate categories. Theology ought to choose other concepts.

H.: May I ask you finally: We've been talking about what separates conservative and modern theologians. What binds them together?

KÜNNETH: There seems to me to exist a common interest in the New Testament.

H.: I should admit that also in regard to Professor X, who has a chair for atheism in Moscow or Jena.

KÜNNETH: Perhaps one would have to go a step farther and say that apparently it is not only an interest, but a directed interest in this sense, that the New Testament has a significance for contemporary man. And *that* the Communists would not say.

H.: You would not want to say that most theologians still have in common a concept of God, hence faith in God?

KÜNNETH: That is a difficult, even a painful question. I want to do no one an injustice and can give no information at all on what others believe. I can only say what they have written. And on that basis I should have doubts about agreeing to your question.

H.: Is this faith not common to all theologians, with *perhaps* one or two exceptions—that Jesus lives?

KÜNNETH: It depends on what is meant by "Jesus lives." Does he live in the kerygma, in some words, or does he live—as my conviction of faith has it—as a personal reality? That is for me the decisive criterion.

12. Is Jesus Risen
as Goethe?

Expanded Version of the Der Spiegel *Interview** *with*
Professor Rudolf Bultmann of Marburg

SPIEGEL: Professor, the heretic John Huss was condemned
at the Council of Constance in 1415, in spite of having
first been given a hearing. You and your students were
condemned at a rally in the Westfalenhalle in Dortmund
in 1966 without a hearing. Since then a Confession
Movement is spreading in the Protestant church against
your theology, called "heresy" by your opponents.

BULTMANN: The charges raised against me in the Westfalenhalle in Dortmund are a matter of complete indifference to me. I do my work in the awareness that we
can do nothing against the truth, but only for the truth.
That's what it says in 2 Corinthians (13 : 8: "For we
cannot do anything against the truth, but only for the
truth.")

SPIEGEL: You have been accused, and are accused, of wanting to liquidate virtually everything in the Apostles'
Creed—from the virgin birth to the resurrection—under
the catch-word "demythologization."

* The conversation was conducted as a *Der Spiegel* interview. In agreement with Professor Bultmann, the version approved and published at that time has been expanded with the
questions and answers marked by an asterisk.

BULTMANN: Demythologization is not a matter of liquidation, but of interpretation.

SPIEGEL: It is current opinion that a Christian distinguishes himself from a non-Christian in that for him the Apostles' Creed is almost a dogma. He accepts it as true; he believes what is expressed there. Do you think that this is a rather correct definition of the Christian faith?

BULTMANN: No. It is an error to say that the Apostles' Creed is a dogma that the Christian must accept as true. Faith is not the accepting of salvation-facts as true. It is rather the answer to the Christian proclamation, which promises men the grace of God. The reception of the grace of God presupposes that man is conscious of his nothingness before God. In that faith submits itself to the judgment of God, it is at the same time obedience, as Paul particularly emphasizes.

SPIEGEL*: But wasn't faith for the Apostle Paul at the same time also the accepting of salvation-facts as true?

BULTMANN*: For Paul there is only *one* salvation-fact, better, a salvation-*event*, which consists in the death and the resurrection of Jesus—and the two build a unity— through which God has reconciled the world to himself.

SPIEGEL*: You appeal to 2 Corinthians?

BULTMANN*: Yes, Chap. 5 : 18f.* In this letter there is also the assertion that the salvation-event continues in the Apostolic preaching, so that it becomes present at any given time**

---

* "All this is from God, who through Christ reconciled us to himself and gave us the ministry of reconciliation; that is, God was in Christ reconciling the world to himself, not counting their trespasses against them, and entrusting to us the message of reconciliation."

** 6 : 1f.: "Working together with him, then, we entreat you not to accept the grace of God in vain. For he says (Isa. 49 : 8): 'At the acceptable time I have listened to you and helped you on the day of salvation.'"

SPIEGEL: At the present time, however, the question raised most often in the congregations is "What is there left to believe of the creeds, still confessed in worship services, if one accepts your 'demythologization,' your criticism of the Bible?" (As it was put by Professor Beckmann, president of the Evangelical church in Rhineland (98/5)). May we therefore ask you specifically whether the confession of Jesus Christ as the "only-begotten son of God" demands of Christians belief in the preexistence of Jesus, that he was a heavenly being that came down to earth? If not, what does the "preexistence" mean when it is demythologized?

BULTMANN: In the Pauline passages about the preexistence of Jesus Christ, the point is that the person and destiny of Jesus do not have their origin and meaning in connection with this-worldly events. Rather, these passages insist that God has acted in the person and destiny of Jesus.

SPIEGEL: When you formulate it that way, could not, must not, even many a conservative theologian agree with you?

BULTMANN: Let me put it in this way. It is a fact that there is a proclamation of the prevenient grace and love, a proclamation authorized by God. This fact is expressed mythologically in talk about the preexistence of Christ.

SPIEGEL*: The expression "true God and true man" is also contested. You once wrote in relation to this formula, as it was decided upon in the year 451 by the Council of Chalcedon, and as it is still recognized today in all Christian churches, that it is "an expression that is now impossible for our thought" (24/286). Do you think that the expression should nevertheless be retained, and how ought it to be understood?

BULTMANN*: The formulation "true God and true man" was fashioned at Chalcedon in the conceptions of Greek thought . . .

SPIEGEL*: . . . as the unity of both natures of Jesus Christ, the divine and the human.

BULTMANN*: The truth that the expression conveys is that a historical phenomenon, the historical image of Jesus of Nazareth, is at the same time the eschatological phenomenon, Christ as the Lord.

SPIEGEL: The Creed says: "Born of the Virgin Mary." The research published particularly by you and Martin Dibelius leads to the conclusion that Jesus was not born of the Virgin Mary, but as the child of Mary and Joseph. What, then, does "born of the Virgin Mary" mean?

BULTMANN: It is the legendary expression for faith's claim that the source of the meaning of the person of Jesus is not to be seen in his natural this-worldly origin.

SPIEGEL: It is often asked, above all by your opponents, that if Jesus is not the divine being descended from heaven to earth, and is not the son of the Virgin Mary, then in what sense is he the Son of God?

BULTMANN: I should like first to ask my opponents what they understand by the phrase "Son of God"?

SPIEGEL: You mean that there is no clarity, no agreement among your opponents on this point?

BULTMANN: I at least have reasons to doubt it. From my point of view, I should say that the divine sonship of Christ consists in the fact that Jesus, in obedience to God as the Father (as the Gospel of John particularly stresses) and in authority, proclaimed the Word of God which still encounters us today as his Word.

SPIEGEL: The Westphalian Confession Movement declares as "anti-Christian" the statement of Professor Hartmann of Dortmund that Jesus was a man and nothing but a man. Do you consider this statement to be Christian, theologically correct?

BULTMANN: Yes, I can appeal to Luther for support.

SPIEGEL: Your colleague Gogarten, in his recently published book *Jesus Christus Wende der Welt*, refers to passages from Luther such as: "The humanity of Jesus would have been of no use if the deity were not in it. But on the other hand, God does not want to be found, nor may he be found, except through and in this humanity." (48/2).

BULTMANN: Gogarten quotes, in fact, the decisive passages of Luther.

SPIEGEL: Luther surely reprimanded the Church for trying from the beginning to separate Jesus from sins and from sinners, in order to make him an example, a judge. From Luther there is also the statement: "If I deny that he [Jesus] is a sinner, I also deny the crucified one" (48/3). But cannot many words of Luther also be cited which make him the chief witness for the conservatives?

BULTMANN: With Gogarten I am convinced that Luther is correctly understood only when one takes to heart his rule about the knowledge of Christ, namely, that the more deeply we can bring him into the flesh, the better.

SPIEGEL: That is important for you. But on the other hand, you have often stressed that it all depends only on the *"that*ness" of the coming of Christ (29a/67). Is that not perhaps the most critical point of your theology? Does not Christ evaporate into an idea, a mythological cipher, if you deny interest in the historical Jesus?

BULTMANN: These questions concern the controversial formulation that the really decisive thing is the *that* of Jesus' coming, not the *what*, that is, not the historically verifiable data of his life and work. Now it is uncontestable that in Paul and in the rest of the New Testament, except in the Synoptic Gospels . . .

SPIEGEL: . . . the Gospels of Matthew, Mark, and Luke . . .

BULTMANN: . . . only the *that*, and not the *what*, plays a role. In the assertion of the *that*, the paradox is maintained that a historical figure, the person of Jesus of Nazareth, is at the same time the eschatological figure, the Lord Jesus Christ.

SPIEGEL: No theologian denies this paradox. However, . . .

BULTMANN: Of course, there is a danger connected with the emphasis on the decisive *that*, that the figure of Jesus will evaporate into a mythical figure or, as you formulate it, into an idea or a mythological cipher. Nevertheless, a historical person is meant with the *that* whose historicity can be verified by means of historical–critical research. Historical–critical research is necessary for Christian proclamation, among other reasons, in order that Jesus might not be misunderstood as a mythical figure. As a historical figure he is the criterion of the proclamation, that which legitimates the proclamation. The Gospel of John proceeds in this way, putting all the weight on Jesus' coming, and handles the historical tradition of the life and words of Jesus with great freedom. However, the Synoptic Gospels handle the tradition of the life and words of the historical Jesus with similar freedom. For they do not write as historians, but place what they say about Jesus in the service of the kerygma . . .

SPIEGEL: . . . of the proclamation . . .

BULTMANN: . . . and in doing this they make clear, in their own way, that paradox of the conjunction of the historical *that* and its eschatological meaning.

SPIEGEL: Few other theologians have written as impressively about the significance of the cross, of the death of Jesus on the cross, as you have. Among your other statements is the one that some consider famous, others infamous: "If the Christ who died such a death was the pre-existent Son of God, what could death mean for him? Obviously very little, if he knew that he would rise again in three days!" (9*/8).

BULTMANN: You are correct in citing this statement in this connection. If preexistence is retained in the traditional sense, then the significance of the cross is weakened.

SPIEGEL: You are accused, however, of destroying the

significance of the cross with a single statement; namely, that "we cannot know whether or how Jesus found meaning in his death. One ought not to ignore the possibility that he simply suffered a collapse."

BULTMANN: I stand by the statement you quote. The Gospels furnish us with no biographical data on the basis of which one could decide what was in Jesus' mind when he went to his death. But one can say that he knew himself to be sent by God and therefore also understood his destiny as determined by God.

SPIEGEL*: The theologians who, as you yourself, practice biblical criticism, have maintained that the virgin birth is a legend, that Jesus did not do many of the miracles which are reported of him, that much of that which stands in the Bible as his word was attributed to him only after his death, and so on. May we ask you what significance the historical criticism has for proclamation? You once wrote that historical research of the New Testament is a "way to grasp the truth of the Christian faith." But one can also read in your writings that for the preacher in the pulpit the Bible can be a book "fallen from heaven," that in the moment when the preacher enters the pulpit, the origin of the Bible determined by historical–critical research means nothing" (23/100).

BULTMANN*: I don't remember having written that first sentence.

SPIEGEL*: We found it in your *Theology of the New Testament*, Vol. II (29a/236).

BULTMANN*: (takes the book in hand): I don't find it.* If I really did write that sentence, then I must admit an error. Instead of "to grasp the *truth* of the Christian faith," I ought to have said to grasp the *meaning* of the Christian faith. The meaning of the Christian faith,

* *Der Spiegel* cited the first edition; Bultmann consulted a copy of the fifth edition, which also contains the sentence, but on a different page.

that is, what Christian faith generally means, we can experience only out of Christian proclamation; and that means out of the tradition in which proclamation not only has its origin, but through which it is also legitimized. But the source of the legitimizing tradition is the New Testament. The proclamation required therefore the interpretation of the New Testament, and this can be achieved through the medium of historical research. Insofar is this the presupposition of a legitimized sermon. The origin of the New Testament investigated by historical criticism has nothing in fact to do with the preacher in the situation of the sermon, inasmuch as historical–critical research of the New Testament as a source serves the reconstruction of a past time, as does historical–critical research of all historical texts, to which the New Testament also belongs.

SPIEGEL*: Certainly the sermon ought not to be a history lesson, but might it not fall into the other extreme and be abstracted from history? You yourself once wrote that the sermon may "make it quite clear what [the] hearers are expected to accept and what they are not" (9*/9).

BULTMANN*: The *reconstruction* must be distinguished from the *interpretation*, namely the effort to get at the essential content of a text. The historical–critical research of the New Testament has, therefore, finally to recognize the meaning—What is Christian faith? As all research, it cannot be uncritical, even with regard to distinctions lying within the New Testament itself. Think of Luther's judgment on the Epistle of James and the Revelation of John.

SPIEGEL*: The Epistle of James he called an "epistle of straw," and he said that the Revelation of John could be thrown in the river Elbe. May we proceed now to that which is said in the Christian creed about Jesus after his death. Do not even your most stubborn opponents seem to have silently demythologized the concepts "descended into hell" and "ascended into heaven"?

BULTMANN: I assume that my opponents, for good or ill, also demythologize these phrases, because they also live with a picture of a world in which there is no above and no below. But in what way they demythologize, I surely do not know.

SPIEGEL: In a widely circulated book, it is maintained that for you Jesus is only "risen as is Goethe" (14/45). If this claim is true, could you call yourself a Christian?

BULTMANN: One can say that Jesus is risen as is Goethe, if one views the person and work of Jesus as a phenomenon of cultural history. For the persons and works of great men remain effective in cultural history, and that goes also for Jesus. But if one understands Jesus as an eschatological phenomenon, and that means—according to Rom. 10 : 4: "For Christ is the end of the law, that every one who has faith may be justified"—as the end of world history insofar as its course is submitted to objectivizing observations, then his presence does not consist in his effect on cultural history, but it happens only in the moment of Christian proclamation and of faith.

SPIEGEL: To believe in the resurrection of Jesus means then . . .

BULTMANN: . . . to allow oneself to be encountered by the proclamation and to respond to it in faith.

SPIEGEL: In what sense is belief in the resurrection of Jesus the criterion for whether someone is a Christian or non-Christian?

BULTMANN: Christian faith in the resurrection believes that death is not being swallowed up into the Nothing, but that the same God, who is always coming to us, also comes to us in our death. In this sense, faith in the resurrection is the criterion for whether someone is a Christian or a non-Christian.

SPIEGEL: People have also been angry about your having written that for Easter faith—therefore, faith in the resurrection—"the historical problem is scarcely relevant" (9*/42). Does that mean that a Christian can judge as freely as a non-Christian about what may have happened after Jesus' death—visions, hallucinations of the disciples, or the bodily resurrection of Jesus?

BULTMANN: Easter faith is in fact not interested in the historical question; for historical research concerning the events after the death of Jesus can fundamentally have its eye on Jesus only as a historical and not as an eschatological phenomenon. The historical method of investigating these events which happened after the death of Jesus is therefore the same for Christians and for non-Christians.

SPIEGEL: What do you think of the fact that belief in the empty tomb and the return of Jesus to earthly life is almost made into the criterion of Christian faith by the spokesmen for the Confession Movement?

BULTMANN: I think it is absurd.

SPIEGEL: There are, roughly speaking, three positions among Protestant theologians concerning the empty tomb. The conservatives say it *must* have been empty. Karl Barth and your student Fuchs, among others, say that it could have been empty, but it did not have to be empty. A third group says that it could not have been empty. Do you consider yourself to be in the third group? In the debate with Karl Jaspers, you once wrote that you were convinced, as he is, that a corpse cannot become alive again and climb out of the grave" (54/62). Is that true also for Jesus?

BULTMANN: My opinion about the empty tomb is, in fact, the one expressed in the sentence you have quoted.

SPIEGEL: In the Gospel of John, Jesus says, while dying on the cross, "It is finished." On the basis of that you have concluded—and we quote—"that with the cross the

work of Jesus is finished, and that it requires no com-
pletion through a bodily resurrection" (25/205). Does
the Jesuit Schiwy interpret you correctly when he expresses the opinion that for you the resurrection of Jesus
is "only the legendary concretization of an idea"
(112/292)?

BULTMANN: He is correct in saying that for me the reports
of a bodily resurrection of Jesus are legends. But with
that it is by no means said that the resurrection of Jesus
is only the legendary concretization of an idea. The
resurrection reports are the legendary concretization of
the faith of the first Christian community in the risen
Lord, the faith that God has exalted the crucified one as
Lord.

SPIEGEL: In the view of your opponents, that position contradicts the New Testament.

BULTMANN: Perhaps it would be useful to point out here
that the Gospel of John uses the word "exaltation" in a
double sense: The exaltation of Jesus on the cross is at
the same time his exaltation into heavenly glory, the
realization of Easter faith.

SPIEGEL: Hans Grass, professor of theology here in Marburg, agrees with you that the Easter stories are legends,
and thinks that just for that reason—for the sake of the
veracity of the sermon—"there is no necessity for the
preacher to preach on every Easter text" (51/281).

BULTMANN: I am in complete agreement with Professor
Grass.

SPIEGEL*: In the Apostles' Creed, it says "sitteth on the
right hand of God the Father Almighty, from whence he
shall come to judge the quick and the dead." Do you
take it to heart when President Beckmann—without
quotation marks and without names, as regrettably has
become customary in the Protestant church—characterizes the following sentence as hazardous: "Christ
is risen in the message of the Church and as such is

also the one coming again, while the biblical expectation of his final advent must be given up as an error of an apocalyptic understanding of the world" (98/9)?

BULTMANN*: I regret that it is characterized as hazardous that I have characterized the biblical expectation of a final advent—return—of Christ as an error, which must be given up with the apocalyptic world-view. If the sentence is attributed to me, that Christ is risen in the message of the Church and as such is also the one coming again, that expresses my opinion. With that is presupposed, to be sure, that the meaning of the Church does not lie in its being a phenomenon of cultural history and a sociological phenomenon, but in this, that it is an eschatological phenomenon—or better, that the proclamation of the Church is an eschatological phenomenon in which Christ encounters us as present, and as final if this proclamation encounters us for the last time.

SPIEGEL: Professor Bultmann, do you consider it conceivable or possibly desirable—as does, for instance, your colleague Barnikol in Halle—that a new "demythologized" creed should be agreed upon?

BULTMANN: It is perhaps desirable that a new creed be formulated. But bound up with it would be a danger to which Wilhelm Herrmann . . .

SPIEGEL: . . . one of your teachers . . .

BULTMANN: . . . once called attention. He thought that the old Apostles' Creed should continue to be confessed serenely in the worship service, because scarcely anyone considers it obligatory to take all its assertions as literally true. But if a new confession were to be formulated, it would consist of sentences that the listeners—or speakers—would think were sentences that they must accept as true, and therefore faith would once again be confused with accepting sentences as true.

SPIEGEL: So in your opinion the creed should continue to

be confessed every Sunday, even though many believing Christians cannot confess it without "ifs, ands, or buts"?

BULTMANN: I personally think that the recitation of the creed in the church service should be renounced altogether. In my home church in Oldenburg at one time the Creed was never recited, and I don't think that the Oldenburg Christians would have to have been worse Christians because of that.

SPIEGEL: Professor Bultmann, we thank you for this interview.

List of Works Cited

Only the literature cited in the text is listed. No claim can be
made, therefore, that the list contains the most important works.
(Whenever possible, citations were given from existing English
translations, which are also listed here—Translator.)

A. BOOKS

1. Adam, Karl. *The Son of God.* Translated by Philip Here-
   ford. New York: Sheed, 1940.
2. Althaus, Paul. *Die christliche Wahrheit.* Vol. 1. Gütersloh,
   1949.
3. ———. *Die christliche Wahrheit.* Vol. 2. Gütersloh, 1949.
4. ———. *Die Wahrheit des christlichen Osterglaubens.*
   Gütersloh, 1941.
5. Asmussen, Hans, and Zahrnt, Heinz. *Ich frage Sie.* Hamburg, 1964.
6. Barth, Karl. *Church Dogmatics* 1/2. New York: Scribners,
   1956.
7. ———. *Theologische Fragen und Antworten.* Zollikon,
   1957.
8. Bartsch, Hans-Werner, ed. *Post Bultmann locutum.* Vol.
   2. Hamburg, 1966.
9. ———. ed. *Kerygma and Myth.* Vol. 1. Translated by
   Reginald Fuller. London: SPCK, 1953. [References to
   this work designated by an asterisk (*) indicate that
   material quoted appears in preface to second edition
   and does not appear in the English edition.]
10. ———. ed. *Kerygma and Myth.* Vol. 2. Translated by
    Reginald Fuller. London: SPCK, 1953.
11. Baum, Gregory. *Is the New Testament Anti-Semitic?*
    Glen Rock, New Jersey: Paulist Press, 1965.
12. Bäumer, Rudolf. *Kein anderes Evangelium.* Wuppertal,
    1966.
13. Bea, Augustin Cardinal. *The Study of the Synoptic
    Gospels.* Edited by J. Fitzmeyer. New York: Harper,
    1965.

14. Bergmann, Gerhard. *Alarm um die Bibel.* Gladbeck, 1965.
15. ―――. *Tagebuch eines Evangelisten.* Gladbeck, 1966.
16. Bismarck, Klaus von, and Dirks, Walter, eds. *Neue Grenzen I.* Stuttgart-Berlin/Olten-Freiberg, 1966.
17. Blinzler, Josef. *The Trial of Jesus.* Translated by Isabel and Florence McHugh. Westminster, Md.: Newmann, 1959.
18. Bornkamm, Günther. *Jesus of Nazareth.* Translated by Irene and Fraser McCluskey with James M. Robinson. New York: Harper, 1960.
19. Braun, Herbert. *Gesammelte Studien zum Neuen Testament und seiner Umwelt.* Tübingen, 1962.
20. Bultmann, Rudolf. *Das Evangelium des Johannes.* Göttingen, 1964.
21. ―――. *Das Verhältnis der urchristlichen Christusbotschaft zum historischen Jesus.* Heidelberg, 1961.
22. ―――. *The History of the Synoptic Tradition.* Translated by John Marsh. New York: Harper, 1963.
23. ―――. *Essays, Philosophical and Theological.* Translated by James C. G. Grieg. New York: Macmillan, 1955.
24. ―――. *Glauben und Verstehen.* Vol. 2. Tübingen, 1965.
25. ―――. *Glauben und Verstehen.* Vol. 3. Tübingen, 1965.
26. ―――. *Jesus and the Word.* Translated by Louise Pettibone and Ermine Lantero. New York: Scribners, 1958.
27. ―――. *Jesus Christus und die Mythologie.* Hamburg, 1965.
28. ―――. *This World and the Beyond: Marburg Sermons.* Translated by Harold Knight. New York: Scribners, 1960.
29. ―――. *Theology of the New Testament.* Vol. 1. Translated by Kendrick Grobel. New York: Scribners, 1951.
29a. ―――. *Theology of the New Testament.* Vol. 2. Translated by Kendrick Grobel. New York: Scribners, 1951.
30. Campenhausen, Hans Freiherr von. *Der Ablauf der Osterereignisse und das leere Grab.* Heidelberg, 1958.
31. ―――. *The Virgin Birth in the Ancient Church.* Translated by Frank Clarke. London: SCM, 1964.
32. Conzelmann, Hans. "Jesus Christus." *Religion in Geschichte und Gegenwart,* Band 3. Tübingen (1959).
32a. Cullmann, Oscar. *The Christology of the New Testament.* Translated by Shirley Guthrie and Charles Hall. Philadelphia: Westminster, 1959.

32b. Dannenbaum, Hans. *Katechismusstunden für Erwachsene.* Wuppertal, 1956.

33. Dibelius, Martin. *Botschaft und Geschichte.* Vol. 1. Tübingen, 1953.

34. ————. *From Tradition to Gospel.* Translated by Bertram Woolf. New York: Scribners, 1935.

35. ————. *Jesus.* Translated by C. Hedrick and F. C. Grant. Philadelphia: Westminster, 1949.

36. Diem, Hermann. *Theologie als kirchliche Wissenschaft.* München, 1951.

37. Ebeling, Gerhard. *The Nature of Faith.* Translated by Ronald Gregor Smith. Philadelphia: Fortress, 1962.

38. ————. *Word and Faith.* Translated by James W. Leitch. Philadelphia: Fortress, 1963.

39. Eckert, Willehad Paul, and Ehrlich, Ernst Ludwig, eds. *Judenhass—Schuld der Christen?!* Essen, 1966.

40. Felder, Hilarin. *Die Beweise Jesu.* Paderborn, 1921.

41. Fuchs, Ernst. *Studies of the Historical Jesus.* Translated by Andrew Scobie. London: SCM, 1964.

41a. ————. *Zur Frage nach dem historischen Jesus.* Tübingen, 1960.

42. ————. *Glaube und Erfahrung.* Tübingen, 1965.

43. Gamm, Hans-Jochen. *Sachkunde zur biblischen Geschichte.* München, 1965.

44. Geiselmann, Josef Rupert. *Jesus der Christus.* Vol. 1. München, 1965.

45. Girock, Hans Joachim, ed. *Himmelfahrt.* Stuttgart, 1966.

46. Gloege, Gerhard. *The Day of His Coming.* Translated by Stanley Rudman. Philadelphia: Fortress, 1963.

47. Gogarten, Friederich. *Demythologizing and History.* Translated by Neville Horton Smith. London: SCM, 1955.

48. ————. *Jesus Christus, die Wende der Welt.* Tübingen, 1965.

49. Goguel, Maurice. *Das Leben Jesu.* Zürich, Leipzig and Stuttgart, 1934.

50. Gollwitzer, Helmut. *The Existence of God as Confessed by Faith.* Translated by James Leitch. Philadelphia: Westminster, 1965.

51. Grass, Hans. *Ostergeschehen und Osterberichte.* Göttingen, 1954.

52. Haarbeck, Theodor. *Biblische Glaubenslehre.* Giessen, 1965.

53. Hasenhüttl, Gotthold. *Der Glaubensvollzug.* Essen, 1963.
54. Hirsch, Emanuel. *Das vierte Evangelium in seiner ursprünglichen Gestalt, verdeutscht und erklärt.* Tübingen, 1936.
55. Jaspers, Karl, and Bultmann, Rudolf. *Myth and Christianity: An Inquiry into the Possibility of Religion without Myth.* New York: Noonday Press, 1958.
56. Käsemann, Ernst. *Essays on New Testament Themes.* Translated by W. J. Montagne. London: SCM, 1964.
57. ————. *Exegetische Versuche und Besinnungen.* Vol. 2. Göttingen, 1965.
58. Keller, Werner. *The Bible as History.* Translated by William Neil. New York: Morrow, 1959.
59. Klein, Günter. *Wunderglaube und Neues Testament.* Wuppertal, 1960.
60. ————. Marxsen, Willi; and Kreck, Walter. *Bibelkritik und Gemeindefrömmigkeit.* Gütersloh, 1966.
61. Koch, Gerhard. *Die Auferstehung Jesu Christi.* Tübingen, 1959.
62. Kretschmar, Georg, and Lohse, Bernhard, eds. *Ecclesia und Res publica.* Göttingen, 1961.
63. Künneth, Walter. *Glauben an Jesus?* Hamburg, 1962.
64. ————. *The Theology of the Resurrection.* Translated by James Leitch. St. Louis: Concordia, 1965.
65. Marxsen, Willi. *Der Streit um die Bibel.* Gladbeck, 1965.
66. ————. *Die Auferstehung Jesu als historisches und als theologisches Problem.* Gütersloh, 1965.
67. ————. *Introduction to the New Testament.* Translated by G. Buswell. Philadelphia: Fortress, 1968.
68. May, Georg. *Katholische Kinderziehung in der Mischehe.* Trier, 1965.
69. Müller, Eberhard. *Conversation on Faith.* Translated by John Doberstein. Philadelphia: Muhlenberg, 1961.
70. Neuner, Josef, and Roos, Heinrich, eds. *The Teaching of the Catholic Church as Contained in Her Documents.* Translated by Geoffery Stevens. Staten Island, New York: Alba House, 1967.
71. Niemöller, Martin. *Ein Welt oder keine Welt.* Frankfurt, 1964.
72. Otto, Gert, ed. *Glauben heute.* Hamburg, 1966.
73. Pannenberg, Wolfhart. *Jesus, God and Man.* Translated by Lewis Wilkens and Duane Priebe. Philadelphia: Westminster, 1968.

74. Rahner, Karl. *Inspiration in the Bible.* New York: Herder and Herder, 1962.

75. ———. *Theological Investigations.* Vol. 5. Translated by Cornelius Ernst. Baltimore: Helicon, 1967.

76. Reatz, August. *Jesus Christus.* Freiberg, 1924.

77. Rengstorf, Karl Heinrich. *Die Auferstehung Jesu.* Witten, 1952.

78. Ricciotti, Joseph. *Das Leben Jesu,* Basel, 1949.

79. Ristow, Helmut, and Mattiae, Karl. (ed.) *Der historische und der kerygmatische Christus.* Berlin, 1962.

80. Robinson, James M. *A New Quest of the Historical Jesus.* London: SCM, 1959.

81. Rodenberg, Otto. *Der Sohn.* Wuppertal, 1963.

82. Sartory, Thomas. *Fragen an die Kirche.* München, 1965.

83. Schelkle, Karl Hermann. *Das Neue Testament.* Kevelaer, 1963.

84. Schlatter, Adolf. *Das Evangelium nach Matthäus.* Berlin, 1952.

85. Schultz, Hans-Jürgen, ed. *Theologie für Nichttheologen* I. Stuttgart–Berlin, 1965.

86. ———. *Theologie für Nichttheologen* II. Stuttgart–Berlin, 1965.

87. ———. *Theologie für Nichttheologen* III. Stuttgart–Berlin, 1966.

88. Stauffer, Ethelbert. *Jesus and His Story.* Translated by Richard and Clara Winston. New York: Knopf, 1960.

88a. ———. *Christ and the Caesars.* Translated by Ronald Gregor Smith. Philadelphia: Westminster, 1955.

89. ———. *Jesus, Paulus und wir.* Hamburg, 1961.

90. Symanowski, Horst, ed. *Post Bultmann locutum.* Vol. 1. Hamburg, 1965.

91. Thielicke, Helmut. *Ich glaube.* Stuttgart, 1965.

92. Wegenast, Klaus. *Jesus und die Evangelien.* Gütersloh, 1965.

93. Zahrnt, Heinz. *The Historical Jesus.* Translated by J. S. Bowden. New York: Harper, 1963.

B. ARTICLES

94. Augstein, Rudolf. "So stell ich mir die Christen vor." *Der Spiegel* 10 (1965).

94a. Bartsch, Hans-Werner. "Historische Erwägungen zur Leidensgeschichte." *Evang. Theologie* 22 (1962).

95. ———. "Weihnachten abschaffen." *Die Zeit,* 31 Dec. 1965.

96. Bea, Augustin Cardinal. "Inspiration." *Lexikon für Theologie und Kirche* 5 (1960).

97. ———. "Das jüdische Volk und der göttliche Heilsplan." *Stimmen der Zeit,* December 1965.

98. Beckmann, Joachim. "Ein anderes Evangelium?" Düsseldorf, 1966.

99. Bergmann, Gerhard. "Was ist die Bekenntnisbewegung, kein anderes Evangelium?" *Licht und Leben,* March 1966.

100. Bieneck, Edmund. "Die Bibel in der Hand des Gemeindegliedes." Kassel, 1965.

101. Blinzler, Josef. "Pilatus." *Lexikon für Theologie und Kirche* 8 (1963).

102. Geisser, Hans. "Viva vox Evangelii in Ecclesia." *Materialdienst des konfessionskundlichen Instituts* 3 (1966).

102a. Ginsberg, Renate. "Unterrichtsskizze über die Jungfrauengeburt." *Der evangelische Religionslehrer an der Berufsschule,* 1958, pp. 183ff.

103. Grosch, Heinz; Wegenast, Klaus; and Hartmann, Walter. "Wundergeschichten der Bibel in der Grundschule." *Evangelische Unterweisung,* February 1966.

104. Haenchen, Ernst. "Jesus vor Pilatus." *Theologische Literaturzeitung* 2 (1960).

105. Heintze, Gerhard. "[Brief] an alle Pfarrer, Pfarrvikare, Pfarrdiakone und Pfarrvikarinnen der Braunschweigischen Evangelisch–lutherischen Landeskirche" (duplicated). Wolfenbüttel, 1966.

106. Knevels, Wilhelm. "Selbstbesinnung des Glaubens zwischen Fundamentalismus und Existentialtheologie." *Deutsches Pfarrerblatt* 2 (1966).

107. Künneth, Walter. "Irrlehre Heute." *Rheinischer Merkur,* 28 January 1966.

108. Locher, Albrecht. "Umdenken in der Glaubensverkündigung." *Stimmen der Zeit,* March 1966.

109. Lohfink, Norbert. "Katholische Bibelwissenschaft und historisch-kritische Methode." *Stimmen der Zeit,* May 1966.

110. Michl, Josef. "Apokryphe Briefe" in *Lexikon für Theologie und Kirche* 2 (1958).

111. ———. "Pilatus-Schrifttum" in *Lexikon für Theologie und Kirche* 8 (1963).

112. Schiwy, Günther. "Die Osterberichte zwischen Rationalismus und Irrationalismus." *Stimmen der Zeit*, April 1966.

113. Schmid, Josef. "Bibelkritik" in *Lexikon für Theologie und Kirche* 2 (1958).

114. Selge, Kurt-Victor. "Zum jüngsten Bibelstreit in Rom." *Materialdienst des Konfessionskundlichen Instituts* 1 (1961).

115. Vögtle, Anton. "Wunder" in *Lexikon für Theologie und Kirche* 10 (1965).

116. ———. "Messiasbekenntnis und Petrusverheiss ung." *Biblische Zeitschrift*, New Series 1 (1957) pp. 252–272, and 2 (1958), pp. 85–103.

117. ———. "Die Konstitution über die Offenbarung." *Herder-Korrespondenz*, April 1966.